THE
PLYMOUTH
BOOK
OF
DAYS

JOHN VAN DER KISTE

I would like to record my particular thanks to my wife Kim for her constant support and reading through of the manuscript; to Brian Moseley's invaluable Plymouth Data website; to the local newspapers and books, all of which have provided so much of the material for this book; and to my editors, Matilda Richards and Jenny Briancourt.

First published 2011

The History Press
The Mill, Brimscombe Port
Stroud, Gloucestershire, GL5 2QG
www.thehistorypress.co.uk

© John Van der Kiste, 2011

The right of John Van der Kiste to be identified as the Author of this work has been asserted in accordance with the Copyrights, Designs and Patents Act 1988.

British Library Cataloguing in Publication Data.
A catalogue record for this book is available from the British Library.

ISBN 978 0 7524 6080 2

Typesetting and origination by The History Press
Printed in India
Manufacturing managed by Jellyfish Print Solutions Ltd

January 1st

1824: On 24 December 1823, the Home Secretary, Robert Peel, granted Plymouth Dock (which had overtaken Plymouth in terms of population) its own identity and allowed the residents to change its name – something they had been yearning for. Eight days later its new name, Devonport, was officially used for the first time. An official proclamation, carried from point to point in the town, was read repeatedly to cheering crowds. Later, a 124ft column, designed by John Foulston, was erected, including a pedestal intended for a statue of King George IV which was to be financed by £20 shares. But it was never built, as several subscribers failed to pay.

* * *

1951: The Royal Parade had its first fatal accident when Mrs Kathleen May, of Laira, was knocked over by a bus; she died on her way to hospital.

* * *

2007: Professor Roland Levinsky (63), vice-chancellor of the University of Plymouth since September 2002, was walking his dog in a field at Wembury during a storm, when overhead power cables came down. Paramedics were called but he was pronounced dead at the scene. A new arts building at the university, opened in September 2007, was named The Roland Levinsky Room in his honour.

January 2nd

1958: A woman shopping in the city centre told her husband that she had come out without her key. He told her what a good job it was that he never did such a thing. As they approached their house in Woodford, he fumbled in his pockets and realised that he had done likewise. He had to force the back door, and, only after getting inside, did he discover that he had left his key in the lock of the front door the whole time.

———◆———

1964: The pianist in an orchestra playing at a venue in the city complained to the management that he was cold, and said that he would like an electric fire. His request was refused with the simple words, 'Nonsense. Tell him to play faster.'

———◆———

1965: Senior Inspector Forward, of the RSPCA, revealed that a fully grown Muscovy duck had been handed in before Christmas and that he, his wife and 10-year-old daughter had looked after it at their home in Peverell. It was occasionally allowed to exercise in the back garden, but they kept it penned up most of the time. The family had also acquired a large white rabbit and a ferret from people who had found them straying over the festive season.

January 3rd

1725: Plymouth's first locally produced newspaper, The *Plymouth Weekly Journal*, or *General Post*, was published for the first time. It was printed, and perhaps edited as well, by Mr M.E. Kent, Southside Street, with a cover price of 1½*d* per issue. Despite its title, it was not really a local newspaper, as it did not cover events in the area but relied on reprinting material taken from London newspapers. The earliest edition still known to exist, No. 36, dated 5 September 1718, is in the British Library. A copy dated 12 March 1725 is held by Plymouth Proprietary Library, but there are no records as to when publication ceased.

———— • ◆ • ————

1860: The first issue of the *Western Morning News*, the city's longest-lasting newspaper, founded by William Saunders and Edward Spender (the first editor), was published. Politically it claimed to be independent, although it was considered more sympathetic to the Liberal cause in its early days. The offices were originally at New George Street, then moved from the city centre to purpose-built premises at Derriford in 1992. From February 1997 onwards the paper was published in tabloid format. The Derriford offices closed in 2010 and from April that year the paper was printed in Didcot, Oxfordshire.

January 4th

1957: Occupants of buildings in Armada Way were annoyed on this particular morning when they looked out of the windows to see ladies distributing bread on the grassy areas in front of the shops and offices – encouraging pigeons, and other birds that came in large numbers, to feed. They complained that the latter were waiting on roofs and façades, leaving a terrible mess. When one irate manager spoke to a woman whom he caught in the act, and suggested that it would be preferable if she scattered the food further away from the buildings, she retorted that in her view the Corporation were neglecting their duties by not employing an official pigeon feeder.

———— • ◆ • ————

1982: A collection of about 1,000 library books, which had been withdrawn from stock, were destroyed in a fire at the Stoke branch library, Albert Road. The blaze was believed to have been started deliberately by children lighting a bonfire. The books were being kept in storage in an air-raid shelter at the back of the library, until a rise in the pulping price made it more viable to dispose of them. Appealing for witnesses, the police particularly asked for help in tracing three youths seen running away from the scene.

January 5th

1945: A wedding reception was held at a café in the city centre. Despite wartime restrictions and rationing, no effort had been spared by the bride's family in making a magnificent two-tiered cake, coated in icing and marzipan. It had been taken to the café the day before, and, after the guests arrived from the church, a waitress brought it out and placed it in front of them. The bride duly cut it, handed slices round, and everyone pronounced it quite delicious. After the guests had gone, more taxis arrived at the door and a second wedding party came in. Casting an eye over the neatly laid table, the bride noticed something missing. 'Where's our cake?' she asked.

1973: In the afternoon a Christmas party was held for about 500 children, aged between 5 and 8, of employees at Tecalemit Engineering in the company's canteen. Among the attractions were star exhibits from Plymouth Zoo, namely Donna, a lion cub; Corky, a sulphur-crested cockatoo, and Charlie, a capuchin monkey. Also on hand to provide fun were Gordon Straight's puppets, and three members of the workforce dressed as clowns and entertainers. A 'Tom and Jerry' cartoon was shown, and Father Christmas gave each child a present.

January 6th

1843: At a monthly meeting of Plymouth Proprietary Library, the committee passed a resolution regretting the inconvenience 'experienced in consequence of the detention of newspapers for a longer time than is compatible with the general accommodation'. They proposed that in the future 'two glasses of fifteen minutes each be provided and gentlemen be limited in the perusal of a paper to that time in case it is required by another member'.

1888: Three young women were charged with 'extraordinary behaviour in the workhouse'. On New Year's Eve, they had climbed over the garden wall and run into the town, and, when brought back by the authorities, 'revenged themselves at the supper table by seizing pannikins [small metal cups] and smashing panes of glass'. They were sentenced to three months in prison.

1954: A man with a splinter in his finger went to see his doctor to have it removed. The practitioner told him it was a case for hospital treatment. The man thought it hardly worth waiting in a queue for two or three hours for something so trivial, so instead he tried a chemist in the city centre, where the splinter was taken out within two minutes.

January 7th

1949: A bus was boarded at Hyde Park by a couple who wanted to go to Peverell. The conductor helpfully told them that they needed a bus going in the opposite direction, as they were heading for the city centre. They would only reach Peverell after stopping first at Royal Parade, Fore Street, Devonport and Milehouse.

'But that's what we want,' they said. 'We're visitors and we're out sightseeing.'

'There's nothing to see in this place,' the conductor insisted.

His views were backed by a passenger, who told them, 'If you come here once, you'll never want to come again.' The couple must have wondered why they had bothered to visit Plymouth in the first place.

———— • ◆ • ————

1953: During a spate of burglaries in the city, one lady returned to her house for something she had forgotten. While she was in her bedroom, she heard someone moving around on the ground floor. She carefully crept down the stairs and, as she reached the bottom, the door of her sitting room opened and she found herself face-to-face with a strange man. 'Good evening,' she said, too surprised to come out with anything else. He wished her the same, opened the front door and left. Only then did she discover that he had taken £8 in cash with him.

January 8th

1788: Plymouth had an unofficial royal visit from the eldest sons of King George III – the Prince of Wales, later George IV, and Frederick, Duke of York – who had come to cheer up their brother William Henry, the future William IV, who was then only a junior officer in the Royal Navy. He was in the town in parental disgrace, having disobeyed orders to spend winter in Québec (he had sailed to Cork instead). He was ordered to the south-west port and was told to stay there until instructed otherwise. The three princes drove in a coach-and-six along Fore Street, with cheering crowds lining their route. After visits to the Citadel, dockyard and Mount Edgcumbe, they attended a grand ball at the Long Assembly Rooms, Stonehouse, where they got drunk and 'were still lustily performing country dances' until after 1 a.m. (*See* May 23rd)

1954: 'I want a bow tie, please,' a customer asked in a clothing store. 'Yes, sir,' answered the female assistant, 'Long or short sleeves?'

1965: It was reported that an elderly lady, in bed at a hospital in the city, used to remove her hearing-aid at night, but always kept her glasses on. When asked why by another patient, she replied, 'Well, I get some very vivid dreams, and I can see them better if I keep my glasses on!'

January 9th

1841: A court-martial was held on board the HMS *San Joseph*, moored off Hamoaze. George Hobbs, of HMS *Pigeon*, was charged with being drunk and disorderly, repeated drunkenness, insubordination and disobedience to orders, and with striking his superior officer – the master of *Pigeon*. After pleading guilty, he was sentenced to be hanged from the yardarm of one of the ships off Hamoaze.

1948: After increasing problems with souvenir hunters removing ashtrays, the NAAFI Club found a solution. New ashtrays of pink and green marble, weighing over 2lb each, were introduced to deter those of a light-fingered persuasion.

1961: A passer-by scolded three small boys for throwing knives at the door of an old church on the Barbican. They assured her that it was 'all right', as it was an old building 'and will have to be knocked down soon'.

1975: Efford Youth Centre, Blandford Road, was offered an old snooker table as a gift, but it was in a hut 500 yards away, and weighed 1½ tons. Leader Vivian Parker had the problem of moving it, preferably free of charge, to its new home. An appeal for ideas and volunteers produced the perfect solution – members of the centre's weightlifting club.

January 10th

1929: Tony Soper, one of Plymouth's most famous naturalists and presenters, and sometimes regarded as Britain's 'Mr Birdwatch', was born. Educated at Hyde Park Elementary School and Devonport High School for Boys, he joined the BBC as a trainee studio manager. He helped to found the BBC Natural History Unit and became its first wildlife cameraman and film producer, as well as presenting several natural history documentary series on television. He was the president of the Devon Bird Watching & Preservation Society in 1969 and 1970, and wrote several books on British and overseas birds, including the international bestseller *The Bird Table Book*, which was first published in 1965 and has been frequently reprinted since.

———◆•———

1956: A gentleman was walking towards Mutley Plain when he met another man, who was rather short of breath, leaning against the wall. 'I wonder if you would mind helping me up the hill?' the breathless man asked. 'It's a bit of a climb for me at my age.' The other man was happy to lend a helping hand.

'Thanks very much,' the old man said afterwards, 'I find this hill very trying nowadays. You see, I'm 72.'

'Oh that's all right,' replied his benefactor, 'I'm only 74.'

January 11th

1886: Ella Fitzroy (20), of Devonport, died from the effects of injuries received while she was changing for a ball on Christmas Eve. A lighted candle had fallen on her dress and caught fire. Her sister Maude (19) had heard her screams and gone to her rescue, but was severely burned herself, and, after lingering in agony, she died from her burns on the evening of Christmas Day.

— ◆ —

1948: A 12-month-old bullock owned by Mr Pudner of Highland Farm, near Roborough, had climbed a bank to drink from a static water tank in a nearby field. In the process it fell in, and the sides of the tank were too high for it to scramble out again. Pudner was informed by a neighbour who had seen it getting progressively panic-stricken. He, his son, and some farm workers were unable to move it while the tank was full. After knocking a hole in the side to drain the water out, they tried to coax, push and pull the increasingly frightened animal out, but without success. They fetched ropes, tackle and a hoisting pulley, wrapped sacks round it and placed a loop of rope over it so they could haul it clear and swing it back to safety.

January 12th

1957: A woman standing in the queue at the Gaumont Cinema, waiting to see the Norman Wisdom picture, *Up in the World*, found herself in conversation with a group of four boys, all aged under 13. Every one of them had a television at home, and they had all been given 1s 6d by their mothers to see the film in the best seats, but none of them had had any dinner. All, the woman reflected, were 'latch-key children', with their parents apparently putting entertainment before proper meals.

———— • ◆ • ————

1973: Several members of the Hare Krishna sect in New George Street – dressed in Indian costume and covered with anoraks to keep the rain and cold at bay – were moved along by police. They were told that they were street traders and were causing an obstruction, as they were offering literature to passers-by and requesting donations to cover printing costs. There were five in the group altogether, with one tapping a drum and the others ringing small bells. They had come to Plymouth from Bloomsbury on the previous Sunday, 7 January, and were staying with a friend at Plymstock. Two of them had come from Plymouth originally, and they had adopted names such as Diaranga and Dhira Shanta.

January 13th

1953: A show at Plymouth Arts Centre, 'Turn of the Century', included among its exhibits an object that had been dismissed as nothing more than an old black box covered in dust. Walton Gale, who brought it to the show, said it had been found by a friend when turning out a garden shed on behalf of an elderly widow, whose husband had died in 1920. He had examined it, realised it was an old camera, and noticed a manufacturer's plate with 'Ross of London' on it. He had sent it to them, and they had returned it with a note confirming that it was a model they made in 1901. The plates were removed and taken to a local chemist, who produced prints of remarkable clarity in view of their age – one showing a family group and another a typical Victorian parlour.

———— • ◆ • ————

1956: St Mary's Church, Plympton, organised a 'talents scheme' by which participants had to start off with a small sum to use as capital, which would enable them to raise funds throughout the year. One lady in the congregation, who always took her husband a cup of tea in the morning, decided that in future she would charge him 1s per week in aid of the fund.

January 14th

2010: Casper, a 12-year-old black and white cat, who became world-famous as a bus commuter, was killed by a driver while crossing the road for his daily journey on the No. 3 First Devon & Cornwall service. His owner, Susan Finden, had acquired him as a rescue cat in 2002 and thought he must have begun life at a haulage yard because of his fondness for large vehicles. She named him Casper, after the friendly ghost. For about five years, he would get on at a bus stop outside the front door of his home in St Budeaux at around 10 a.m. every morning. He'd curl up on a seat throughout the full 11-mile route to the city centre, travelling for up to an hour before arriving back at the same stop. Mrs Finden was puzzled when he began to disappear regularly but was amazed when she found out he had become a regular passenger. Drivers on the service were advised to look out for him and ensure he got off at the right point. During the five years or so, he travelled an estimated 20,000 miles on the bus before his nine lives ran out. After worldwide media coverage of his life and death, Mrs Finden published his story in *Casper the Commuting Cat* later that year.

January 15th

1898: Yealmpton station, the terminus of the Yealmpton to Plymouth Railway branch line, was opened by the Countess of Morley. It carried passengers and freight, but with the increase in car ownership after the First World War, passenger traffic was reduced and ceased on the line altogether in 1930. The services were restored in 1941 during the Second World War, as Yealmpton was one of the outlying villages being used as a dormitory town by people in the city during the worst of the air raids. In 1947, the line was again used for freight only until its closure in 1960. The station was demolished and the site was used for housing.

1954: A notice was displayed in city buses: 'Bus passengers. Do you realise you are made to pay £30,000,000 a year in fuel tax. What are you doing about it?' Pencilled underneath on one were the words: 'Paying my share!'

1957: A Plymouth shopper, having made her purchases, was handed them by the assistant in a large paper bag with a rather sharp corner. As she walked out, it accidentally caught and pricked another assistant in the leg. When the latter complained, the customer told her crossly, 'Well, it's your bag!'

January 16th

1890: Devonport was badly affected during a national epidemic of influenza. On this day about forty new cases were reported at the military hospital, which now had seventy-two patients altogether. Stonehouse had twelve new cases, making a total of seventy-four in the hospital. The Mayor of Plymouth, Mr Waring, was also confined to bed with the virus.

1948: A 16-year-old girl had gone to apply for an office job in Plymouth, saying she was qualified as she knew 'a bit of shorthand'. She wanted £2 10s per week to start with, adding, 'Of course, I must have my own room. I need plenty of air.' Her exasperated would-be employer then replied, 'I'm afraid this job won't suit you. You'd better join the land army.'

1953: One man's patience was eventually rewarded. Several weeks previously, he had advertised his car for sale in the newspaper, but with no reply. He had almost given up hope when he received a letter from a man who had stopped with his wife for fish and chips. They got home, unwrapped their package and noticed the ad. A successful sale was the result.

January 17th

1906: Samuel Tope, of Chapel Street, a naval pensioner who worked in the dockyard, was summoned at a court before the mayor, charged with persistent cruelty to his wife Charlotte. Her defence counsel said that she left him after he had threatened her with a chopper on New Year's Day, and on a previous occasion had run after her with a knife. She denied provoking him by drinking to excess, but nevertheless the case was dismissed.

1956: A city doctor was being pestered by a family who frequently rang him at around 2.30 a.m. each morning; it was nearly always regarding some trivial complaint which could easily wait until later in the morning. One night he went out to a party, which went on very late. On his way home, he was passing the house where his patients lived, and decided it might be a good idea to stop and call on them. He parked the car, got out and rang the bell. A bleary-eyed man in pyjamas and dressing gown answered the door. 'I'm sorry to disturb you,' said the doctor brightly, 'but I was passing this way, and as this is about your time, I just dropped in to see if everybody was all right.'

January 18th

1956: A man whose interests included campanology was walking along Durnford Street when he heard what he thought was a particularly fine peal of bells, coming from St George's Church. He went inside and asked the verger if he would be allowed to come in and do some bell-ringing there in the future. The verger had to decline his request, pointing out that what he had just heard was a tape recording of bells from a church in London. St George's sadly had no bells of its own, having lost them during the war.

———◆•———

1961: An exhibition of French Impressionist paintings was being staged at the City Art Gallery. One of the groups who visited on this day was the crew from a French fishing boat which had recently docked in Sutton Pool. The men wore wooden sabots, which they discarded as soon as they entered the door; they left them in a little row inside the building, then walked around in their stockinged feet. A spokesman said that the fishermen were regular visitors to these displays as they enjoyed the paintings so much, and they carried out the same little ceremony every time they came to the museum.

January 19th

1956: Even in midwinter, Plymothians, and those who were considering a visit to the city later in the year, were starting to get holiday fever. The city's holiday guide was already in great demand, hotels were taking bookings for the summer, and huts by the Hoe were also being booked up. The prize for being well-prepared in advance, however, went to the man who walked into a chemist and asked for three tubes of sunburn cream.

—————•◆•—————

1957: The Plymstock firemen were used to holding their annual dinner dance at the Beacon Hill Hotel, Newton Ferrers. It was due to be held on this night, but it had to be cancelled because of the petrol shortage, or at least postponed until the situation eased. Others were inconvenienced by the situation in different ways. Later that week a motorist, just outside the city, encountered a garage attendant who offered him 2 gallons at 8s per gallon. He eagerly took advantage of this offer; he then had a difficult drive and arrived at his regular Plymouth garage with the engine sputtering badly. When the tank was inspected, the 'petrol' was found to be fifty per cent paraffin. (*See* November 30th)

January 20th

1916: Mrs Moore, of Torrington Place, celebrated her 105th birthday. She died ten weeks later.

———— ◆ • ————

1945: Several Plymouth firms were reporting how short-staffed they were, with members of the workforce suffering from coughs and colds. Errand boys seemed particularly susceptible, with one firm reporting six absentees out of twelve at one stage during the week. Managers had to deal with a variety of excuses, some less convincing than others. One boy took a day off because he wanted to go to the pictures. When it was pointed out to him that the cinemas were not open that morning, he hastily said he needed a rest first.

———— ◆ • ————

1954: A whale – a 29ft lesser rorqual – was washed up at Langdon Beach, Wembury. It proved to be a job for the bomb disposal squad from HMS *Defiance*, who needed twenty 1¼lb canisters of plastic dynamite. Experts estimated that the carcass must have weighed about 4 tons, and if it had been easily removable it would have provided a good supply of fertiliser or pig food. But, as it was difficult to access and impossible to remove whole, the only alternative to blowing it up would have meant about £50 in removal costs.

January 21st

1957: The Odeon booking office opened for tickets for two concerts on a nationwide tour by Bill Haley & the Comets. Prices ranged from 1 guinea for the 250 front seats, to 5s 6d for the cheapest. Within three days, every seat was sold for the second house, and the rest for the first went soon afterwards. The wife of a well-known businessman bought a ticket for her housemaid who loved rock'n'roll. Taking her place in the queue at the box office, she was rather alarmed when a press photographer came and took a picture in which she would clearly occupy a prominent position. Terrified that she would be branded 'a crazy rock'n'roll fan', she was relieved when the picture was never published.

Shortly after the concerts, a local girl sported a white sweater, with BILL HALEY embroidered in black on one arm and THE COMETS on the other. Across the front was a bar of music. When her friend asked if it was one of his hits, she said she did not have a song book, so she had taken it out of a hymn book. It turned out to be the first bar of 'Arise my Soul'.

January 22nd

1850: Thomas Moon (85), founder of Messrs Moon & Sons Ltd, piano manufacturers and music retailers, died in Plymouth. A former choirboy, he had originally set himself up as a cabinet maker in a shop in Butcher's Lane, later moving to larger premises at Treville Street and in due course to George Street. He and his family expanded their business to include the manufacture and selling of musical instruments and sheet music, providing music lessons and a piano tuning and repair service. With the advent of recorded sound and broadcasting, they also added gramophones, records and radiograms to their merchandise. By the time of the Second World War, the firm had branches in Exeter, Exmouth, Barnstaple, Truro and Bugle. The premises in George Street were destroyed during the war; the company dispersed to various smaller shops around the city until opening a new double-fronted shop in New George Street in 1956. Just inside the entrance, the shop displayed a television screen on which customers could see themselves arriving at the store – at the time, one of the earliest demonstrations of closed circuit TV. In 1963 the premises were taken over by Messrs J. & F. Stone, a London lighting and radio firm, but later closed.

January 23rd

1933: An inquest was held on leading aircraftman Alfred Slatter (20), who was killed on 12 January when his RAF flying boat sank after colliding with a naval dockyard launch in Plymouth Sound. John Wilcox, who had been in charge of a tug on the water at the time, told the inquest that he saw the flying boat on the water travelling very fast, and thought he heard the engine making a spitting sound, before seeing it swerve violently to port. The accident was ascribed to engine failure.

———— • ◆ • ————

1948: A journalist called at a friend's house and was amused to find a cat fast asleep in a large dish on top of the kitchen dresser. The owner explained that his feline friend had more or less made it his permanent bed since Christmas, when he had been given his first taste of roast turkey. The dish had been used to bring the turkey to the table on Christmas Day, and the cold carcass was left on it for several days afterwards. Having developed a taste for the turkey, the cat had associated the dish with it ever since, even though it had been thoroughly washed and scoured. He would sleep nowhere else.

January 24th

1871: The Devonport School Board was formed, the first in the Three Towns to be established under the Elementary Education Act of 1870 (which provided the opportunity of education for all children up to the age of 10). Plymouth followed suit a week later, as did Plymstock a few months after that, and other districts over the next few years. Each body was given the authority to set up elementary schools if there were not sufficient voluntary or endowed schools within the borough. By 1901 there were 4,900 children registered in attendance in Devonport, and 8,959 in Plymouth. A new Education Act was passed in 1902 and School Boards were replaced the following year by Local Education Authorities.

———— ◆ ————

1964: A young woman in Plymouth, who had recently become engaged and was planning her wedding, declared that she wanted to hold the ceremony at St Jude's Church, although she was living in another parish. When asked why, she explained that parking would be much easier there. Her own church was situated in a busy thoroughfare with several 'No Waiting' notices, and she presumably wanted to ensure that there would be maximum convenience for her guests who were coming by car.

January 25th

1904: The Drake Institute, or the Church of England Soldiers' and Sailors' Institute, near Stonehouse Bridge, was officially opened by Lieutenant-General Sir William Butler. Work on the site had begun in May 1903 and the foundation stone was laid by Princess Henry of Battenberg, Queen Victoria's youngest daughter, on 25 July. The Drake Institute was destroyed in the Blitz during the Second World War.

———•◆•———

1954: During the start of a cold spell, snow arrived in Tavistock Road at about 10.30 a.m., 3in deep – on top of a covered lorry. The lorry had a Leeds business address on the windscreen, and had obviously come through several counties. Nevertheless, expectations of a snowfall in Plymouth were not to be realised that winter.

———•◆•———

1990: Winds with a speed of up to 120mph tore across Devon and Cornwall. Several people were injured and at least ten Plymouth schools were closed for at least a day, as their roofs were lifted off and classroom windows were blown in. At Vauxhall Court, the roof was blown off a block of council flats. A lorry was blown over on its side while crossing Tamar Bridge, and, with all three lanes blocked, commuters were delayed for over two hours.

January 26th

1786: Benjamin Robert Haydon was born at Wimpole Street, Plymouth. He studied painting at the Royal Academy in London, and became known for painting historical pictures and portraits. Frequently in debt, he had little success with his work – apart from the sale of a picture to King George IV – and he lectured on art in order to supplement his meagre income. He was not highly regarded by his contemporaries, and, according to Charles Dickens, 'he most unquestionably was a very bad painter, … his pictures could not be expected to sell or to succeed'. After years of disappointment and severe depression, he committed suicide in 1846, cutting his throat alongside a canvas on which he had been working.

———— ◆ ————

1956: A middle-aged lady went into a city hairdresser to speak to the proprietor. 'My son has his hair cut here,' she said. 'You never cut it short enough.' The hairdresser assured her that this would be remedied on his next visit, and asked if the lady would give him a note to bring. She said that to do so would be rather awkward.

'In that case, Madam,' the proprietor suggested, 'can you give us a description so that we shall know him?'

'Why, certainly,' was the answer. 'He's aged 30 and beginning to go thin on top.'

January 27th

1874: Sylvanus Sweet had an argument with his wife Elizabeth at their home in Clifton Place. He struck her repeatedly over the head with a cutlass, and within a few minutes the wounds had proved fatal. When he took a cab, walked into the nearest police station and gave himself up, admitting he had killed her, the officers thought his behaviour was very odd, and one of them asked the police doctor to examine him first. On being questioned, Sweet said he was convinced that she and several other people, including Sir Edward Bates, the local Conservative MP, were trying to have him sent to a lunatic asylum. He was charged and tried for her murder at Exeter in March, and it emerged that he had frequently suffered from epileptic fits. He and his wife had married almost six years previously, but had separated after about a year together and had begun divorce proceedings, which were never finalised. She had recently given him another chance and gone back to live with him. There was a history of madness in his family, and he was found guilty but insane at the time of the killing. He was sentenced to detention at Her Majesty's pleasure.

January 28th

1945: A Plymouth businessman was having some trouble with his car and thought he probably needed new valves for it, but with wartime shortages he was not sure of how to obtain any. His wife had a solution: 'Why don't you try some of the wireless shops, dear?'

1956: A Scotsman embarking on the liner *Venus* at Plymouth, for a holiday in Las Palmas, remembered just in time that he had far more cash on him than the then current regulations permitted him to take abroad. Shortly before he was due to sail, he ran into the nearest office at the docks, waving a bunch of notes, and asked the clerk to look after them until his return. Too late he realised that he had left neither name nor address.

1964: Alec Cumming, director of the City Museum, attended a sale at Sotheby's, London, hoping to acquire a bell-shaped mug and saucer to add to the collection of Cookworthy porcelain pieces already in the 1,400-strong collection, valued at £250,000. Sadly, he came away empty-handed. He had been prepared to bid up to £200 for the mug (which realised £370) and up to £50 for the saucer (realised £200). At a sale in 1938, the same mug had only fetched £37.

January 29th

1961: On a day of exceptionally windy weather and severe gales throughout the West Country, the junction of Royal Parade and Armada Way, adjacent to Dingles department store, was recognised as the draughtiest corner in Plymouth. In two separate incidents, a man and a woman were both blown over and taken to Greenbank Hospital suffering from head injuries, but were discharged after treatment. A news vendor, who had sold newspapers from the site for some years, had to anchor his stand to a sturdy sapling in order to prevent it (and himself) from being blown away.

———————•◆•———————

1966: Frederick Vosper (74) died at his home in Stoke. He was the former chairman of Vosper's Motor House (Plymouth) Ltd, which was founded by his son Frank after the Second World War. From humble beginnings at a garage in Russell Street, they moved their main premises to Princess Square and later to Union Street, where they became the sole Ford dealer in Plymouth, with workshops at Cremyll Street. They also ran a rental and contract hire business, and were the major dealers for the area in Honda motorcycles. Before the war, Frederick Vosper had run a radio business in Russell Street.

January 30th

1913: At a very well-attended afternoon concert at the Guildhall, featuring Dame Nellie Melba, the *Western Evening Herald* wrote that:

> … she amiably maintained her position as the foremost soprano of the day. The delightful timbre, freshness, and flexibility of her glorious voice have perhaps never been heard to greater advantage, when her perfect vocalisation, grace of expression, and dramatic verve pronounced her the great artist.

Her repertoire included a duet with Mr Edmund Burke, the 'rich and resonant baritone', and music from *Lucia di Lammermoor* and *La Bohème*.

———— •◆• ————

1949: Several people walking along North Hill on this morning were bombarded by clods of earth. They thought that somebody was deliberately trying to irritate them – until they looked up at the rooftops. The culprits were half a dozen jackdaws, apparently doing the house owners a favour by clearing out debris from the gutters.

———— •◆• ————

1957: An interesting case of mixed metaphors was overheard at a business reception in the city: 'I rather think that I was helped to find my feet in my new job by the fact that I was obliged to plunge headfirst into it.'

January 31st

1938: A lady in Stoke answered her doorbell, and was horrified to find herself face-to-face with a tall stranger. He sported a long, red beard which descended to his waist, had a silk hat on his head, and had white rims around his eyes; he was demanding money. She slammed the door, but he kept on ringing until she telephoned her neighbours for help. Only the cook and the housemaid were at home, and they came round to help but ran off when they saw the extraordinary character outside. The police were called, and a constable caught the man further down the road. He was a young naval officer in disguise, doing a door-to-door collection for the Three Towns Nursing Association. Once he was advised to go back and apologise to the lady, the episode ended in laughter and she made a suitable donation.

———— • ◆ • ————

1959: Police squad cars went to investigate after receiving reports of an apparent break-in at Pearl Building. A window had been found open by the caretaker, but when the premises were inspected there was no sign of a burglary or any other crime. It was then assumed that the window had probably become unlatched during working hours, and the wind had blown it open overnight.

February 1st

1896: The Barbican Fish Market was opened. Construction of the building and sewers, and dredging part of Sutton Harbour, had taken four years. A temporary market had been held on the Parade, but it proved unpopular with nearby residents as fish slime soaked into the earth between the cobblestones and produced an overpowering smell.

———•◆•———

1956: Singer David Whitfield was appearing on a variety bill at the Royal Cinema. When the advance booking office opened in January, one eager fan booked six seats for the first house on the opening night, and another six seats for the second house, explaining that the family would be there for both shows. Then, as an afterthought, she added, 'You'd better give me some tickets for the Saturday night too. We love him, you know.' When David arrived by car for his first performance in heavy snow, fans waiting outside the stage door with autograph books helped him remove the ice from his windscreen. Disliking large hotels, he stayed in a pub in Stonehouse while in Plymouth. Signing records for more fans in Dingle's, he was delighted to meet a former mate with whom he had served on the *Black Swan* in Hong Kong during the war.

February 2nd

1906: Daniel McCoy, a hawker of Rendle Street, was charged at Plymouth Police Court with stealing an oilskin coat and six sou'westers from Arthur Skewes's shop, in Old Town Street, on the previous day. The theft had been witnessed by Skewes's assistant, William Nicholls, who had seen McCoy and a friend calling at a pawnbroker's shop in Gibbon Street with two pairs of trousers, which were refused. Nicholls had followed them to another pawnbroker in Duke Street, where the clothes were refused a second time. The men then went to Drake Street, where McCoy was seen to remove the items. Nicholls reported the theft to Mr Skewes. McCoy, who already had a police record for theft, pleaded guilty and was sentenced to three months in prison.

———— •◆• ————

1961: A motorist was caught by radar traps on Elburton Road, a long, straight stretch notorious for drivers exceeding the speed limit. When he was stopped by the police for going too fast, he protested that he should have been given some warning. The policeman told him that he had been warned, and when the driver disputed this, the policeman pointed to a nearby circular sign with 30 in the middle.

February 3rd

1949: Towards the end of a meeting in Plymouth, evidently of a Temperance Society or some similar gathering, one of the speakers declared that if he had his way, he would pour all the beer and whisky there was into the river. Proceedings then concluded with the singing of a hymn, 'Shall we gather at the river?'

———— ◆ ————

1982: A warning was delivered to the City Council by county estates surveyor Andrew Smy, who claimed that plans currently under discussion for the future use of empty land on Roborough Industrial Estate could be detrimental to job prospects for the city. It was one of three sites being investigated as a temporary solution to the problem of travellers camping illegally at Lipson Vale, on land where the county was intending to build a new £5,250,000 comprehensive school. Smy, whose duties included planning industrial estates and boosting employment prospects, told the committee that he could not think of a worse way to change the prestige of Roborough than to 'introduce gypsies', especially as he was in the process of making arrangements to show the site to some major national firms who were potentially interested in investing there.

February 4th

1949: Complaints regarding insect damage to about fifty Corporation houses at Swilly and Mount Gould were discussed in a report from the Housing Manager to the Housing Committee. The problem was caused by old timber having been used; nearby houses built around the same time, between 1919 and 1925, were subsequently going to be inspected to see if they had a similar problem. Chairman Alderman W.A. Miller said they would spray affected woodwork, which could be done without having to move tenants. Nevertheless, the problem had not been sorted by the summer, with one Swilly resident declaring that their bedroom suites had been ruined by insects. They had lost most of their possessions in the Blitz and had purchased new furniture with war damage compensation, only to see it ruined. They feared they would never have the money to replace it, and demanded further compensation from the Corporation.

An anonymous letter was received in June by the Housing Department, advising residents of affected houses to place a large bowl of beer in the middle of the floor at night, with sticks leading from the bowl to the floor. In that way, when the beetles climbed to the top of the stick, they would fall in the bowl and drown, and all would be thus disposed of within a week.

February 5th

1880: A sailor from HMS *Valorous* who had come ashore was arrested for theft. As the officers led him away, they were set on by a crowd of other sailors, soldiers and women. Although some law-abiding marines came to the assistance of the police, they were considerably outnumbered by the mob and were overpowered. Some tried to drag the sailor into a nearby stationer's shop and help him escape, but the crowd followed them, and the place was soon wrecked. Several people on both sides suffered serious injuries, before police reinforcements restored order and arrested some of the ringleaders.

———— • ◆ • ————

1915: Lily Ford (22), 'an unfortunate', was charged by Plymouth magistrates with concealing a deserter. Thomas Jenkins of the Royal Marines, who had previously served a sentence for living on Lily's improper earnings, pleaded guilty to deserting and was handed over to the military authorities. He had been living in her room for five weeks, and was found concealed in a cupboard when a policeman went to search the house. His uniform was discovered underneath Lily's bed. She pleaded guilty to the offence and was sentenced to fourteen days' hard labour.

February 6th

1960: A Plympton schoolmaster asked his class if they would write an essay on 'Things I am thankful for'. One boy wrote in his, 'I am thankful for my glasses. They keep the boys from hitting me and the girls from kissing me.'

1961: Tombola games at St Boniface Church, St Budeaux, were stopped after anonymous complaints were made by a parishioner to the Bishop of Plymouth, Dr Norman Clarke, about games of chance being played for prize or reward. The bishop declared that he himself was opposed to any form of gambling sponsored by the church, although he denied claims that he was prepared to disassociate himself personally from the parish if they continued. The tombola had been launched the previous summer, and, according to the Revd John Porter, vicar at St Boniface, it had proved very popular. In an average week, it was generally raising about £15 for parish funds. He said he was 'not personally in agreement' with the bishop's views on what he called controlled gambling, which he was at pains to stress was always supervised by the Social Committee 'with the utmost scrutiny'.

February 7th

1959: Messrs Bowden & Sons, one of the longest-established Plymouth jewellers, closed their shop at Mutley Plain and moved to Royal Parade. The business had been founded in 1869 when Frederick Bowden acquired a watch-making firm at George Street from Jabez Shepheard and expanded it to include jewellery retail and repair. Towards the end of the century, two of Bowden's sons joined him, and they moved to larger premises in the same street in 1903. They remained there until the shop was destroyed in the Blitz, and, after working from temporary accommodation for eight years, they moved to Mutley Plain in 1951. Bowden's remained a family-run concern until another Frederick Bowden, great-grandson of the founder, retired in 1989 and sold it to another local jewellery business, Messrs Michael Spiers.

———— •◆• ————

1960: One of the members of Plympton Rotary Club overheard a conversation between his wife and Denis, their 9-year-old son. 'Denis, you use more hair cream than Daddy does,' she told him. 'I know,' he replied, 'I've got more hair.'

February 8th

1953: Offers of free car washes for the first customers to purchase new branded petrol soon drew large queues to a garage in the city. One man even arrived on a bicycle to ask the pump attendant if it was true. When told that it was, he pedalled away and returned a little later to take his place in the by now ever-growing queue – in a mud-bespattered car.

———◆———

1954: A group of students from Royal Naval Engineering College, Manadon, went to see *Aladdin*, the pantomime playing at the Palace Theatre. One of them threw a firecracker on the stage, which landed perilously close to the foot of one of the drapes. Nat Jackley, who was playing the Dame, singed his hand after removing it. The youngsters had already interrupted the show by firing peas from peashooters at the principal performers, who were said to be 'exposing tempting anatomical features'. One of the party had a soda water siphon with him, but, fortunately, thought better of using it. However, after the firecracker incident, a member of the management came and ordered those responsible to leave immediately, and they were threatened with disciplinary action.

February 9th

1957: At a Golden Jubilee celebration dinner of the Dickens Fellowship, Mr W.J. Oats, Lord Mayor, said (in reply to Miss Pryor who had proposed the toast) that he was amazed at those who advocated retaining the 'hovels of the Barbican'. Visitors and tourists, he maintained, did not go to see old buildings, but wanted to see the Mayflower stone, the Hoe, and have their photos taken under Drake's statue. To retain the Barbican's old dwellings would be to degrade the city. In other speeches, he declared that the 'hovels will have to come down', and it was 'time to stop this nonsense of preserving something because it was built in the Elizabethan era'.

Not everyone agreed with him. In March, while addressing the Devon & Cornwall Liberal Federation, John Foot said that the city fathers were 'pulling down the Barbican merely to lay their hands on a few miserable subsidies'. For the next few weeks, arguments raged for and against preserving the Elizabethan quarter, and in June the Old Plymouth Society received an assurance that the Housing Committee would recommend the City Council to accept proposals to preserve houses of historic interest in New Street and Looe Street. Later that year, the Plymouth Barbican Association was founded with this very aim in mind.

February 10th

1950: One item of mail delivered to the Corporation's offices was a postcard sent from Birmingham, Alabama, addressed to 'Government of Plymouth, England', demanding the execution of 26 million people on religious grounds. The writer had 'annotated' the stamps, marking one of President John Adams, ATHEIST, and one of President Thomas Jefferson, INFIDEL. Needless to say, the card went speedily into the right place – the bin.

———— ◆ ————

1959: Pasley Street, Stoke, was known as 'the happiest street in Plymouth'. The street parties, which had been held to commemorate the Queen's Coronation almost six years earlier, had been such a success that they inaugurated what was to become something of a local tradition. Since the summer of 1953, a committee of residents had continued to organise an annual party for children, which included entertainment and a present for everyone attending, followed by a dinner for all the adults. Even people who had moved out of the street kept in touch with their friends and returned for the occasion every year, bringing their children along to share in the fun.

February 11th

1860: The town's first Co-operative opened in an upstairs room in Catte Street. Initially it was only open on Saturday and Wednesday evenings, but as its popularity increased, it opened on additional evenings. On 19 September, it moved to new premises at Kinterbury Street. This better accommodation included a ground-floor shop, a storeroom, and a first-floor room for use as an office, committee room and a library.

———•◆•———

1938: North Road station witnessed an unrehearsed 'pageant of politics' as the Cornish Riviera Express arrived this afternoon. Lady Astor, MP for Plymouth Sutton, stepped out from the rear of the train, while Colonel Henry Guest, MP for Plymouth Drake, emerged from one of the middle compartments, and Jimmy Moses, his predecessor, boarded to go and visit Camborne, the constituency he planned to contest at the next general election. (In the end, Moses did not do so, partly owing to ill-health and partly as the outbreak of war delayed the election for five years.)

———•◆•———

1954: Overheard at St Budeaux, a woman who had found a novel way to get the housework done: 'I've finished all my spring cleaning. No trouble at all. I just had one or two of those vacuum demonstrators in, dear.'

February 12th

1944: The Manadon Field Hospital, Manadon Vale, was opened. Built by the United States Construction Battalion the previous year, when the US Army arrived in Devon to prepare for the D-Day landings, it had accommodation for 250 patients. Facilities for dental and general surgery, X-rays, and orthopaedic and traumatic injuries, were provided by equipment imported from America. Casualties were less than expected and it became more of a general hospital. It closed in August 1945, reopening two years later as a temporary hostel for British and Polish workers. The buildings were demolished in the early 1950s.

———◆———

1957: A lady had just been shopping and was putting the purchases in her car. While arranging everything on the back seat, she put a couple of items on the roof and then forgot about them. Walking down the street a few minutes later, she remembered that she had left a pound of mushrooms and a bag of tomatoes on the car. As it was raining, she did not want them to get any wetter than they must be already. She dashed back to find the tomatoes where she had left them, but somebody had evidently helped themselves to the mushrooms.

February 13th

1953: A member of the Young Wives' Association, Crownhill, who used to run tea parties and social events for the elderly, called on one lady to ask if she would like an invitation to their next do. She eagerly accepted, then asked with some hesitation whether she could have a ticket for her boyfriend as well. Two tickets were immediately issued and the lady duly turned up with said boyfriend on her arm. To the member's astonishment, both of them were the same age – 91.

———— • ◆ • ————

1978: It was rumoured in the city that the statue of Sir Francis Drake was about to be replaced by one of Sir Walter Raleigh. Visions of 'Raleigh Circus' and the 'Raleigh Cinema' were conjured up. A very surprised City Council spokesman said it was 'news to him', and doubted it would meet with much support, if any. The story had its origins in a letter which William Bartlett of Plymstock had published in the *Illustrated London News*, commenting on and correcting a recent article which had suggested that Puritans 'would strongly have approved Walter Raleigh's playing at bowls as he waited for the Spanish Armada'.

February 14th

1931: The Bishop of Plymouth officiated at a special evening service at St Gabriel's Church, Mutley, during which he dedicated the recently completed carved sanctuary panelling. Created and erected in memory of past members of the congregation, it consisted of carved panels in a reredos around the walls, with a canopy for the Cross.

1938: Mr J. Harding's aquarium shop, in Mutley Plain, took charge of the largest importation of goldfish by a local business in Plymouth. Over 3,000 arrived from Italy, coming by way of Newhaven. Although they had been four days in transit, there were no casualties. They were packed in tins of about 3ft in diameter, which were covered with straw and protected by blankets. In size they varied from small to half-pounders for putting in garden ponds. They had to be starved before transportation, and were purged before leaving Italy, so they would arrive in better condition. At Newhaven their water was changed, but they were given no food. This time of year was regarded as the best for importing them. When they were bred in England, said Mr Harding, they remained a brown colour until about eighteen months old, but the Italian ones were 'gilded from the earliest youth'.

February 15th

1948: Hugh Dalton, who had been Chancellor of the Exchequer in the first post-war Labour government (until he was asked to resign after leaking budget secrets to the press three months previously), came to Plymouth so he could see how the reconstruction of the city centre and outlying areas was taking shape. He was still smarting after recent criticism from the opposition leader, Winston Churchill, for his 'profligate expenditure'. In a party political broadcast on the radio, delivered on 21 February, he referred to what he had seen while walking around the city. 'Plymouth was as badly blitzed by the Germans as any city in the country,' he said. He then continued:

> Plymouth has a Labour Council now. I visited some of their splendid new housing estates. I went into the houses and talked to the tenants. I saw happy faces there and healthy children. That famous city is rising from the ruins, more spacious, more beautiful and better planned than ever it was in the old days. These new houses get a larger subsidy and cheaper loans under this Labour government than ever before. Profligate expenditure? No, homes for brave men and women who stood up to Hitler.

February 16th

1948: A small boy came home from school after having just had his first lesson in Civics. Having learned how Plymouth Corporation provided them with gas, electricity, water, buses, education and other services, he was most impressed. 'Daddy, I've been wondering,' he asked his father, 'who does most for us, God or the City Council?'

1953: Notice spotted in a butcher's window: 'Pre-war sausages for sale.'

1957: A schoolboy claimed that he had been watching a flying saucer, at cloud level, over houses in Mannamead. He said it had no lights and was making no noise, and had a diameter twice that of the moon.

1958: A group of people were enjoying a country walk along a narrow lane near the River Yealm, when one began listening attentively as they reached a corner. 'Better stand in near the hedge,' he told the rest of them. 'There's somebody coming on horseback.' The group duly came to a halt and stood close to the hedge, waiting for the riders to appear, but none did. The 'riders' that they had heard turned out to be two teenage girls wearing stiletto heels.

February 17th

1956: While carrying out its spring window dressing, a large city department store was filled with bird music from BBC records played on concealed gramophones near the entrances. Shoppers, and a ginger cat who wandered in, were extremely puzzled at being unable to see any evidence of birds.

———◆·———

1957: Several people walking on the Hoe were annoyed to see green stains on the base of the Naval War Memorial. Students from the Plymouth and Devonport Technical College were blamed, though they were innocent as the marks turned out to be verdigris. The students had, however, already attracted adverse publicity that week. The Lord Mayor, Alderman Oats, was to have reviewed the Rag Parade on the previous day, but boycotted it after what became known as the 'night of paint brushes'. Several hundred pounds' worth of damage was caused when traffic signs, zebra crossings, Belisha beacons and war memorials in and around the city centre were daubed, some with the giveaway slogan 'Don't gag the rag'. After the Rag Committee was threatened with prosecutions for the costs of paint removal, students were sent out with supplies of turpentine to carry out a clean-up operation. Raymond Dodd, the Rag Committee president, said it was the work of 'unauthorised students'.

February 18th

1866: Charles Bazeley, aged 2 months, was baptised at Stoke Damerel parish church. He later became a baker, but was best remembered as a rather eccentric busker in the years immediately following the First World War. He wandered around the Devonport streets, entertaining the public with his performances on various instruments, assumed to be mouth organ, Jew's harp, or pennywhistle – or possibly all three. It is assumed that he was self-taught, and 'the noises that emanated from the instrument(s) could never be set to music'. Nevertheless, he was something of a local character, and would end his performances declaring, 'Oh be careful, oh be careful, be careful where there's none,' or 'I'm Billy Muggins, commonly known as Old Juggins.' His act would then finish with a little dance or a handstand against a nearby wall, after which he would quickly remove his cap and hold it out to the audience for any coppers they could spare. He died in 1923, aged 57.

* ◆ *

1948: A gift from the people of the Fiji Islands, in the shape of 6,000 tins of pineapple, were distributed to pensioners in the wards of Crownhill, St Aubyn, Nelson and Compton, on production of their old age pension books.

February 19th

1938: For a while, throwing tramp parties had been proving very popular in Plymouth. Everybody dressed up in old, tattered clothes to attend, and a good time was had by all, despite the occasional difficulties – such as getting to the house in which the party was held without being recognised by one's friends. However, on this evening, one such party resulted in a joke which might have killed the evening stone dead if not handled properly. A policeman rang the doorbell and complained to the host that he had just seen a number of very suspicious characters entering the house, and requested an explanation. Just in time, he revealed that he was not a genuine member of the force, but a neighbour who had chosen to dress up as something other than a tramp.

———◆———

1949: While watching Plymouth Argyle playing Blackburn Rovers at Home Park, Joseph Sammells (40), of Pennycross, collapsed and was taken to hospital, later dying after suffering a heart attack. After the same match, Arthur Jones, of Ladysmith Road, collapsed in the car park and was also rushed to hospital, but was sent home after treatment.

February 20th

1856: William Vaughan, who had been consecrated Bishop of Plymouth the previous summer, bought a portion of Fivefields, Eldad Hill for £3,904, intending it to be the site for the new Plymouth Cathedral. The Church of St Mary and St Boniface, Wyndham Street West, had been elevated to cathedral status when the Diocese of Plymouth was created in 1850, but Vaughan decided that a larger building was needed. After a tender of £3,904 from the architects Joseph and Charles Hansom was accepted, work began on 22 June, though there were construction problems, in the early days, with subsidence (caused by a naval officer who fired new heavy Turkish man-o'-war guns in Plymouth Sound). The clergy moved in in September 1857, and the cathedral was opened at the Feast of the Annunciation in March 1858.

———◆———

1907: The Prince and Princess of Wales, later King George V and Queen Mary, arrived at Devonport for a three-day visit, during which they stayed at Admiralty House. On the second day, they opened an extension to the dockyard, and were presented with a solid gold casket containing an illuminated plan of the extension on vellum. In the evening, there was a grand military tattoo on Mount Wise, and, on the last day, the Prince inspected the Royal Marine Light Infantry.

February 21st

1864: A Service of Consecration took place at the synagogue in Catherine Street; it is the oldest Ashkenazi synagogue of central European origin in the English-speaking world. Some Jewish families had settled in Plymouth in about 1740 but had to wait for their own place of worship for over twenty years, when a lease was granted to Samuel Champion in 1762. The building was delayed by financial troubles but was completed in 1784. Fifty years later, the freehold was transferred from the mayor and commonalty to seven members of the congregation for the sum of £100.

———•◆•———

1957: Mr and Mrs Rees bought a bunch of bananas from a fruiterer in the city. When they took it home, they found it contained a cocoon with a colony of ninety-eight baby spiders. Curious to know more, they took it to the City Museum where it was examined by Mr C.V. Adams, keeper of Natural History. He reported that only three were still alive. Only ¼in across, they were too small to survive in a colder climate. Had they lived, they would have grown into 'huge hairy tropical spiders of the type generally associated with tarantulas', but would not have been particularly dangerous.

February 22nd

1956: Plymouth Central Library, the interior of which had been destroyed in the Blitz of 1941, was reopened by Peter Scott, the naturalist and son of Plymouth-born explorer Sir Robert Falcon Scott ('of the Antarctic'). As there was no room large enough in the building to accommodate all the councillors and guests who had been invited to the ceremony, Scott opened it formally from the North Gallery in the museum next door, after which everyone went out and into the library. The public were admitted on the following day.

1956: Two newly-married couples were among those leaving on board the motor liner *Venus* for holidays in Madeira and Tenerife, the bridegrooms being aged 69 and 61 respectively. The younger couple, from Leeds, had married in the Leeds Register Office the previous day and had left their passport there, only realising after they had boarded their train for King's Cross. As the express went through Doncaster, the couple threw an SOS on the platform, and the stationmaster passed it to the police. The police obtained the passport from the register office, put it on the train, and the couple picked it up from London in the nick of time before taking the boat train for Plymouth.

February 23rd

1832: James Tregear, a licensed Devonport postmaster, appeared at the Guildhall, 'convicted in mitigated penalty and costs, £6 19s, for neglecting to attend to pass and pay his Post Horse Duty Accounts, at the time and place specified on the front of his stamp office weekly account.' In default of payment, he was committed to Exeter Gaol for six months.

———◆———

1956: A quotation displayed on a board outside a church in Mutley Plain, opposite a pedestrian crossing, read, rather appropriately: 'THOSE WITHOUT VISION WILL PERISH.'

———◆———

1957: John Gilbert, of Plymouth Philatelic Auctions, Lockyer Street, offered for sale, at auction, a book of postage stamps which had originally cost 3s 9d. They had been purchased a few weeks earlier at a local post office by a man who lived just outside Plymouth, and who was careful to preserve his anonymity, even to the extent of deliberately not coming to the auction. What made the book so remarkable was that it included one pane of six imperforate 2½d stamps. Bids had been anticipated from collectors in the USA and Canada, as well as throughout Britain, and after fierce bidding the item was knocked down at £525.

February 24th

1956: The Traders Road Transport Association held their annual dinner at the Duke of Cornwall Hotel. Providing the entertainment was a band playing appropriate tunes for each course. While the guests tucked in, the band played 'Three Little Fishes'; for the roast chicken, 'Chick Chick Chick Chick Chicken'; for the fruit salad, 'Yes! We Have No Bananas'; and for the demitasse, 'They've got an Awful Lot of Coffee in Brazil'. During the mushroom soup course they played a selection from *South Pacific*, as the conductor could not come up with anything suitable. He said afterwards that he had considered 'Cool Water', but thought that might be verging on the libellous.

———◆•———

1995: Animal rights campaigners claimed victory after their protests halted shipments of livestock from Millbay Docks to the Continent, and MT Shipping announced it would withdraw from the trade forthwith. Protesters had gathered there since November 1994, and by the time they called off their action, the cost of policing had exceeded £235,000, taken 18,000 man-hours, and involved 150 officers at a time. Most of the action was peaceful and law-abiding, though violence had flared on two occasions when rocks were thrown at lorries. Protest organisers claimed that troublemakers, rather than genuine animal rights supporters, were to blame.

February 25th

1992: There was general surprise after Alan Clark, Conservative MP for Sutton, announced that he intended to stand down at the end of the then current parliament. Having represented the constituency since February 1974, where he was defending a majority of 4,013, he said in a statement that he felt it was time for a change. There was speculation that while his abrasive style had been admired by Margaret Thatcher, the previous Prime Minister, her successor John Major, did not share her view and Clark did not see any ministerial future for himself at Westminster. There were also rumours that he had been irritated by insinuations that he had not pressed the Ministry of Defence strongly enough on securing the eagerly coveted contract to refit the Trident submarine for Devonport. The constituency party selected Gary Streeter as its candidate, and, in the following general election, held in April, he held the seat with a considerably increased majority. Clark later regretted having left the political fray, and returned to Westminster in 1997 as MP for Kensington and Chelsea, but died two years later from a brain tumour at the age of 71.

February 26th

1880: A serious gas explosion occurred at a shop belonging to Mr Rowse, ironmonger, at the junction of East and Old Town Streets. An assistant had taken a naked light too close to a leaking gas pipe. The shop front was completely blown out, with the premises and stock completely destroyed, while several other assistants were badly burnt or injured, and had to be taken to hospital. The windows of most other shops and a hotel in the neighbourhood were also broken.

———◆———

1956: Alola (23), a Spanish girl working at Chipperfield's Circus during its Plymouth season, had previously been a human shell, being fired out of a gun during performances. Now presenting a wild animal act, she was thought to be the only woman trainer of wild cats in England. She was devoted to lions and tigers, even to the point of keeping Ruth, a 6-month-old lion cub, in her own caravan. He had been born at Chipperfield's Farm, and she described him as a perfect pet, no more trouble than a cat, sleeping on her bed at night and being fed with milk from a bottle every morning. The only animals of which she was not fond, she admitted, were mice.

February 27th

1952: Thomas Eames (31) killed his wife Muriel (26) with a table knife which he had sharpened into a two-edged dagger at his place of work. He had married her bigamously in 1947 and they had a child, but the relationship soon deteriorated and she left him for another man. She returned home briefly to tell him that she intended to marry the new man in her life, and, as she moved towards him to say goodbye, he put his arm around her and stabbed her in the back. Found guilty of murder, he was hanged at Bristol on 15 July, the last man to be sentenced to death in Devon and go to the gallows.

———— ◆ ————

1960: A goldfish was swimming in its pond in a Mannamead garden one morning, when the family cat scooped it out and left it for dead alongside. The sorrowing small boy who owned the fish found a suitable box in which to bury it. Four hours later, at teatime, he suddenly had second thoughts and wondered whether the fish really was dead. His father exhumed the little coffin, looked inside, saw the fish wriggling, and returned it to the pond where it carried on swimming.

February 28th

1957: A baker in St Budeaux was asked by a customer if he could make a suitable 'divorce cake' for a party that he and his ex-wife were planning. He had never had such a request before, but soon hit on a novel way. He made a round cake, cut it in two, and placed the halves back-to-back. He then iced it and applied the man's name in blue on one half and the woman's in pink on the other. Between the segments he made a small plaque, inscribed, 'Here's To Freedom'.

———— • ◆ • ————

1960: The City Museum & Art Gallery was staging a major exhibition of the works of Victorian animal painter James Ward. After walking round and viewing the pictures, several visitors approached the curator to point out that they were sure one item in the catalogue must have been hung upside down. 'Curing Hams', a watercolour of hams hanging by chains from a beam, definitely looked somewhat wrong. On close examination, the picture was revealed to have been displayed correctly after all – but the artist's signature was upside down in the top left-hand corner. He evidently had it wrong when he signed it.

February 29th

1888: The Corporation held a ceremony outside the Guildhall to accept delivery of a steam fire engine which had been donated to the town by the Western Insurance Company. It was christened 'The Western' by Mrs Perossi, wife of the company chairman, and then handed over to Superintendent Wreford of the Plymouth Fire Brigade, who tried it out by discharging several streams of water over the Guildhall. Costing about £650, the engine was capable of raising steam from cold water in about six or seven minutes. It weighed only 20cwt and could thus be drawn by a small group of men or a pair of horses if it needed to go a long distance. It carried a wide selection of suction and delivery hoses, which could be connected to high-pressure water mains in the street, and was capable of throwing 360 gallons per minute up to a height of 150ft. Plymouth had had a civilian fire brigade since 1863, with a station in Tavistock Road, but there had been several major fires in the towns and West Country in recent years, and the coroner had commented on the lack of a well-equipped service, particularly after the Exeter theatre fire tragedy of 1887, which claimed 186 lives.

March 1st

1945: A woman travelling from Paddington asked the naval officer in her compartment to tell her when they reached Plymouth. 'You won't miss it, Madam,' he assured her, 'because when we get there it will be raining.' He was right.

———◆———

1956: A woman sent in a claim for damage to clothing which she alleged had been set alight while being aired in front of the kitchen fire. An insurance official came to visit her in her third-floor flat, where she showed him the bathtub full of charred remains of underclothes. He made a list of everything, with approximate replacement values, and left. On his way out of the building he met another tenant, who stopped him and asked if he had been seeing 'Mrs So-and-so' about the fire. When the official said he had, she told him that no such thing had taken place there. 'The fire was in my own flat,' she insisted. 'As I am not insured, I threw all the burned clothing out in the backyard. That's where she got it from.' The official went back to inform the opportunist claimant that she would not receive a penny, and she was lucky not to find herself facing prosecution for fraud.

March 2nd

1945: It had been several months since the last air raids, when the sound of a wailing siren broke over the city early on this evening. Several part-time personnel from the Plymouth Report Centre rang to ask if they would be required for duty. In one cinema the film stopped, and a sign flashed on the screen to announce that the air-raid warning was being sounded. Several people immediately left the cinema, and a little later the programme was halted again for the 'All Clear' message. At another cinema, the manager put the 'Air Raid' slide on the screen, but two minutes later realised it was a false alarm, and followed it up with the 'Raiders Past' sign. It was later established that the warning had been accidentally activated by somebody at the Report Centre. At least one member of the public believed it meant the end of the war.

———— •◆• ————

2004: A survey by Unilever found that Plymouth was the wettest city in England. A former meteorological office confirmed this finding, saying that prevailing winds across this country were from the south and south-west. When winds blew from the area or depressions came in, they picked up much moisture over the Atlantic, and south-west England therefore received much of this rain.

March 3rd

1942: Six City of Plymouth police and fire officers attended an investiture at Buckingham Palace where they were presented with the British Empire Medal for bravery and gallant conduct during the bombing raids of the previous year. They were Inspector Herbert Beswick, Constable Robert Eakers, Aircraftman (formerly Constable) Alan Hill, William Edgecombe, Arthur Larson, and Pte Leslie Stephens, a former messenger in the fire brigade. Stephens was, at that time, the youngest person ever to have received an award at an investiture.

———— ◆ ————

1953: The Revd C.H.D. Grimes, vicar of Newton Ferrers, reported in his parish magazine the tale of two ladies who took their dog for a walk on the road alongside the cemetery at Efford, where a burial was in progress. The animal, with a ball in his mouth, could not resist joining the mourners around the grave. As the vicar pronounced the words of committal, and the earth was thrown in, the dog dropped his ball in the grave. Nobody could retrieve it, or perhaps they thought it inappropriate to try and do so. On subsequent walks in the area he would return to the same spot, running and scratching around the grave, trying to locate his missing toy.

March 4th

1953: A Plymouth schoolmaster returned from a few days away over half-term. His break had not gone according to plan. He had arranged to meet a friend at Weston-super-Mare, and, on arrival at North Road station to catch his train, found he had left his money at home. There was just time to dash back and collect his wallet. As he settled down for the journey, he found that he had left his tobacco and pipe behind. Deprived of one of his major comforts, he arrived at his hotel in a less than benign mood, and went to spruce up for the rendezvous – when he discovered that he had also forgotten his comb and razor. Having replaced them, he set off to meet his friend, but when he arrived at the appointed place there was no sign of him. After making a telephone call, he found his friend had forgotten the date and could not come until the following day.

———— ◆ ————

1954: At a dinner dance, an eliminating quickstep took place. About thirty couples were still left on the floor after various eliminations. The MC then requested that all couples who had not been to church the previous Sunday go and sit down. Only one couple remained.

March 5th

1906: 'Ahrensmeyer', a cowboy hypnotist, was the star attraction at the Palace Theatre of Varieties all week. To advertise the show, he drove blindfolded through the streets of the town.

———•◆•———

1954: When Maison Terry, a hairdresser's at Tavistock Road, was fitting out its premises, the lighting went up in two stages – with the second part of the sign illuminated first. The shop then received a call from a prankster, asking if Mr Maison had just died.

———•◆•———

1957: A visitor to the city centre on a torrentially wet day asked where he could find the nearest pub, and was told of a very good one around the corner. When informed that it was called Noah's Ark, he answered, 'And it's about time you Plymothians got round to building one!'

———•◆•———

1965: Plymouth Chamber of Trade and Commerce reported several rather odd enquiries they had recently received. These included a letter from America requesting 'a genuine sample of Gulf Stream water as it reaches the English coast', which was referred to the Marine Biological Association, and one from Italy asking for a list of toy factories in the Plymouth area, as 'we are much interested in little soldiers of all types and materials'.

March 6th

1945: Although the war had been synonymous with food shortages in the city, at last a glut was reported – Seville oranges. Several city fruiterers had piles rotting in their windows, to the point where some were considering throwing up to half of them away. The impediment to greater sales was a shortage of sugar, the vital ingredient which housewives needed in order to make marmalade with them. The Ministry of Food was advised to send no more to Plymouth for the time being. One shopkeeper said:

> I've had mine in for ten days and sold only 50 per cent. The percentage wouldn't have been as high as this if a number of people hadn't bought them with the intention of trying to eat them. I don't know how they got on but they didn't come back for more.

Among remedies which had been suggested were removing the pips, cutting up the oranges, boiling and bottling them with the juice and then sealing them the same way as one would with other fruit. Or, for the lucky ones who were still managing to get any sugar, preparing them for breakfast the night before, just as they would with grapefruit.

March 7th

1791: A double tragedy occurred at Buckland Monachorum, when Mr W. Good and his daughter were crossing a ford on horseback. The horse lost its footing and Miss Good fell off. Her father tried to save her, but both were swept away by the water and drowned.

———◆———

1950: At a City Council meeting, Alderman Bert Medland, who had been Labour MP for Plymouth Drake until retiring at the general election the previous month (when his seat was abolished in boundary changes), spoke on the state of the Corporation's Barbican properties, alleging that some members had been unduly penny-wise. 'And that is a point for the chairman of the Finance Committee,' he declared, raising his voice as he pointed at a relaxed-looking Alderman Randolph Baker on the Conservative side. 'Are you addressing me?' Baker asked. 'Then don't shout.' Medland apologised to the Lord Mayor. 'I thought he was asleep. He was looking like a dormouse.'

———◆———

1953: As an influenza epidemic swept the city, it was reported that one infected married couple hit on a novel way of deciding who did the cooking. They kept a thermometer by the bed, and agreed that it should be the job of whoever had the lower temperature.

March 8th

1954: Chipperfield's Circus was at Central Park for one week from this day, and attracted about 80,000 visitors. Everything went smoothly apart from one minor hitch before the second house on the first day, when a lorry bringing the cannon into the arena became bogged down in mud and the show was delayed for fifteen minutes.

When the cavalcade stopped at a Plympton garage on its way to Central Park on Sunday 7 March, 95 gallons of petrol were purchased, and the subsequent parade brought out vast crowds in the city, comparable to those normally seen at a royal visit.

Long queues formed at Dingles for tickets, with one lady waiting patiently for over two hours. It was assumed that she was taking her grandchildren, until she said that it was her 83-year-old mother who wanted to go. Meanwhile, a gang of youngsters collected a pile of free newspapers issued by the publicity department, and sold the lot at 2d each by going door-to-door around Pennycomequick.

One evening, two smartly dressed ladies, one in a fur coat, were seen leaving the circus ground and stopped outside Salisbury Villas. They removed their shoes and scraped the mud off their soles – on the bumper of a parked car.

March 9th

1949: A Labour councillor in the city calculated that he had had 1,700 callers at his home during the previous four years. This had not been achieved without some wear and tear on the fittings in the house, and his wife had just put in an estimate for a new carpet.

———— •◆• ————

1974: The highlight of Plymouth students' Rag Week, raising money to provide a holiday for underprivileged children, took place. Activities included 'silly walks' (inspired by the anarchic TV comedy show *Monty Python's Flying Circus*) in the suburbs, twelve men in white coats cleaning the zebra crossing in New George Street, and others doing likewise at nearby bus stops. Four more ambitious souls, wearing helmets and rucksacks, used ropes to climb 'Mount New George Street' and successfully reached the summit, the flagpole by the Civic Centre. At the top of the street, entertainment for shoppers was provided by the Tone Deaf Choir. During the previous month, the Rag Committee had tried to book an excursion train to London and back, on the basis that hiring a 'rag special' would cost £1,000, and with a full load of 450 passengers would make a profit of £250. The break-even figure would have been 300, but only 100 people were interested in going.

March 10th

1945: It was revealed that Plymouth had been hit by a wave of practical jokers, with the Electricity Department being 'impersonated' by an unknown individual ringing up residents in Hartley, saying, 'This is the Electricity Department speaking. We are testing the lights in your neighbourhood. Would you mind going outside and seeing if the street lamps are on?' At least two such requests were reported to the Electrical Committee from Vapron Road. One woman was suspicious and summoned her nephew to the telephone, at which point the mystery caller vanished.

Mr H. Midgeley, the City Engineer, told a *Western Independent* reporter that the public should be warned. The idea was ridiculous, as there was no street lighting in the area; moreover, the lighting was not controlled centrally, and any testing would be done locally with somebody on the spot to note the results. Additionally, the department would not go around testing by ringing up private individuals. A similar incident was reported, in which a local businessman apparently received a call from the Telephone Department asking him to step back a couple of paces from his phone and whistle. He did, only for the caller to thank him and promise to send a packet of canary seed.

March 11th

1956: There was a happy ending for the black and white spaniel taken into the home for dogs and cats at Prince Rock. He was thought to be a stray after he was found by police wandering around Camel's Head early in February. The staff reckoned he was aged between 6 and 8, and called him 'Old Man'. He was becoming ill with grief, howling and whimpering all day, then lying down motionless with apparent exhaustion. He showed every sign of having come from a good home, was well groomed and used to being fussed over, and they decided that if the owner did not come forward within a week or so, they would have to try hard to find another home for him – otherwise there was a risk that he might pine to death.

Luckily, after his picture appeared in the papers, 'Gyp' was recognised by his master and they were soon reunited. He would have been returned home but his collar was missing. There had recently been several cases of children befriending dogs, then stealing their collars and selling them. One woman in Prince Rock had had to buy no less than six new ones for her dog in only ten months.

March 12th

1836: The house of Fort-Major James Watson (70), at the Citadel, was destroyed after a fire started just before midnight. It was probably caused by a servant who had put some wood to dry on the hobs of the parlour grate. It was a windy night, and, after a sudden gust came down the chimney, flames spread everywhere. After the alarm was raised, most of the people inside managed to escape – including the Major's blind son (who was helped to safety by the servants), three of his daughters and the family surgeon. Tragically, the Major tried to rescue two of his daughters from their bedroom on the second floor, but all three were overcome by smoke and burned to death. By the time dawn broke, only the bare walls and fireplace remained.

———— • ◆ • ————

1956: A boy at Kings Tamerton had planted a bulb in a cocoa tin filled with earth, kept it in a warm place, and watered it until green shoots began to appear. Presenting it to his mother as a gift on Mothering Sunday, he apologised for the daffodil not having yet come into flower. The recipient did not have the heart to tell him that the bulb was actually an onion.

March 13th

1787: The transport ships *Friendship* and *Charlotte*, carrying male and female convicts bound for Australia, set sail from the Barbican. They left to join the rest of the fleet at Portsmouth, from where they departed on 13 May. They landed with nine other ships from England on 28 January 1788 at Port Jackson, which became Sydney, New South Wales. A first British colony was established under the command of Captain Arthur Phillip, who is regarded as the father of modern Australia. The sailing from Plymouth was commemorated by a plaque near Mayflower Steps, unveiled on the 200th anniversary.

———•◆•———

1960: A man turned up for service at Plymouth Coroner's Court for an inquest on a road victim. After consulting the papers, he said, 'I ought not to be here, I'm dead.' He waved the form summoning him as a member of the jury, on which his name had been written in the space reserved for the name of the deceased.

March 14th

1973: Brazilian footballer Pelé, real name Edson Arantes do Nascimento, played Plymouth Argyle at Home Park, with his team Santos, as part of their European tour that month. Brazil, winners of the 1970 World Cup, were the then world champions, and Pelé was regarded as the greatest footballer of his day. In front of a crowd of 37,639, the match almost did not take place. Twenty minutes before kick-off, officials ordered the Santos players to remain in their dressing room while they made a last-minute demand for £2,500 more than was stipulated in the contract. Argyle chairman, Robert Daniel, initially refused, but when told bluntly that it was a case of 'no money, no match', and looking at the excited waiting spectators, he had no choice but to concede, although he refused to hand over the additional money in cash until both teams attended an after-match reception at the Holiday Inn. The game still failed to go smoothly, with the home team winning 3-0 by half-time and members of the Santos team threatening to walk off if the referee was not replaced at half-time. It took all Pelé's powers of persuasion to restore equanimity. During the second half, he and another member of his team each scored, but Argyle remained the victors, 3-2.

March 15th

1913: The steamship *Niagara* left Plymouth on her maiden voyage to call at Durban and Sydney. Among those getting on board before she left were a man and his mother, who had just arrived by train from London. The man recognised his wife and small daughters, plus a male companion, among the second-class passengers. He confronted them, struck the companion in the face, and appealed to his wife to return home, but she refused. Sobbing bitterly, the little girls were taken away by their father and grandmother, who took them back to London while their mother and companion continued their voyage.

———◆———

1957: A Devonport woman took her cat Timothy to the vet for treatment, left him there for several hours, then called back and took him home. He behaved strangely, did not seem to have any of his old habits, and would not settle in his usual chair, or eat the same food. When she looked at him she realised that he looked similar – but different. Wrapping him in a shawl, she caught the next bus for the vet again. On the journey, another woman stared at her, and then said, 'I believe that's my cat you've got there!' She was on her way to the same destination.

March 16th

1945: The NAAFI (Navy, Army and Air Force Institute) Club was opened by A.V. Alexander, First Lord of the Admiralty, at a ceremony also attended by the Lord Mayor and the Bishop of Plymouth, who performed the dedication. Established in 1921, the NAAFI had been formed to run recreational facilities for men of the armed forces and to sell goods to their families. In Plymouth, the club was situated in Nissen huts on the site of what had been the Royal Hotel on the corner of Lockyer Street. Among facilities provided were lounges, bars, a barber's shop, a dance hall, a restaurant and a reading room. The institute later became known as the Plymouth Hoe Service Club, but, after years of financial losses, it closed in September 1969.

———— • ◆ • ————

1949: A Conservative Party candidate was canvassing in her ward. To keep warm during the cold snap, she was wearing a fur coat. Calling on one woman voter, she started, 'I'm a Conservative … '. 'Oh, I can tell that,' was the reply. 'You see, the difference is that the Conservatives don't mind going round in their fur coats before the election, but the Labour Party wait until it's over before they put theirs on!'

March 17th

1768: William Cookworthy, regarded as the father of English porcelain, took out a patent for the manufacture of 'a kind of porcelain, newly invented by me, composed of moorstone or gowan, and gowan clay'. Until he discovered china clay in Cornwall in 1746, porcelain was imported from China. He took some samples back to Plymouth with him, and in 1766 set up a small factory. There is some doubt as to its location, which may have been in High Street or perhaps in the China House at Shepherd's Wharf, Coxside – although the latter was perhaps only a storage unit. Never very profitable, in 1774 he sold the business, which was amalgamated with another at Bristol as Messrs Cookworthy & Co., but he received a small royalty on every item produced there. He died in 1780 and was buried in the family vault at Westwell Street near St Andrew's Church.

1945: Seen chalked on the back of a wedding car in the city: 'AISLE ALTAR HYMN.'

1950: A Plymothian wrote his bank manager a rather wordy, pompous letter (the contents of which might have been interesting to know), asking what the current bank rate was. Back came the reply, 'The bank rate is 20 customers per hour.'

March 18th

1838: Four of the 'Tolpuddle Martyrs' sailed into Plymouth near the West Pier on the Barbican. In 1834, six Dorset farm workers were convicted for forming a trade union, and were deported to Australia for seven years' hard labour. After much lobbying on their behalf, they were pardoned and allowed home after serving just over half their sentence. James Loveless, James Brine, Thomas and John Stanfield stepped ashore at Plymouth, a regular point for former convicts on transportation ships to be brought home. A plaque was erected on the sea wall in May 1956.

1960: Prince Philip, Duke of Edinburgh, was appointed Lord High Steward of Plymouth. The wand of office was originally a broomstick costing 4*d*, painted black, adorned with a silver badge. It had been damaged during the Blitz in 1941, and, when it was presented to him, he said in a speech of thanks, 'I understand that I have to hand the wand back to the Lord Mayor for safe keeping, but it doesn't look as if you have done a very good job up to now!' On a subsequent visit to Plymouth in 1965, he was again presented with it, and said that his duties were hardly onerous: 'I am not even allowed to carry the wand.'

March 19th

1938: A mystery airman was seen giving displays over Saltram estate. In the afternoon he circled over the grounds several times and did a hazardous falling-lead impression of a machine completely out of control, before vanishing into the blue. Nobody knew who he was, but people in Plympton and Billacombe were kept very entertained.

———— ◆ ————

1954: Illusionist and conjuror Edward Victor brought his shadowgraph act to one of the Plymouth theatres. While he was staying in the city he met an amateur magician, who was keen to exchange ideas and tricks with him. After one of Victor's evening shows, they were driving home from the theatre when the other magician began to discuss one of his latest ideas. Intrigued, Mr Victor asked him for a demonstration. They stopped the car, got out, and the man began to explain his trick with much moving of hands and arms in front of the headlights, with Victor faithfully copying him. It presented a rather extraordinary spectacle to anyone passing by, and within a few minutes a police car drove up. The officer got out and enquired if there was any trouble. He thought the driver must have been the victim of a hold-up.

March 20th

1941: King George VI and Queen Elizabeth visited Plymouth for a tour of the dockyard and an inspection of the Civil Defence and Voluntary Services in Guildhall Square. The royal train arrived at Millbay station at 1.30 p.m. When a warden told the Queen 'we are keeping our chins up,' Her Majesty replied, 'It is only by keeping our chins up, as we are doing, that we shall win the war.' They left the city at about 5.30 p.m.

Just over three hours later the alert was sounded, in what was to be a prelude to the Plymouth Blitz. In less than three hours, some 125 enemy aircraft bombed the city, leaving 336 dead, fourteen of whom were babies. Overnight Plymouth became the most heavily blitzed city in Britain, and by midnight the city centre was ablaze. Fire brigades from neighbouring areas arrived, their sole navigational aid being a huge orange glow in the night. When they arrived, they found that they were only of limited help when it came to extinguishing fires, as their equipment was incompatible with that already being used in the city, and they had to rely mainly on the ordinary water mains. Further bombing raids over the next four weeks brought the death toll to 926.

March 21st

1929: The French liner *Paris* left New York for Plymouth and Le Havre. On inspection, prior to departure, one of the engine room ventilators was checked, to reveal the emaciated body of a man aged about 50. At an autopsy, the ship's surgeon said that the man had been dead for about five or six days. He had presumably stowed away in the ventilator, was overcome by fumes and heat from the engine room, and starved to death. Papers in the name of Giuseppe Panetta were found in the pockets of the discarded clothing – he was buried at sea.

1931: The *Western Evening Herald*'s 'Talk of the City' column featured a comment on the inadequacy of fire fighting, signed 'Citizen':

> Behind the news story of the local fireman who got a lift on a motor hearse to expedite his attendance at a fire is a quite serious reflection. I wonder whether the Chief Constable is perfectly satisfied with the present arrangements for manning the fire brigade.

Although he conceded that the system had worked for a number of years without any major disasters or preventable loss of life, he pointed out that it was unwise for the authorities to rely on what was obviously 'a very skeleton force of men'.

March 22nd

1880: Edward Tate, a soldier who was stationed at Bovisand, booked himself into May's Dining Rooms, Fore Street, Devonport, telling the staff he expected to stay for a week. After dinner he complained to the proprietor, Mrs May, of feeling unwell, and said he would go up to his room to lie down for a while. When he did not reappear for his tea, she went to check on him and was aghast to find him lying on the floor with his throat cut, and a razor lying nearby. She could still feel a faint pulse, and at once she called a surgeon and the police. He died a few minutes later. A suicide note was found on the body, alongside a letter stating that he was to appear before the Military Board prior to being discharged from the services.

———— ◆ ————

1884: David Davies, master of the Aberystwyth brigantine *Dreadnought*, was charged before the local Marine Board at Plymouth with drunkenness and defacement of the official logbook. The court suspended the ship's certificate for six months, and decided to report Thomas Davies, the mate, for aiding and abetting him by concealing evidence and cutting out a page from the logbook.

March 23rd

1885: The transport ship *Tamar* reached Plymouth this afternoon, at the end of an eventful journey of 25,000 miles around the Cape, returning via Suez. Several hundred passengers were on board, including a large contingent of naval prisoners. Shortly after leaving Gibraltar on the final lap, the *Tamar* was caught in a heavy gale, and one of the engines stopped working after the piston rod became bent. An official inspection was made on her arrival, prior to her final voyage to Spithead in the evening.

1948: When Stanley Leatherby (64) died, the flag on the Corporation mast was flown at half-mast. During his years in Plymouth public life he had served as mayor 1934-5, and chairman of the Education Committee for some years, as well as working on behalf of the Methodist Church and as a staunch fighter for local fishermen's rights. It was said that he enjoyed getting his name regularly in the newspapers, and he had admitted that he always loved seeing his own name in print, referring to himself as a 'blushing violet'. When he was the president of the Rotary Club, a colleague suggested that he might give an address on Modesty, a suggestion he found hilarious. His funeral took place on 27 March at St Catherine's Church.

March 24th

1938: In the morning, three film stars arrived in Plymouth from the ship *Ile de France* – Paul Lukas, Charles Butterworth, and Popeye the Sailor. The last-named was a life-sized rubber model of the spinach-eating cartoon character. On the next day, he was exhibited at Regent Cinema before being taken to London. Hollywood had despatched Popeye on a goodwill tour. As one of his sponsors said, 'You couldn't send Greta Garbo to every country in the world as a messenger of goodwill, but you can send Popeye. And Popeye is a film star.' With him he carried an autograph book which the Lord Mayor, Solomon Stephens, signed at the cinema. Butterworth agreed to pose with him for a photo, but Lukas insisted he had no wish to be photographed with Popeye.

———— ◆ ————

1949: The craftsman who cut the marble to make the pedestal for a bust of Sir Robert Falcon Scott at Devonport Technical College decided to call in and have a look at it for old time's sake, as he had not done so for many years. He met the caretaker at the entrance and told him whom he had come to see. 'And what class is he attending?' asked the caretaker helpfully.

March 25th

1865: The slightly scorched bodies of four children, Charlotte Keynes (12), her brother William (10), and their younger sisters, Bessie (4) and 18-month-old Emma, were found on their bed after flames swept through their house early on this morning in King Street. They had died from suffocation. Their widowed father, a market trader, had gone to Launceston on business the previous evening, leaving Charlotte in charge. A neighbour had been asked to keep an eye on the family, and saw them in bed late in the evening. At midnight a light was noticed in the bedroom, and it was thought that the fire must have broken out, probably in a cupboard, about an hour later. According to the *Western Morning News*: 'It was a sad scene – snow was falling without, four naked corpses were within, and the house being thronged with very poor but warm-hearted Irish, was filled with the sounds of lamentation.'

1953: A boy of 15 who had taken a clerical job in a Plymouth office a fortnight earlier gave notice. He told his boss that since coming to work for him, he had realised he did not know enough, and was going to go back to school.

March 26th

1954: A National Exhibition of Children's Art at the City Art Gallery attracted about 8,000 visitors. All appeared satisfied except for one, who evidently missed the point. On admission, he looked around him and exclaimed, 'What rubbish! I'm not going to waste time seeing that! It's just childish!'

———•◆•———

1962: Dr Richard Beeching, chairman of the British Railways Board, opened the new Plymouth station, also comprising an office block, Intercity House. It had originally opened in March 1877 as Plymouth North Road, a joint station for GWR (Great Western Railway) and LSWR (London & South Western Railway), with two platforms. Following expansion in 1908, a major rebuilding scheme (begun in 1938) was put on hold until after the Second World War. Passenger traffic increased in 1941 when Millbay Road station was closed after being destroyed by a bombing raid in 1941; work was resumed in 1956. The old LSWR Friary station was closed in September 1958 and North Road station was renamed Plymouth station. Poet and author John Betjeman was unimpressed, calling it in his introduction to *The Book of the Great Western*, 'the dullest of stations and no less dull now that it has been rebuilt in copybook contemporary'. (*See* April 2nd)

March 27th

1938: According to one breathless newspaper reporter, 'the most amazing thing which happened in Plymouth' this week (starting on this day) was the presentation of a striptease act at the Palace Theatre – and without any protests from the city's moral guardians. Miss Rosemary Andrée was 'disrobing' twice every evening as she appeared onstage in a short series of statuesque studies. 'On the face of it,' according to the *Western Independent*:

> This act was so daring that it might have roused a storm of criticism. That it did not is due to two facts. One was delicacy, and reticence with which the turn was staged, and the other the 'quiet' manner in which it was announced beforehand.

The advertisements discreetly called it 'a posing display'. The theatre management said that it was absurd to call her performance striptease, as to use such a term suggested American and French shows 'of a less artistic nature'. British 'disrobing' on stage was clearly an art form, far superior to anything America or France could possibly produce, and the star of the show invariably did so in an indisputably inoffensive manner, in 'a frame at the back without any exhibitionism whatever'.

March 28th

1896: About 200 medals were distributed among the crew of HMS *Phoebe* at Devonport, in recognition of their services in Benin in 1894. The crew had been part of an operation by the navy and Niger Coast Protectorate forces in the West African kingdom when they invaded and destroyed the town of Brohomi, on the Benin River.

1926: The police recovered two valuable horses allegedly stolen from a stable which had been broken into in the Laira district. Two youths had been seen riding them towards the countryside just outside Plymouth. A car was commandeered, and, after the area had been thoroughly searched, a witness showed the direction in which they had gone. The alleged thieves were overtaken as the chase developed 'into a race somewhat after the style of the Wild West "thrillers" beloved by kinemagoers'. Once they realised they had been outwitted, the thieves dismounted and fled across the fields, but police said they were confident of catching them. Meanwhile, the horses were recaptured and returned unharmed to the stables.

1957: Ernest English, of the Plymouth Council of Social Service, was paid a compliment by a woman praising his work for the elderly. 'You'll have one of the most wonderful funerals ever!'

March 29th

1904: Alderman John Pethick (76), a Justice of the Peace and Mayor of Plymouth between 1898 and 1900, died after an accident in his horse-drawn carriage in Lockyer Street. He was at the reins when he lost control. A former carpenter and builder, his firm Pethick Bros later built the City Museum & Art Gallery. He had been a director of the Plymouth Tramways Company.

1968: During an unseasonably warm day, a window was opened in Plymouth Magistrates' Court. A bumble bee flew in and a police officer struck it with a file. 'That was rough justice,' remarked Chairman Geoffrey Leatherby. 'We haven't tried him yet.'

1997: Yachtsman Pete Goss sailed into Plymouth Sound on his 50ft-boat *Aqua Quorum*, escorted by a flotilla of smaller craft, to the welcome of thousands on the waterfront. He had risked his life to rescue Raphael Dinelli, a French sailor competing in the Vendée Globe round-the-world yacht race. During a storm in the Southern Ocean, Goss spent two days sailing into hurricane force winds to find Dinelli, a feat for which he was later awarded the Légion d'Honneur.

March 30th

1956: It was Good Friday, and when Llewellyn Davis, proprietor of the 200-seater Lee Mill Estate cinema, applied for a licence to show the film *Kiss Me Kate* on this day, the Plympton Bench dismissed his application on the grounds that the film was unsuitable. The solicitor's plea that it was a perfectly innocent musical comedy fell on deaf ears. None of the magistrates had ever seen the film or stage play of the same name, and presumably neither they nor anybody else in court was aware, or thought it fit to mention, that it was unlikely to corrupt the morals of local movie-goers, as it was based on *The Taming of the Shrew* by a rather well-known British playwright.

———◆———

1958: Bretonside bus station, which replaced the old one in Union Street, was opened. The City Engineer, J. Paton Watson, promised it would be the finest in Britain. As it was a Sunday, business was quiet. The first passenger to use the facilities at their new location was Eric Watson, who lived on the Hoe. He was the only person to board the 5.05 a.m. Western National service No.88, as he left for Ivybridge on his way to work at Moorhaven Hospital.

March 3-1st

1861: Mr Hulm, a commercial traveller from Birmingham, had taken rooms in a lodging house in Adelaide Road. Between 10 and 11 p.m. he jumped out of the bedroom window into the balcony below. Still conscious, he was assisted upstairs and into bed. A surgeon was called to examine him, and found no evidence of broken bones or any other problems. However, by 3 a.m. the next day he was dead from internal injuries. Witnesses testified that he had seemed very depressed about business problems during the previous few days.

———◆———

1961: A shop in Frankfort Gate was seen displaying the notice 'FOREIGN GOODS' above a plate of Cornish pasties. A reporter mused whether this implied that Cornwall was a foreign country.

———◆———

1964: A headmaster was having second thoughts about the wisdom of having allowed horticulture to be included on the school syllabus. Two of his 10-year-old pupils had a gardening period, and too late did he discover that they had dug up all his spring cabbages. To add insult to injury, one had presented some of the cabbages to a teacher, who had rewarded him with some sweets for his kindness and hard work.

April 1st

1878: Devonport Prison, opened in 1849 at Pennycomequick, was closed – a result of the Prison Act of 1877 bringing all gaols under state control. The remaining inmates were moved to Plymouth Prison, next to the workhouse at Greenbank. This prison closed at the end of August 1878 and all prisoners served their remaining time at Bodmin Gaol.

———◆———

1937: The Guinness Clock at Drake Circus was erected by the Electric Sign Company Ltd. It had a diameter of 10ft, with an advertisement 50ft by 13ft. 'Guinness Time' was permanently illuminated, whilst each individual letter of 'Guinness is good for you' lit up in sequence; the complete sentence then flashed. The lights all switched off automatically at midnight. Damaged in the Blitz and badly rusted (though the hands and electric motor still worked), the clock was dismantled just before Drake Circus was demolished in 1960. It was kept in storage for some years, then was disposed of at Chelson Meadow rubbish tip.

———◆———

1949: A Plymouth solicitor received a telegram, apparently from a well-known local agricultural firm, informing him that 10 tons of farmyard manure would be delivered at his house that morning and asking him to make arrangements to store it. He was horrified – until his wife reminded him of the date.

April 2nd

1849: South Devon Railway opened the town's first station at Millbay, on the site now occupied by Plymouth Pavilions. The station was built of wood and the platforms were fully covered by train sheds. The two through platforms were supplemented by additional ones in 1908. A bombing raid in 1941 resulted in the station's closure. (*See* March 26th)

2008: A time machine similar to the Tardis appeared on Plymouth Hoe, and a Cornish country squire stepped out. It was Plympton medium and storyteller Carrington Marshall, dressed up as his grandfather Squire Coleridge Connock Marshall. Carrington stated that he and his wife Sharon had gone in the time machine to May 1938 to Treworgey Manor, Cornwall, to put out a fire which would have destroyed the ancient manor house. Having succeeded, he had sent his grandfather back to meet the Plymothians of 2008. It was all in a good cause, as the stunt was in association with Jeremiah's Journey, the city's charity for bereaved families. Carrington said he would use the time machine for educational and charitable purposes during the next year.

April 3rd

1946: Florence Jarrett (18), of Mount Gould Road, was found lying dead on the scullery floor in her home, with her head on a cushion near a gas copper pipe. At the inquest on 13 April, it was said by those who knew her that she had a 'strange nature and jealous temperament', and had been a difficult pupil at school. Her foster-mother, Mrs Sarah Vinecombe, unable to cope with her, had asked for her to be taken to another home. Arrangements for this were in progress when she died. She had originally been placed under the care of the local authority when she was a few months old, as she had been abandoned by her mother and her father's whereabouts were unknown. A verdict of death by carbon monoxide was recorded. Beside her body was a note, reading:

Dear Mum, So I go but not in the way you expected. I am sorry. It is better this way and at least my mind is at peace … Remember me sometimes, but honestly I cannot stand life any longer. These last few weeks have literally killed me. Thank you for what you have done. I give you my love, but I have never really had yours.

April 4th

1911: John Buglehole, a labourer of Pier Street, West Hoe, was charged with 'indecently assaulting' women the previous evening. The police had been receiving complaints about him for some weeks, and had kept him under observation. Three ladies, having seen and recognised him, chased him to Bath Street, where he was arrested by Constable Bernard. He was sentenced to six weeks' hard labour.

———•◆•———

1947: This evening the telephone rang at a flat in Mannamead. 'Good evening,' said the caller. 'I hope you had a satisfactory lunch today. You lunched at the --- restaurant, didn't you?'

The man said that he had. 'But who are you?'

'I have a favour to ask,' the voice continued. 'Would you mind if I wore your raincoat home this evening?'

The man went to make sure his coat was still in the hall. In its place was one of a similar cut and outer appearance, but newer and with unfamiliar lining. He had picked up the wrong coat as he left the restaurant. The caller, left with the wrong garment, had checked the pockets and found a Westminster car park ticket bearing the car's registration number. It was not a Plymouth number, but he had telephoned the police, who gave him the coat owner's name and address.

April 5th

1915: Rosetta Peaton (37) was found dead in bed at her home in Constantine Street by her widowed mother, Sarah Neal (60). Later that day, Mrs Neal was likewise found dead on her bed. At the inquest the next day, Dr Branton said the daughter's death was due to heart disease and chronic alcoholism, while that of her mother was caused by cirrhosis of the liver and fatty degeneration of the heart, probably accelerated by the shock of her daughter's death.

1929: A group of fifteen Corporation workmen were laying an electric cable this morning when a wall, 14ft high and 25ft long, collapsed at Elm Villa, a large house in Mannamead. Those who could dropped their tools and ran, but those in the trench had no chance and were buried underneath several tons of rubble. The noise was so loud that neighbours thought there had been a gas explosion. Frantic efforts were made to dig the men out, and by early afternoon three bodies had been recovered. Five were killed and a sixth was seriously injured, while some men in the rescue operation were also admitted to hospital, suffering from exhaustion. Police were kept busy trying to control the crowd who had gathered to watch.

April 6th

1874: Major Duperier, a former officer of the 80th Foot Regiment and churchwarden at St Andrew's Church, died by his own hand. He had suffered from depression for some time, and feared he was losing his mind and would be sent to a lunatic asylum. On the previous morning, he got up early while his wife was still in bed and shot himself with a pistol, lingering unconscious 'in an utterly hopeless state' for twenty-four hours.

———— •◆• ————

1911: Workmen were removing some temporary roofing at Plymouth Gas Works. One of them, William Nicholas of Alvington Street, aged about 40, slipped from the scaffolding and fell about 40ft, landing on his head. A doctor could do nothing more than confirm that he had died instantly.

———— •◆• ————

1938: A well-dressed black gentleman walked into the reference library. After consulting some books, he began to hold forth to the assistant about the virtues of education and his own particular interest in educational establishments in the West Indies. He then paused, to ask if she knew who he was. She shook her head. 'I'm the King of Jamaica,' he informed her.

April 7th

1840: About sixty new shipwrights in the dockyard went on strike. They were protesting about having been placed in the third class, and receiving wages of 3s 6d a day. Recently they had learned that if they were employed at the private yards in the port, on their old work, they would have received 4s and a quart of beer. Having withdrawn their labours, they appointed a deputation to meet Rear-Admiral Superintendent Warren and lay their case before him. He heard their grievances and undertook to ensure that they would be paid second-class wages immediately, thus adding an extra 6d per day to their wages, until the matter could be laid before the Lords of the Admiralty for their decision. The men then returned to work at once. Afterwards it was pointed out that they were only to be placed on the third class for twelve months (a probation period). With respect to the differences of pay in the national and private yards, it was noted that as 'government artisans', after a certain number of years' service they had the advantage of a pension in the event of sustaining serious injuries during the course of their work, which those in private yards did not.

April 8th

1957: A Plymouth dairyman received a letter from the Inland Revenue demanding his tax return, addressed to '_____ decd.' He replied:

No 3 Harpist
(second Row)
Celestial Orchestra

Dear Sir,
A form has been addressed to a deceased person, requesting a return of my income for the past year.
As one of the reasons for leaving down below was to escape this kind of thing it seems a little unreasonable that a poor persecuted taxpayer is not allowed to rest in peace even in this realm above. Perhaps you would ascertain if the form has been correctly addressed. It may assist in your researches to know that I am still the maker of heavenly ice cream.
Yours in spirit…

———◆———

1995: Eleven Ladbrokes shops in Plymouth took on additional staff and opened their premises an hour early in anticipation of extra business, on what was being dubbed at the time 'the biggest betting day in history', with an estimated £100 million being waged nationwide. Punters in Plymouth had a choice of major sporting events on which to bet all at once, including the results of the Grand National, the Argentina Grand Prix, the FA Cup semi-finals, and the Golf US Masters.

April 9th

1947: Police advised Plymouth residents to take their fibre doormats indoors after dark and keep porch doors locked, after an increase in the theft of what was at the time a scarce commodity. A furniture shop assistant said they had been unable to obtain any new supplies for several months and were not expecting any for some time. 'The owners tell the police,' she said, 'but it is hard to trace a worn fibre mat.' One shop reported having a few extra large doormats selling at over £2 each – a substantial increase on pre-war prices – the first they had had for a long time.

———◆———

1948: An amateur gardener went into a Plymouth shop to purchase some seed, and asked the shopkeeper how many packets he needed. 'I always recommend three,' was the reply. 'One for the slugs, one for the birds, and one for yourself.'

———◆———

1965: Edward Leadbitter walked out of a shop in Notte Street with a bag of fish and chips, then crossed the road towards Hoegate Street. When he stepped on a manhole cover, he was hurled into the air and landed on his back. A policeman promptly summoned an ambulance and he was taken to Freedom Fields, suffering from shock but otherwise unharmed.

April 10th

1929: Mrs Ruth Berthon, of Crapstone, appeared at Plymouth Magistrates' Court. A policeman had discovered that her driving licence had expired six months previously. In mitigation, she said she thought that the licence would last her for life; she was fined £1.

At the same session, Reginald Pentecost, a 31-year-old electrician, was fined £10 or six weeks' imprisonment for 'a public offence' at Tinside on 3 April. Evidence was given by two small girls, aged 12 and 9. He explained that he was having a sunbath at the time.

———— ◆ ————

1960: Gerard Fisher, who had come to Britain from Vienna in 1938 and worked in Plymouth as a newspaper librarian, was also a successful writer of thrillers. The picture on the dust wrapper of his newest title, *It's Your Turn to Die*, showed a woman about to fall to the ground with a bullet in her side, while a man grimly stood in the doorway with a smoking pistol in his hand. 'It was a very nice picture,' he remarked, 'but in my story the lady wasn't shot. She was strangled. However, my publishers have assured me that this mistake will not affect sales.' As they say, you can't judge (or even interpret) a book by its cover.

April 11th

1957: On 1 April, BBC's *Panorama* had featured a story about spaghetti growing in Switzerland, with strands being plucked from trees, laid out in the sun to dry, and then harvested every year. It was soon revealed to be an April Fool. Ten days later, it was announced that several people in Plymouth had rung up Broadcasting House, convinced that if it was on TV it must be right, asking where they could buy the bushes. Some people were rather indignant that the BBC had misled viewers in this way, and a local teacher said it was especially unfair to children, who could hardly be expected to realise it was a joke.

———— • ◆ • ————

1963: The first self-service petrol pumps in Britain were installed in Turnbull's Garage, on Charles Cross roundabout. Three pumps, designed in Sweden, divided the petrol into five intermediate grades from Regular to Super, while the other six produced the standard grades. Prices ranged from between 4*s* 3*d* and 4*s* 11*d* per gallon. As only one attendant was required in a control booth, the garage was able to sell fuel at around 2*d* or 3*d* per gallon cheaper than its nearest rivals in the city.

April 12th

1890: The *Alexandra*, a Devon and Cornwall Tamar Steam Packet Company boat, arriving at Devonport on market day with a large load of passengers and merchandise, hit the landing stage so hard that everyone on board was thrown off their feet, and the deck was covered with butter and broken eggs. The captain responsible for steering the ship had not heard the call to stop the engine. Nobody was injured, but the Company was liable for structural repair to the landing stage, repair to the vessel, and doubtless reimbursement for lost dairy produce.

———— • ◆ • ————

1957: An elderly couple were backing their car into their garage at the back of Peverell Park Road, when a man riding a bicycle too fast came round the corner and collided with them. Without apologising or explaining, he picked his machine up and found the handlebars had jammed, so he continued his journey on foot as he pushed it. A minute later, while the lady was standing behind her car, a second cyclist came round the corner and knocked her over. To her surprise he was a policeman. Very apologetic, he explained that he had been trying to catch the first offender. Luckily she was unhurt. 'Just like a film comedy, isn't it?' she smiled.

April 13th

1957: Trudy, an Alsatian, was back at home and reunited with her owner, Mr Fred Semmens, at The Parade, after having run wild in Forder Valley since the previous December. Mr Semmens had just moved from Derby to Plymouth, and Trudy had got away within twelve hours of arrival. For four months she had defied all efforts to recapture her as she roamed the fields, feeding off scraps from dustbins at the Tecalemit factory, refusing to allow any human being to approach her. She became friendly with a herd of cattle owned by a farmer at Great Woodford Farm, moving from field to field with the beasts and sleeping among them. Inspector W.J. Mullard of the RSPCA took charge of the operation, and, with the aid of several local dog lovers, plus a piece of doped meat, Trudy was caught. About three hours after eating it she became unsteady on her feet. She was caught while in the middle of the herd, tied up and then reunited with her owner in sound health, although a little thinner after her ordeal. Mullard estimated that over the previous two months, he had spent sixty-three hours at Forder Valley on the exercise.

April 14th

1821: An unspecified sum, said by the *Royal Cornwall Gazette*, *Falmouth Packet* and *Plymouth Journal* to be 'to a considerable amount', was won by an officer of one of the regiments stationed at Plymouth, who had undertaken a wager to go begging from door to door over a fortnight. During this time he assumed several different characters, but acted mostly as a broken-down salesman, and a seller of matches.

———◆———

1951: A man who lived near Freedom Park returned from a fair in Central Park having won a goldfish in a competition. He placed it in its bowl on a shelf. Immediately Willie, a 3-year-old ginger tom, was fascinated. He squatted beside it, trying to catch it with his paw, and was barely able to take his eyes off it. Over the next few days he was obsessed and would not leave the shelf. As he had eaten nothing since its arrival, he was getting thinner. If he was removed from the shelf, he still refused to eat and just returned back there. Then somebody accidentally knocked the bowl, it fell off the shelf, and the fish lay on the carpet. Willie swooped, scooped it up in his paw and swallowed it, then went back contentedly to his food.

April 15th

1920: Ruby Hodge (14) was working at the Co-op laundry, Peverell, on 20 January. While putting a collar through the rolls on a polishing machine, her hand was drawn into the feed and so badly damaged that it had to be amputated. The fault was traced to a broken wire which was liable to stretch and fray. Surprisingly, the court accepted the company's defence that 'if you make a machine entirely foolproof, you make it so that it cannot be worked', and the case was dismissed.

———— • ◆ • ————

1953: A Plymouth butcher was asked by a young lady if she could have a tooth from a calf's head. He duly extracted one and handed it to her. When he asked why, she explained that she was an architectural student and needed it for her studies. All was revealed some days later, when a draughtsman who worked in a drawing office in the city told the press that the tooth of a calf, horse or bullock was often favoured by architects to rub over the spongy surface of paper after erasures had been necessary. It restored firmness to the texture of the paper, so that if ink was used on top it would not run.

April 16th

1929: An inquest was held on Sidney Williams (3), who had died at the Royal Albert Hospital the previous night after falling over on the beach at Devonport. His elder sisters, who had been playing with him, had taken him home and put him to bed. After a restless night he was moved to hospital, but worsened throughout the day. Death was due to cerebrospinal meningitis, which was thought to have been aggravated by the fall.

———◆———

1938: As a lady in Mannamead was preparing a salad for the evening meal, she took her diamond engagement ring off her finger and put it on the table. Later, she threw the lettuce oddments in the bin. Only after the dustmen had been did she realise that she had also accidentally thrown the ring out as well. She immediately contacted the sanitary department to ask if it was possible to recover her precious ring, and was told that it would be possible to have all the refuse that had been collected that day from that particular district hand-picked at Prince Rock, on payment of a fee of £10. As there was no guarantee that the item would be found, she felt there was no point in throwing good money after what might be a lost cause. It had been a very expensive salad.

April 17th

1953: A party of four were eating out one evening at a Plymouth restaurant. One of them was struggling with an unusually tough steak, and eventually had to admit defeat. Loath to waste food which they had paid for, another of them called out to the waiter, 'Bring us a piece of paper and we'll wrap it up and take it home for the dog.'

———•◆•———

1997: Leigham School suffered severe damage, estimated at over £1 million, when fire swept through the junior and infants school. Nobody was injured, although several rooms were completely destroyed, as well as a large number of records and much of the pupils' schoolwork. Within a couple of days, the pupils were able to return to their classes in neighbouring schools, until temporary classrooms could be erected on the site. Classes began in September 1999 on a new £1.8 million school built on the original site; though, according to the junior school head teacher Barry Harding, development plans for the grounds would probably take about ten years to complete. The police and authorities suspected arson, and an incident room was set up, but nobody was ever convicted of causing the blaze.

April 18th

1911: At around midnight, Constable Body was patrolling the area around Plymouth Hoe when he heard groans coming from one of the shelters near the bandstand, and discovered a man on the seat in terrible agony. He had cut his throat and the razor was lying on the ground beside him. An ambulance was called from the police station and the man was taken to the Homeopathic Hospital, where he was put under watch. After being treated, he gave his name as W.H. Grant, aged 59, of London. He had been staying for several weeks with his niece at Brixham, and had only recently come to Plymouth. He was receiving an army pension. His condition improved and a few days later he was discharged.

———◆———

1956: The Chancellor of the Exchequer delivered his annual budget. One woman had been so sure beforehand that the cost of posting a letter was going to be raised from 2½*d* to 3*d* that she made a special visit to the main Plymouth post office and bought a large quantity of stamps. She was convinced that by doing so she would 'beat the budget'.

April 19th

1954: Trevor Francis was born in Boxhill (now Pennycross). He joined Birmingham City FC while in his teens and became Britain's first £1 million player when he joined Nottingham Forest in 1978. After retiring, he became a football manager and TV sports pundit.

———◆———

1956: An elderly gentleman visiting Plymouth saw an exhibition of old local theatre bills in the library entrance hall. He noticed a programme from the Theatre Royal (demolished in 1937) for 'The Grand Equestrian Drama of MAZEPPA, and DICK TURPIN'S RIDE TO YORK'. 'I want to see that show,' he told the staff. 'I remember my father talking about it. He saw it in 1864. Can you direct me to the Theatre Royal?'

———◆———

1962: Plymouth Zoo at Central Park, built at a cost of £300,000, was opened by the Deputy Lord Mayor of Plymouth, Mr W. Ivor Thompson. During the first hour almost 1,000 visitors were admitted, with charges of 1s 6d for adults and 1s for children. Opening hours were from 10 a.m. until dusk daily. It closed on 8 January 1978 due to falling visitor numbers and was converted into a skateboard park. The animals were transferred to Longleat House and Bournemouth Zoo.

April 20th

1938: The 120-strong BBC Symphony Orchestra, conducted by Sir Adrian Boult, played its first concert in Plymouth at the Guildhall. The audience was treated to a programme which included Mozart's 'Symphony in G Minor' ('with its cascades of string music'), Strauss's 'Till Eulenspiegel'('great fun – a glorious romp'), and the finale from Wagner's 'Ride of the Valkyries'.

———◆———

1948: At a meeting of Plymouth pharmacists, chemist Fernley Wallis told how a 73-year-old lady had recently come into his shop and asked him if he would remove her wedding ring, which was too small for her finger. When he took it off, he found another ring underneath. After removing that, a third ring was revealed. 'I've lost three husbands,' she told him, 'but I would marry again if I had the chance.'

———◆———

1957: *Mayflower II*, a replica of the original *Mayflower*, was built in Brixham and launched there in September 1956. She then sailed around to Sutton Harbour, from where she left, on this day, under the command of Captain Alan Villiers, to make the same voyage as her illustrious predecessor. She took fifty-three days to pass the Nantucket Lightship, sailing 5,500 sea miles. *Mayflower II* took thirteen days less to complete the journey than the original ship had done in 1620.

April 21st

2005: Plymouth's most famous lottery winner, antique furniture exporter Michael Antonucci, put his last remaining asset up for sale. Antonucci had bought and built up from scratch The Cooperage, Vauxhall Street – his restaurant and music venue – a couple of months after he had borrowed £10 from his mother for tickets and won the £2.8 million jackpot in July 1995. It attracted just one bid – for 1p and the cost of stock – despite his hopes that it would sell for at least £1 million. The Cooperage had been just one purchase in a spending spree which also included a recording studio, two Mercedes convertibles, a powerboat, designer clothes, a jet ski and gym equipment, and a no-expenses-spared wedding in the Bahamas to a 22-year-old model whom he had met in a Plymouth nightclub – a marriage which lasted just three months before he was locked out of their marital home in the city, and ended in an acrimonious divorce with his wife keeping the house. Yet as he went back to his old job in antiques, he was prepared to put everything down to experience, telling the press, 'You don't want to die as the richest man in the graveyard. You have to spend some and enjoy it.'

April 22nd

1953: Edgar Trout and his agent Donald Steel were in Whitleigh, canvassing for the forthcoming elections in the Tamerton ward, when they came across a lady in evident distress. She was a housewife who had gone into the garden to throw some water on a flowerbed, only to find the front door had slammed and she was locked out, having left the kettle boiling, and dinner in the oven – and did not expect her husband back for at least two hours. Mr Trout promptly climbed on to his agent's back and went through the bathroom window so he could open the front door. Overcome with relief, she assured both men that that was certainly worth a vote.

1954: It was a man's world. At a wedding reception in a Plymouth café, after the cake was duly cut, handed round and eaten, and the normal expressions of goodwill had been made to the assembled company, the entire male presence – groom included – went 'down the road' to the nearest pub. The bride and other doubtless astonished ladies were left behind to continue celebrating at the café.

April 23rd

1965: There were ongoing discussions in the news concerning the renaming of the area long known as Swilly. There were debates about the origins of the name, with people saying it meant 'place with a stream' or 'hollow place in a gutter washed out by the soil'. Others claimed that the name was taken from the Saxon word 'swylle', or said that the area had been the site of a pig farm at the turn of the century. Some residents and officials, including the City Housing Manager, Mr C. Sanderson, were adamant that nobody wanted to live in an area with such a name. The chairman of the Housing Committee, Eric Nuttall, said that many considered the name unfortunate because of its connection with pigs. Others, including City Librarian Bill Best Harris, argued that it represented a historical tradition and there was no need for any change. It was pointed out by another source that the name derived from the long-demolished seventeenth-century Swilly House, owned by explorer Captain Tobias Furneaux, a friend of Captain Cook. 'The origin without a doubt is ancient and honourable,' the press concluded, 'and there is no call to mess about with it.' Nevertheless, the renaming lobby eventually had their way, and a few years later it became North Prospect.

April 24th

1920: Henry Gent (41), a labourer from North Street employed by Gladys Lawrence of Herschell Lazarus, a furniture dealer in Frankfort Street, was charged at Plymouth Police Court with embezzlement. Gladys had asked Gent to take a chair to a customer in the town and collect the money, and when Gent returned to the shop afterwards he said he had not been paid for the item. When asked, the customer stated that he had handed over the money as requested. Admitting the offence, Gent was given twenty-eight days' hard labour.

———◆———

1980: One of the anchors from HMS *Ark Royal* was presented to the city by Lord Hill-Norton, Admiral of the Fleet, on behalf of the Board of Admiralty. It was unveiled at the junction of Armada Way and Notte Street. This Royal Navy aircraft carrier launched in 1955 and was based at Devonport. The first such vessel to have an angled flight deck (which allowed landing and take-off to be carried out simultaneously), she underwent several refits at the dockyard, which she entered for the last time in December 1978. She was decommissioned two months later. Plans to preserve her came to nothing, and in March 1980 it was announced that she would be scrapped.

April 25th

1938: A large store in Ebrington Street, which specialised in selling umbrellas, had to put some of its counter staff on to other work as there had been such a slump in sales. The proprietor said that, with hardly any rain since Christmas, and a drought in the Plymouth area for fourteen weeks, he could not remember anything like it for forty years. During the previous weekend there had been a threat of rain, and something of a rush for new umbrellas, although it had only lasted until blue skies and sunshine returned. The only compensation was that the dry weather had resulted in heavy demand by customers for walking sticks. Yet it would only need a good day's rain to do a roaring trade in umbrellas once more.

———◆———

1957: A new £5 banknote had just come into circulation. In a Plymouth pub, a customer produced one in payment for a whisky. Another man at the bar noticed, said he had not seen one yet, and asked the barman if he could have a look. It was duly passed over for inspection, and then someone else wanted a look – and someone else after that. The barman never saw it again.

April 26th

1962: The Tamar Bridge was officially opened by Queen Elizabeth the Queen Mother, who cut a tape on the Plymouth side and was escorted across the bridge to meet the Mayor of Saltash on the Cornish side of the river. Local businessmen had first suggested the building of a bridge early in the nineteenth century; they even discussed the possibility of having a tunnel underneath the river. Increasing traffic on the Saltash ferry led, in 1924, to suggestions that the Torpoint and Saltash ferries should be replaced by a bridge. Plans were drawn up but the project was regarded as uneconomic – particularly during the post-war reconstruction of the city, when other work had to take priority. In 1950, a committee was formed to examine the proposal and a detailed survey was undertaken. Plymouth City Council and Cornwall County Council decided to finance the project jointly as no funding was made available by central government. The building work began in 1959, and the bridge was declared open to traffic on 24 October 1961 when a Western National No. 76 bus crossed shortly after 5.30 a.m. on its journey to Callington. However, the official ceremony did not take place for another six months.

April 27th

1944: A Plan for Plymouth was published – the joint work of the City Engineer James Paton Watson, and Professor Patrick Abercrombie of London University. The City Council had long realised that when peace was restored after the Second World War, Plymouth would need to be completely redeveloped, and a Reconstruction Committee was formed to oversee the project. The Town and Country Planning Act, passed by parliament earlier in the year, made it possible for the council to make compulsory purchase orders for land devastated by enemy action, as well as adjoining areas – some of which had been regarded as little better than slums. Although the publication bore the date 1943, it officially appeared on this date the following year. Professor Abercrombie had already been working on a reconstruction plan for the similarly devastated areas of Greater London, when he was asked by Lord Astor, Lord Mayor of the city, to play a similar role in the future of Plymouth. He was paid a consultancy fee of £800 for his work. The Plan, largely based on the simple use of the contours of the land, was approved in principle by the council in August, and the task of reconstruction began in 1947.

April 28th

1941: Mass burials of those who had been killed in the Blitz during the previous few weeks took place at Efford Cemetery in the afternoon. A service was held, during which the graves were draped with Union Jacks and floral tributes, from official wreaths and crosses to posies of primroses. Among those taking part were the Bishops of Plymouth and Exeter, the Roman Catholic Bishop of Plymouth, representatives from the Salvation Army, and officers from the army, navy and RAF. Reporting on the ceremony, the *Western Evening Herald* noted:

> Here, in a setting of beauty and peace, which looks out over a wonderful panorama of the Devon hills, this company of Plymothians who were called on to make the supreme sacrifice rest together – men, women and children.

———◆———

1961: A young couple were shown a Plymouth flat, liked it, and were on the point of taking it. They told the landlady of their decision, and then she referred to a remark they had made in conversation with each other which had aroused her suspicions. 'Are you anything to do with television?' she asked. They said they were. 'Then you can't have the flat,' she snapped. 'TV means parties, and we don't want that sort of thing here.'

April 29th

1902: The Devonport Sailors' Home was opened at Morice Square, Devonport. It had originally been founded in St Aubyn Street in 1852 to provide board, lodging, medical attention, education and nautical training for sailors, marines, yachtsmen and merchant seamen. Moving to Duke Street a few years later, it soon outgrew these premises and a new site was purchased in 1899. The building was financed by a grant of £2,000 from the Admiralty. In 1949 the name was changed to the Royal Fleet Club, later becoming a hotel open to the public, before its eventual closure.

———◆———

1961: Westward Television began broadcasting from a transmitter at Stockland Hill, near Honiton. The company was based at purpose-built studios in Derry's Cross, with a London office and a sales office in Bristol. The first chairman was Peter Cadbury, who had left the board of Tyne Tees Television in order to make what proved to be a successful bid for the south-west franchise. He named the company after the golf course at Westward Ho!, where he played regularly. The symbol was a silver model of Sir Francis Drake's ship *Golden Hind*. Westward later lost its franchise to Television South West, which began broadcasting in August 1981, retaining the old name until its official launch on 1 January 1982.

April 30th

1944: The final aerial attack during the Second World War came after an alert sounded at 3.15 a.m. Eighteen were killed and seven were seriously injured in the Oreston area. At the Western National Omnibus Co. depot at Prince Rock, three firewatchers were killed and several buses were destroyed. An Anderson shelter was hit, resulting in the loss of six lives, and a public shelter nearby was struck, killing nine. Also hit were several roads in the Milehouse area, the Rising Sun public house in Crabtree, Laira railway sidings, the Tothill recreation ground and the Gas Company's recreation ground.

———◆———

1954: Mrs Pat Treleaven, Labour candidate for the Drake ward in the municipal elections, was out asking people for their vote. A little girl, who was watching, asked the lady what she was doing. 'I am canvassing for the election,' she answered.

'Are you going to canvass our house? Mummy says that all ours is wearing out and wants doing badly.'

During the same campaign, *Honicknowle Parish News* wrote, 'We believe that some of you would vote against the kingdom of heaven if the wrong party brought it in!'

———◆———

1956: A Plymouth motor firm's calendar was displaying the date 31 April.

May 1st

1970: Five months of Mayflower '70 celebrations were launched to mark the 350th anniversary of the Pilgrim Fathers' voyage. About 60,000 converged on the Hoe and the city centre, undeterred by grey skies and the threat of rain. The official opening by Senator Leverett Saltonstall, who was representing the governor of Massachusetts, where the Pilgrims settled, was followed by a pageant performed by 500 children from the city's primary schools. The senator, one of whose ancestors was among the pilgrims, then inspected the guard of honour with the Lord Mayor, who delivered a speech of welcome and presented him with a sword as a gift from the city to the commonwealth of Massachusetts. A re-enactment of the pilgrims' departure, performed by members of the Plymouth & West Devon Federation of Townswomen's Gilds and Western College Players, was followed by a march of children, a mile-long carnival with over 120 floats, and luncheon in the Guildhall for over 300 guests. Afterwards, there was a fireworks display, dancing on the Hoe to live music provided by local rock band The Earth, a civic reception at the Guildhall, a charity ball, and a procession organised by Plymouth Round Table of over 1,000 people carrying lighted flambeaux from the city centre to West Hoe Park.

May 2nd

1914: A provisional order for the amalgamation of Devonport and Stonehouse with Plymouth was issued by the Local Government Board, and a Local Act which received the Royal Assent three months later, on 10 August. During the previous century, the steady expansion of the Three Towns (Plymouth, Devonport and Stonehouse) had made amalgamation inevitable and desirable, with calls for them to unite as one from 1888 onwards. A meeting of the Plymouth Town Council on 24 November 1913 had pressed strongly for negotiations to be opened for amalgamation. On 28 January 1914, an inquiry was opened at Plymouth Guildhall by the Local Government Board Inspector, requesting an application by Plymouth Corporation for a provisional order for the amalgamation of the county boroughs of Plymouth and Devonport, and the Urban District of East Stonehouse. Representing the Corporation, Honoratus Lloyd stated that there were three local authorities, but only one town; there was no physical boundary between them, and in all respects but their government they were as one. The Borough Council held its last meeting on 29 October 1914 and amalgamation came into effect from 1 November. The new united Borough of Plymouth covered an area of 6,100 acres, with a population of 212,000 and a rateable value of £1,025,000.

May 3rd

1831: Sir George Cockburn and Sir Thomas Byam Martin were both elected as MPs for Plymouth. According to the *Standard*, Sir George 'was hissed, pelted, and loaded with every opprobrious epithet, and with some difficulty escaped a more severe handling. He was removed from the scene of action through a back way'.

———•◆•———

1950: The Guild of Social Service announced that it would distribute gift parcels to those couples in Plymouth who had been married for fifty years. This prompted one woman to write and ask whether she would be entitled, as she had been married for fifty years – but to two husbands.

———•◆•———

1957: A young woman from New Zealand, aged about 25, was walking along Royal Parade wearing a tight sweater and tartan trousers. She was approached by an elderly woman who told her off, complained about her clothing, and told her she was 'a disgrace to her sex'. Until then, the visitor had been reflecting on the ultra-modern atmosphere of the new shopping centre. 'I was just thinking how new and up-to-date everything was looking,' she told a journalist, 'when I suddenly had this reminder that not all the Pilgrim Fathers, or at least the Pilgrim Mothers, had sailed on the *Mayflower*.'

May 4th

1935: The Repertory Theatre, in the building which formerly housed the Mechanics' Institute, Princess Square, closed for the last time. Opened in 1915 by George King and Mr H. Parry, joint owners of the Grand Theatre in Stonehouse, its final production was the play *Devonshire Cream*.

———•◆•———

1949: In Compton, a Conservative candidate in the elections was touring the housing estates in a van with a loudspeaker attached, asking if anyone had any questions. One man came out of his front door with an unexpected one: 'When are you going to move to the next street?' he demanded. 'I've got some studying to do.'

———•◆•———

1958: A dead liver and white spaniel was found in woodland near Puslinch. According to his collar, his name was Jewell and his address was William Street, Morice Town. Closer examination revealed that he was not only deceased but had been stuffed. After this was reported in the press, the information was volunteered that about forty years previously he had been kept in a glass case over the fireplace in the back room of one of the city pubs; he had presumably been discarded more recently by a subsequent owner of the premises.

May 5th

1982: The Theatre Royal was officially opened by Princess Margaret, with a gala performance commencing with Leonard Rossiter and featuring the Melody Attias Dancers, Dickie Henderson, Keith Harris and Orville, Iris Williams, Diana Montague from the Royal Opera House, and Gene Pitney. *Western Evening Herald* critic Harvey Crane, never easy to please, was less than impressed by the proceedings, noting in his report the next day:

> After all the euphoria over the grand opening, we expected a super spectacular with scenic effects and glittering performances and presentation. However the production was minimal, coloured stage lighting almost non-existent, and the brilliance and the glitter lay mostly around the Royal guest and the audience.

An earlier Theatre Royal, opened in 1813, suffered badly from the rise in cinema-going after the First World War and was demolished in 1937. A new theatre for Plymouth and the surrounding area was proposed in the 1943 Plan, but, owing to lack of finance, building did not begin until 1979. The main theatre had seating for 1,300 and the building included a smaller studio theatre, the Drum, for more experimental productions. Later, a production and education centre was opened (Theatre Royal 2), on the reclaimed waterfront site at Cattedown.

May 6th

1935: City status was conferred on Plymouth, in commemoration of the Silver Jubilee of King George V. This was the result of much lobbying by Mr Leslie Hore-Belisha, MP for Devonport and Minister of Transport, and the Town Clerk, Mr R.J. Fittall, whose cause had been supported by the Prince of Wales, Lord High Steward of Plymouth. The announcement was made that morning to take immediate effect, thus raising the position of Chief Magistrate to that of Lord Mayor. An official ceremony was held three days later in Guildhall Square, where the new Lord Mayor, Alderman J.E. Pillar, listened while Mr Fittall read out the proclamation, which had been received from London that morning.

———◆———

2005: Twelve members of Plymouth Trident Ploughshares, an anti-nuclear campaign group, set up a peace camp in an empty building on Drake's Island, which they declared a nuclear-free state. They erected banners saying 'Ban the Bomb' and 'Scrap Trident', claiming that Britain had breached the Nuclear Non-Proliferation Treaty by refitting nuclear-powered and nuclear-armed Trident submarines at Devonport Dockyard. The group were also concerned about the permitted discharge of the substance tritium in the River Tamar. One member claimed that they had squatters' rights, and said they would stay there until a court granted an order to remove them.

May 7th

1948: The last German prisoners of war in the Plymouth area left the camp in Chaddlewood, Plympton. There had been other camps at Bickham in Buckland Monachorum, and Hazeldene in Elburton. Some prisoners had also been housed in former Nissen huts used by American troops in the build-up to D-Day, in the grounds of Chaddlewood House, and in Saltram and Marsh Mills. Chaddlewood had been the headquarters for all prisoner-of-war working camps in south Devon. The prisoners' tasks included farm labouring, clearing debris from streets destroyed in the Blitz, helping the elderly tend their gardens, repainting railings at the barracks in Devonport, and sawing firewood. One group at Plympton formed a choir, which gave concerts in the area for about eighteen months. Because of the shortage of labour, some were employed to help lay the foundations of temporary prefabricated houses and shops.

———— • ◆ • ————

1954: Rex Charlesworth, who had come from Cheshire to work as the Branch Library Superintendent and had just been appointed Deputy City Librarian, had the distinction of being the tallest member of the Corporation staff. At 6ft 4in, he joked that he had entered the library service as he could reach the top shelves. Entering most doorways was difficult, but he had an advantage when it came to watching Plymouth Argyle.

May 8th

1957: An 8-year-old boy near Plymouth complained of persistent earache. The doctor prescribed ear drops, but they failed to give more than temporary relief. His mother consulted several other doctors but none of them could offer a solution. Eventually, she decided to take a syringe and give his ear a thorough rinse. As he held his head over the basin and the water came out of his ear, so did a screw from a Meccano set.

———◆◆———

1995: On the Hoe, crowds of an estimated 200,000 joined to celebrate the 50th anniversary of VE Day. They observed a national two-minute silence at 8.38 p.m., Lord Mayor Walter Ainsworth lit a ceremonial beacon, and there was a large firework and laser display, fired from barges moored by frigate HMS *Argyll*. Earlier in the day, 800 had taken part in a street party on Royal Parade (one of several parties throughout the city), with people dressing up in wartime costumes and 1940s'-style music playing in the background. Veterans paraded through the streets, while pensioners and schoolchildren gathered at war memorials to pay their respects to the dead. Some of the parties had a wartime menu, and guests displayed souvenirs, including their old ration books.

May 9th

1945: The news that VE Day would be celebrated on 8 May proved a mixed blessing for Plymouth's pubs. Eighty per cent had either sorely underestimated the demand of their customers or had failed to obtain all they needed, and had to close early as they were out of beer. At least one house had sold out by 8.30 p.m. on 7 May. The licensee expected a delivery the next day, but as 8 May had been declared a holiday, no new supplies were delivered.

1956: Spooners department store had just opened at its new premises, but not everybody was impressed. One elderly regular shopper asked to be directed to the upper floor. When shown towards the new escalator, she demanded to know where the stairs were. She looked around and said that clearly the building was not finished yet, 'and I suppose you've put that old thing in temporarily.'

1957: A Plymouth typist startled her employer when she told him that she had washed her hair the night before and dried it in the electric oven. Although she owned an electric hair dryer, she found the oven was much more effective. 'All the family use it,' she said, 'and that includes Grannie, who is 82.'

May 10th

1956: A woman living in Stoke kept poultry in her backyard. In the morning, at feeding time, she lifted up the lid of one of the nesting boxes as usual, only to find it occupied by the family cat, who had decided that the soft straw was a good place for her to give birth to a litter of kittens overnight. Perching placidly on top of the feline mother was the hen.

1958: A candidate canvassing in Sutton asked another woman for her support in the forthcoming elections. 'I can't tell you how I'm voting,' the woman said. 'I've got to ask my husband which way he's voting first.'

'But surely you have a mind of your own?' asked the canvasser. 'You're not going to let your husband have everything his own way?'

The undecided voter agreed, explaining that she was not too pleased with him at the moment. 'I want to find out how he's voting and then vote the other way.'

1958: An elderly lady at a department store in Royal Parade said she was not going to use the lifts as she wanted to try 'those moving alligators'.

May 11th

1907: John Collings (15), of Martin Street, and Samuel Britton (12), of Stoke Road, were charged at Plymouth Police Court with breaking open a gas slot meter at King Street and stealing 11*d*. Britton admitted breaking open the meter with Collings and sharing the proceeds with him. Collings had already been before the Bench eight times on similar offences, while Britton had last been in court on 29 April and had been given six strokes of the birch for stealing. This time the magistrates fined Collings 5*s*, or five days in prison, and sentenced Britton to another nine strokes of the birch.

❖

1916: Sarah Barrow, who kept a shop in High Street, Stonehouse, was charged with assaulting her neighbour Annie Williams. The latter said that trouble had arisen and she was now 'refusing further business relations'. On 8 May, Mrs Barrow had been dancing on Annie's doorstep, drunkenly singing a song with the refrain, 'I wouldn't have a wife like you.' Mr Williams had ordered her to go away, which she did – but she returned later, demanding a drink of ale. She then swore at Mrs Williams and threatened her with a gold chain and a bottle of sweets, then hit her, accusing her of being drunk herself. Mrs Barrow was fined 10*s* or sentenced to fourteen days in prison.

May 12th

1946: It was reported that Edwin Pain, landlord of the Penrose Inn, Penrose Street, had a pâpier maché cat sitting behind the bar which had been presented to him at the time of the Blitz. Customers (who had possibly had a drop too much) would be startled by the sight of this feline apparently moving – until all was revealed. The cat contained a mechanism which caused its head and tail to move in lifelike fashion when triggered by a sudden incursion of air, such as when the bar door was opened.

1964: Stephen Wightman, founder of Messrs S.A. Wightman, died at his Mannamead home, aged 76. Born in London, he came to Plymouth in 1929 and opened an optician's shop in Old Town Street. The premises were damaged by enemy action during the war, but the equipment was saved and trade continued almost uninterrupted despite the Blitz. His grandson, Colin Lee, joined the business as a teenager in 1954, opening and developing the retail photographic department and studio with which the name is most associated. In 1963, Lee became Managing Director and the business moved to Market Way. It ceased trading about thirty years later, shortly before Lee's death in 1995.

May 13th

1938: The first crop of strawberries this year, sent by Breton growers, was unloaded at Millbay Docks this afternoon. The season was not due to begin for another week, but lack of rain and much sunshine had ripened the fruit unusually early. Farmers had to charter a French vessel, *Alma*, at Brest, as the steamers were not ready, and it was important to bring the fruit to England as soon as possible in case it proved a short season this year. Further consignments arrived the following week, but drought had made the strawberries rather poor, and they fetched lower prices than in previous years. Not only the cultivated fruit was affected; two days later, a large wild strawberry was picked in a lane at Tamerton.

1978: A letter to the *Western Evening Herald* attacked the Junior Chamber of Commerce's plan to organise a pipe-smoking contest in which the entrant who kept puffing away the longest would be the winner. This ironically coincided with the publication of statistics showing increased death rates from lung cancer related to smoking. 'Could not members put their brains to better use (as in the past) and invent some more entertaining and less pointless, irresponsible plan for celebrating Lord Mayor's Day?' asked the correspondent.

May 14th

1868: A petition was presented to the Court of Chancery for the winding up of the Plymouth Exchange Company. Built in 1813 in Woolster Street, between Batter Street and Vauxhall Street near Bretonside, the company stood on the site of what had been the Old Mitre Inn, and before that the fourteenth-century Franciscan Friary, which did not survive the Dissolution of the Monasteries under King Henry VIII. The premises included a hall for sales and public meetings, subscription reading rooms, a bar, coffee rooms, and nine offices, including those of the Fishermen's Mutual Insurance Society, the Port of Plymouth Ship Masters' Society, the Board of Examination of Masters and Mates, and the Trustees of the Merchant Seamen's Hospital Fund.

It had, however, proved an expensive organisation to maintain. By the end of the nineteenth century, most of the building was empty, although a few commercial organisations continued to maintain offices there until the Second World War. It was severely damaged during the Blitz and the remains were demolished after the war.

———— • ◆ • ————

1964: The survey ship *Owen* sailed into Plymouth after an eight-month general service commission on the Middle East station. As well as the crew, on board was a 2cwt tortoise from the Seychelles.

May 15th

1856: Men of the 3ʳᵈ Jagers Corps, stationed at Bovisand, complained of the severity of the drill to which they were subjected by their colonel. Their sergeant wrote a letter of complaint to the commander of the western district, and, when he was arrested, they grounded their arms and refused to do duty. The sergeant was court-martialled and sentenced to fifty lashes.

———◆———

1907: Albert Knapman, a blacksmith who lived in Stonehouse, was charged by Plymouth Magistrates with assaulting a policeman on the previous evening. Constable Higman told the court that at 7.25 p.m., when he was on duty in Durnford Street, the prisoner ran up to him, pulled his coat off, challenged him to a fight, and struck out at him left and right. He became increasingly violent and had to be taken to the police station. Superintendent Crooke said that in October 1905, Knapman had been remanded to the workhouse as 'a wandering lunatic', and was certainly 'a very excitable man'. The chairman said that Knapman had gone out of his way to assault one of the most respectable men in the community, who did his duty in a very satisfactory manner, and was therefore fining the blacksmith 10*s* plus costs, or fourteen days' hard labour.

May 16th

1920: Private W.G. Freeman (19) had been awarded fourteen days' detention and was being escorted with Private Welford, another soldier, to Granby Barracks. As both men from the 1st Battalion, Royal Munster Fusiliers, were being marched on their way, Freeman gave Welford a sign, a tap on the hand, and they both ran off. They were soon recaptured, and taken to the barracks on a transport wagon. When they were brought before the military court, Welford admitted that it had all been his idea, and he was prepared to take the blame. They had decided to try and escape as he did not think they had been given a fair trial before being punished. They were both given an extra week's detention.

1947: A woman purchased a balloon costing 7d for her little daughter at a Plymouth market stall, and asked the assistant if she would mind blowing it up for her. The woman promptly did so, taking a 1s coin in payment and not giving any change back. 'I thought you said the balloons were 7d!' the mother said. 'So they are,' was the reply, 'but when they're blown up we charge a bob.'

May 17th

1954: Stan Laurel and Oliver Hardy had been touring Britain and were booked to play their last shows at the Palace Theatre. The production was *Birds of a Feather*. Playing on the same bill at the time were Harry Worth and 'Wonder Horse Tony'. Unfortunately, Hardy had had a severe bout of influenza and was also still suffering from the after-effects of a mild heart attack. After managing to perform on stage for the opening night, the show was cancelled, and he spent the rest of his stay in Plymouth recovering at the Grand Hotel on the Hoe. The duo's career, therefore, ended in Plymouth. Hardy's failing health put an end to any plans for further work and he died three years later.

———— • ◆ • ————

1964: During the Whitsun weekend, a teenager who used to work in Plymouth but had since moved to London reported to a journalist friend that she had just paid a brief visit back to her home city. After the frenetic round of activity in the capital, she found it very dull. 'People just amble along regardless. There is little lively conversation. Everybody and everything seems too slow. And most people go to bed too early.' You can't please everybody all of the time.

May 18th

1948: The battleship *Howe*, which had been taking part in Home Fleet exercises off the Norwegian coast, arrived at Devonport Dockyard for a refit. It was anticipated that this would provide employment for the workforce for some considerable time.

— ◆ —

1957: An auction was held at Stoke Damerel Parish Hall to raise funds for the church in Paradise Road. One of the oldest surviving churches in Plymouth, it was in urgent need of structural repairs. There were 131 lots on offer, including an ivory vase which raised £7 10s, a Jacobean skillet (£4 10s), an ornamental Pekin tree on a jade stone foundation (£10 5s), and a set of six Georgian silver dessert spoons (5 guineas). Joan Vickers, MP for Devonport, bought several items, including an invalid wheelchair for £1, which she said she would probably donate to the Red Cross. Perhaps the most unusual item on offer was Charlie, a tan kitten raised in Devonport, who was curled up fast asleep in his basket while he went under the hammer – figuratively speaking – to the Earl of Mount Edgcumbe for £1 10s. Some 200 people, including auctioneers and dealers, were in attendance, and £245 was raised.

May 19th

1923: The Plymouth War Memorial on the Hoe was unveiled by the Earl of Derby, Secretary of State for War. During the ceremony, the mayor deposited a roll of honour in a casket, which was then placed beneath the memorial.

1945: A woman on the top deck of a bus was heard asking the lady beside her what she had in the paper parcel on her knee. 'I'm taking this home for my cat,' the other lady replied, opening the package and holding up the contents – a huge dead rat.

1975: Plymouth Sound, Britain's eleventh commercial radio station, was launched on air at 6 a.m. by 9-year-old Plymouth schoolboy Master Andrew Knight. Founded jointly by Bob Hussell, the first Managing Director, and broadcaster David Bassett, the station's premises were in a former organ factory at Earls Acre. The first programme, Sunrise Sound, a four-hour show of music, news, traffic information and local topics, presented by Colin Bower, was followed by Bassett's Phone Forum, and Louise Churchill's Tradio, 'an on-the-air market'. Plymouth Sound was rebranded as Heart Radio on 23 March 2009.

May 20th

1848: In a message from the mayor, James Moore, the local papers announced:

ALTERATION OF TIME: BOROUGH OF PLYMOUTH: THE COUNCIL of the BOROUGH of PLYMOUTH, considering the Advantage of a Uniform Computation of Time, and following the example of other large Towns possessing communication by Railway, have resolved to adopt LONDON TIME as kept by all Railway Stations in regulating the arrival and departure of Trains. Notice is therefore hereby given that from and after Twelve O'Clock at Noon, on MONDAY, the twenty-second day of May instant, London Time, being 16 minutes earlier than Plymouth Time, is appointed to be kept for all purposes within the Borough of Plymouth.

1953: Tiddles, a 6-month-old female Persian cat, was reunited with her owner Mrs Caines at Salcombe Road, Lipson. Four days earlier, a couple from Coleridge Road had visited their son at Swilly Hospital. While driving away they heard mewing in the car, and had stopped to check – to find Tiddles crouched in the toolbox. Thinking she had come from the hospital and crawled in while they were there, they drove back and left her in the grounds. Two days later, Tiddles's owner told friends and neighbours that her pet was missing. A nurse reported finding the cat crying nearby, and traced her to Mrs Caines.

May 21st

1982: HMS *Ardent*, a frigate built by Yarrow Shipbuilders, Glasgow, was sunk during the Falklands War – the first ship from Devonport to be lost in the conflict. She had been protecting transport ships carrying the men to shore in San Carlos Bay, when she was bombed, on 21 May, by planes from the Argentine Air Force. The damage was extensive and the crew had to contain the fire, look after the wounded, and try to counter any further attacks. The *Ardent* sailed to Grantham Sound, where she sank. Twenty-two men were killed and thirty were injured.

A memorial service on 7 August at St Nicholas' Church on the Royal Navy shore base, HMS *Drake*, Devonport, was attended by about 600 people, including the survivors, their families and the relatives of those killed. Also present were Captain Brian Turner, president of the board of inquiry into the loss of the ship, and the captain, Commander Alan West. The Revd Bernard Marshall, the naval chaplain who had the grim task of telling those at Plymouth of the loss of their loved ones, paid tribute in his address to those who had died bravely, 'upholding a principle and serving their country. We hope and pray their sacrifice may bear fruit abundantly.'

May 22nd

2001: During the campaign for the general election on 7 June, former Prime Minister Lady Thatcher spoke at a rally at Plymouth Pavilions, which was attended by an audience of about 500 Conservative supporters. She was fiercely opposing any move by Britain to join the euro, and voicing her suspicions that Prime Minister Tony Blair was expected by other European nations 'to lead Britain by the nose into the single currency'. The greatest issue in the election, if not the greatest issue before the country, she declared, was whether Britain would remain a free, independent nation state or be dissolved in a federal Europe. She said:

> There are no half-measures, no third ways and no second chances. A country which loses the power to issue its own currency is a country which has given up the power to govern itself. Such a country is no longer free. And it is no longer democratic – for its people can no longer determine their own future in national elections. To surrender the pound, to surrender our power of self-government, would betray all [that] the past generations down the ages lived and died to defend.

She received a standing ovation from those present, though her comments later received a mixed reaction from other senior party members.

May 23rd

1786: Prince William Henry accepted the Freedom of Plymouth from four senior aldermen and 'common council men'. Two months earlier, he had been initiated into 'the ancient and honourable Society of Free and Accepted Masons' at the Prince George Inn in Vauxhall Street. (*See* January 8th)

1863: A fire broke out at Mr W.G. Emmett's grocery in Tavistock Street, Devonport, at about 9.15 p.m. Emmett had been asked for a quart of highly inflammable cazeline oil. Due to its hazardous properties, he would not allow any of his assistants to fetch it from the cellar, but insisted on doing so himself. He went down the steps with a lighted candle in his hand, and almost at once there was an explosion, followed by flames which spread to adjoining properties in very little time. It took a combination of civilian, naval and military manpower nearly four hours to get the situation under control. Several nearby business premises in Tavistock Street and three private houses in Princess Street were destroyed, as well as the grocery. Emmett had been killed at once, and all that was left of him were a few charred bones, which were dug out of the ruins on the following morning.

May 24th

1839: On Queen Victoria's 20th birthday, the British Orphan Asylum for the Female Orphans of Sailors, Soldiers and Marines was founded at Stoke. A Devon and Cornwall Asylum had been established in 1834 by Mrs Mary Tripe, but, because of the large number of applications for places, she had decided to found another, which would undertake the responsibility of supporting and educating female orphans of seamen, soldiers and Royal Marines, especially those who had lost their lives in the public service. When the Queen agreed to become the patron in October 1839, the prefix 'Royal' was added to the title. Funds came entirely from voluntary contributions. Girls were supported from the age of 5 until 12, when they were of an age to go into service. In May 1840, a house in St Michael's Terrace at Stoke was rented to provide further accommodation; when that became inadequate, larger premises in Albert Road were acquired. Further extensions were built later in the nineteenth century, and in July 1895 there were 200 inmates. After the Second World War, numbers declined sharply. The asylum closed in February 1974 and the remaining residents were moved to Alexandra Home, St Budeaux.

May 25th

1892: Beaumont Park, the town's first recreation ground after the Hoe, was officially opened to the public with a civic procession from the Guildhall. The mayor used a silver key to open the gate, and crowds were invited in to wander around the grounds while the Royal Marines Band played. Thomas Bewes of Beaumont House had bought the land as an extension to his garden. He was a bachelor, and, being without any heirs to inherit the property, he stipulated in the deeds that the land was to be held until taken over by the Borough of Plymouth with the rest of the Park. After his death, the house and land were sold by his Trustees to the Corporation for £26,000. The house was briefly the local museum, then became a chest clinic, and later a solicitor's office.

1951: A notice was spotted in a children's playground at Efford, saying 'No children under five allowed on slide'. As several youngsters went out unaccompanied by their parents, it was wondered how many of them could actually read it.

1956: Advertisement placed in a local newspaper: 'To Let: Unfurnished 3-Roomed Flat, Mutley area. Only plasterers need apply.'

May 26th

1919: During the evening Frances Thompson, aged 42, of St John Street, Devonport, was arrested by Constable Williams, for being drunk whilst in charge of a child. She had been found in Edgcumbe Street with the infant, wandering around and abusing passers-by. When she appeared in court the next morning she pleaded not guilty, but it was her twenty-first conviction for such an offence, and she was fined 10s.

1921: Eliza and William Clarke of Summerland Street were charged with assaulting Mr and Mrs Whiteman, their neighbours. The Clarkes had returned home drunk one evening and had broken open the door of the complainants' house whilst they were in bed. There had been bad blood between the families for a while, and the Clarkes alleged that Irish-born Mrs Whiteman 'tried to carry o' the Sinn Fein system', though they did not explain what they meant. Magistrates considered the evidence inconclusive and dismissed the case.

1953: Mrs Clarke, of the cats' and dogs' home at Prince Rock, received a telephone call from a motorist who had just driven some distance into Plymouth and had stopped at a petrol station in the city. When the caller had opened the bonnet, he had found a cat crouching underneath. Mrs Clarke came to meet him and took the cat to the home. Within an hour it had produced four kittens.

May 27th

1953: As part of the celebrations for the forthcoming Coronation of Queen Elizabeth II, two 16ft-high effigies depicting Queen Elizabeth I and Drake, designed by the College of Art, were placed on St Andrew's roundabout. Some passengers on a passing bus were heard to comment that it looked nothing like the Queen, as the nose was all wrong. They had presumably thought that the wire mesh and plastic figure was meant to be her present Majesty and not her Tudor namesake.

———◆———

1965: Local dentist Roy Mawton, who had purchased a book on Sir Francis Drake, published by Nicholas Breton in 1581, from a London bookseller in 1951 for a few pounds, sold it by auction through Sotheby's. An American buyer secured it with a winning bid of £5,000.

———◆———

1999: The Warner Village Leisure Complex at Coxside, on the site formerly occupied by the old gasworks, was opened by film critic and broadcaster Jonathan Ross and supermodel Caprice. Developed by Citygrove Leisure at a cost of £40 million, it included a £15 million fifteen-screen cinema, had seating for 3,577, and a THX sound system – the first in Britain outside London. The first film, *Notting Hill*, was seen by 400 winners of a local newspaper competition.

May 28th

1960: At a dinner, a Plymouth alderman told the story of a small boy who was taken to the city's child guidance clinic, as his parents were worried about his apparently low intelligence. Maybe they need not have feared after all, as the lad was not impressed when he came out. 'They asked me what two and two were and where milk came from,' he said in disgust. 'They're all nuts in there.'

———— ◆ ————

1967: Francis Chichester sailed *Gipsy Moth IV* into Plymouth at the end of his single-handed circumnavigation of the world, which saw him cover about 24,000 miles in 274 days. Crowds had gathered on the Hoe to see him depart nine months earlier, and 40,000 came to welcome him on his return. The spot where he came ashore at West Hoe Pier is marked by a memorial, which was unveiled by the Duke of Edinburgh on 25 July 1997.

———— ◆ ————

2008: Beryl Cook, the artist renowned for her comic paintings of Plymouth life, died. She and her husband had moved to the city in the 1960s to run a boarding house, but after a local exhibition of her work was mounted in 1975, and her paintings were exhibited in London a year later, she became one of the best-known artists of her time.

May 29th

1860: Mary Ann Luke (18) had an argument with her father at their house in Union Street. He slapped her, struck her with a rope and sent her to bed. Later that evening, her sister Emily (14) saw her throw herself out of the window. Her skull was badly fractured and she died next day. At the inquest, Emily said that a few days earlier, Mary Ann had shown her a bottle of oxalic acid and a bottle of laudanum, threatening to take them 'if father is told', though what was to be kept a secret from him remains a mystery.

———— ◆ ————

1884: The Promenade Pier, 420ft long, 60ft wide, was officially opened. Guests gathered at the Council House for refreshments and formed a procession to the pier where the mayor, John Greenway, was presented with a key to unlock the gate. The ceremony was watched by about 30,000, with the Royal Marines Band playing. A plan to build a pavilion which could hold up to 2,500 people was initially abandoned when objections were raised that this would block out the view of Drake's Island, but, as a compromise, a slightly smaller one was added and completed in 1891. It was destroyed during the Blitz.

May 30th

1929: In the general election, Plymouth returned its first Labour MP, Jimmy Moses, a former shipwright at Devonport Dockyard who had also been the town's first Labour mayor. A former Liberal who had joined the Labour Party in 1918, he stood for the Drake division, and defeated the sitting Conservative MP Arthur Shirley Benn. Five months later, an election petition was presented alleging bribery and corruption on the part of his agent. If it had succeeded, his election would have been declared void, but, after an eight-day hearing, Moses and his agent were cleared of all charges and the MP was awarded £3,000 costs. Moses was defeated at the next election in 1931.

———◆———

1949: The Earl and Countess of Athlone arrived in Plymouth for several days of public engagements. Alvin Gamble, an antiques dealer on the Barbican, had kept aside a souvenir mug bearing a portrait of the Countess's aunt, Princess Alice, Queen Victoria's second daughter, as she had arranged to call at the shop with Lady Astor later in the day. He had refused to let anybody else touch it in case of accidents – and ironically dropped it himself, leaving it beyond repair. Fortunately, he had a similar piece that would do just as well – one showing the Queen's eldest daughter Victoria, Princess Royal, later the German Empress Frederick.

May 31st

1919: The NC4, an American seaplane with a wingspan of 126ft, weighing 14 tons fully laden, arrived at Plymouth Sound. It was one of three planes which had taken off on an Atlantic crossing from Long Island, New York, on 8 May, but the only one to reach the Azores. From there it flew to Lisbon and then Plymouth, becoming the first plane to fly between North America and Britain.

2002: Mrs Marie Dorothy Hanika died at Rowcroft Hospice, Torquay, aged 103. Since 1931 she had managed Genoni's Restaurant, George Street, which she had taken over on the death of her father, Aldo Genoni. He and his brother Clement had run the restaurant since 1895, when it was the Grand Swiss café in Union Street. For some years it was the only restaurant in town which stayed open after 7 p.m., and was the first in town to provide candle-lit tables and suffused lighting. During the inter-war years it attracted a clientele which included Lord Louis Mountbatten (when his ship HMS *Kelly* was in port), Clement Attlee, T.E. Lawrence, Noel Coward, John Mills, Michael Redgrave and Robert Donat. The restaurant was badly damaged in the Blitz, and closed after business had finished with a last-night party on 15 August 1959.

June 1st

1935: Government House in Mount Wise, Devonport, built in 1820 as the private residence and military offices of the lieutenant-governor of the Plymouth Garrison, was taken over by the Admiralty and, as the new Admiralty House, became the new offices of the Commander-in-Chief.

———— • ◆ • ————

1961: The newly rebuilt Athenaeum Theatre was opened by the Lord Mayor, Arthur Goldberg. The theatre had seating for 350, and it also contained a library. It had its origins in the Plymouth Institution for the Promotion of Science, Literature and the Liberal Arts, which was formed in 1812 by Henry Woollcombe. Permanent communal premises were sought and the original Athenaeum, consisting of a lecture hall and rooms in front, was opened in 1819. It was later extended, and a museum was added. Destroyed during the Blitz, the old building was completely demolished in 1959.

———— • ◆ • ————

1964: A service of exorcism was held in a flat at Clifton Place, North Hill, by prebendary J.G. Burnell. The family living there was sure it was haunted. They reported pieces of coal flying around the room, and, when they left for a night, they came back to find that glass tumblers had been moved, although not broken.

June 2nd

1975: The new West Devon Record Office was opened. A year earlier, in April 1974, Plymouth City Council had been placed under the control of Devon County Council; at this time, the Archives Department of Plymouth City Council became the West Devon Record Office. In May 1975, the archives were moved into new accommodation in the basement of the Central Library, which thus became the legal point of deposit for public records, manorial records and parish records, with facilities for private institutions to preserve their documents. The new accommodation left much to be desired, though; a public records inspector reported to the council in December 1980 on the cramped, overcrowded storage premises with poor working space for staff, while humidity in the basement and the damp at an auxiliary storage place in Crownhill meant that preservation of the documents could be at risk.

A modern industrial warehouse at Coxside was converted at a cost of £26,000, providing a large storage room, search room and room for meetings and lectures. It was opened to the public on 1 March 1982 by the Devon County Council chairman, George Creber, in the presence of the Lord Mayor of Plymouth, Reg Scott, three months later.

June 3rd

1904: 'Buffalo Bill', real name Commander William Frederick Cody, visited Plymouth, bringing with him a troop of Red Indians who were touring with him as part of his Wild West Show. It was assumed that, until then, the town's sole experience of Red Indians had been through reading about them. The spectacular was staged at Exhibition Fields, Pennycomequick, and special arrangements were made for extra trains to bring people, as well as animals, into the area. Three special trains were needed to transport the 800 horses taking part from show to show. The highlight of the programme was a re-enactment of the defeat of General Custer at the battle of Little Big Horn.

1954: Alex Cumming, curator of the City Museum and of Buckland Abbey, where he lived, received a cheque for 5 guineas, to be used for the benefit of the museum. It was signed 'Francis Drake'. All was explained by the accompanying letter, headed Mystic, Connecticut. Drake was an American citizen who had recently visited the abbey and had called outside visiting hours. Cumming had been reluctant to admit him at first, but, on hearing his name, felt he had to let him in. His efforts were evidently appreciated by the visitor.

June 4th

1876: An inquest was held at the Guildhall on the death of the illegitimate child of Edith Luke, a domestic servant. Medical evidence showed that the baby, for whose maintenance the mother paid *2s 6d* per week to a Mrs Shovel, had starved to death. Eleven members of the jury intended to return a verdict of manslaughter, but as they were not unanimous, it was considered impossible to charge both women with criminal neglect and they escaped with a severe censure.

———— • ◆ • ————

1916: Erik Samuelson, a Norwegian sailor, was a stowaway on the French ship *Treport*. He was discovered as she was sailing to England with one too many on board. When brought before the captain, he said he wanted to go to Liverpool, but his ship had sailed without him because he got drunk on his 18th birthday. He was sentenced to fourteen days in prison.

———— • ◆ • ————

1956: During the weekend, a drought in the area came to a sudden stop with a heavy downpour. Almost an inch of rain fell in twenty-four hours in Plymouth. Groundsmen at the Hoe Bowling Green were seen watering the grass with a hose almost as soon as the rain stopped. Amazed passers-by were told that the rainfall was not enough to water the fertilisers in properly.

June 5th

1958: The Drake Cinema, the only new cinema to be built in the city after the Second World War, was opened by the Lord Mayor of Plymouth, Alderman George Wingett. It had a seating capacity of 1,644, and a large model of Sir Francis Drake's ship, the *Golden Hind*, over the entrance. The day's programme, shown on a 66ft x 27ft screen, comprised the Movietone News film *Plymouth Story*, followed by a charity premiere of *South Pacific*. The first full programme featured Pat Boone and Shirley Jones in *April Love*, with a supporting programme of *Thundering Jets* and again *Plymouth Story*. Admission prices were 4s and 5s for the circle, 2s and 3s for the stalls. *South Pacific* returned on 17 July and stayed for six months.

The cinema closed on 1 March 1975, reopening four weeks later as the Drake Film Centre after a conversion enabling it to take three screens. After further renovations, and an upgrading to five screens, in 1991 it became the Drake-Odeon Cinema. With falling numbers and competition from the Warner Village, it closed on 31 October 1999 after a final showing of the film *Big Daddy*, to an audience of eight men, one woman, and twenty-five members of staff.

June 6th

1866: The closing lecture of a series on doctrines and practices of the Roman Catholic Church, delivered by Mr Murphy, of the London Protestant Electoral Union, was given at St George's Hall, Stonehouse. This last lecture, 'On the Infallibility of the Church of Rome and the Worship of the Cross', was interrupted shortly after it began by about 150 Irish men and women, many armed with cudgels, who tried to attack the audience. Thanks to swift action by several marines present, nobody was injured, the rioters were ejected, the meeting was closed and Mr Murphy was escorted home.

———◆———

1928: 'Plymouth, the centre of maritime excursions, with steamer trips, run daily', read Mr Dobell in court, from a 1928 guidebook. He represented Luke Dampney & Co., who had paid for an advertisement in the book. The judge pointed out that there were no steamers in Plymouth any more. When the company paid for the advert in September 1926 in the 'Saltash Three Towns Steamship Company' guide, they were assured repeatedly that it was going to press, but by the time they received a copy, it was out of date. A publisher's representative stated that under the terms of the contract, there was no guarantee of a time limit for its appearance. Nevertheless, undisclosed costs were awarded to the plaintiff.

June 7th

1838: The Devonport Teetotal (later Temperance) Society was formed at a meeting in the Wesleyan Association Chapel, Cannon Street, where a committee was elected. The Society established its headquarters in a room in Cherry Garden Street three months later, and founded the first Temperance Hall in the Plymouth area in Fore Street, which opened in 1852.

———•◆•———

1949: At a City Council meeting, the matter of the overpowering stench at Camel's Head Creek was raised. The problem was blamed on the new housing estates built there within the last two or three years, which had resulted in an increase in sewage. People had been complaining as they could not open their windows without being assailed, and it had been particularly intolerable during the exceptionally sunny weather over Easter. The area had been plagued with blowflies, and one resident who had lived there for almost thirty years said that she had never known the smell to be as bad as it had been that spring. A snap of slightly colder weather since April had come as a welcome relief.

———•◆•———

1956: A Plymouth solicitor received a letter from one of his lady clients, referring to her possible impending divorce: 'Shall I be entitled to acrimony money?'

June 8th

1965: A few years before the advent of colour television, when the idea was still a novelty, a TV and radio shop in New George Street had a set showing a colour film of Queen Elizabeth II on a royal tour of New Zealand. It was clearly visible from the doorway, and a few people gathered round to watch. One or two made enquiries as to the price, but on being told it was 133 guineas, said that it was too dear for them. Only later did the salesman reveal that it was not what it seemed but merely a sales gimmick designed to arouse curiosity. The set was actually a cabinet without any works inside, with a colour film being relayed onto the screen by an ordinary film projector.

That same day, another sign of times gone by could be observed in a nearby Plymouth café, where a large notice was displayed: 'In the interests of hygiene, customers should refrain from smoking.' The staff had thoughtfully left ashtrays on the tables, in case their clientele were unable to abstain from the weed. Sure enough, there were several customers inside at the time – and all of them were smoking.

June 9th

1948: A Plymouth butcher was asked why he was standing outside his own shop one morning in a queue of thirty people. He said that by the time the customers had all been served, his morning supplies of sausages would be exhausted, so he was standing there to stop more people queueing and then finding there was nothing left for them. Most of them appreciated the gesture, but one woman said crossly, 'What do you mean? I can see them in the shop.'

———— • ❖ • ————

1953: The manager of a Plymouth cinema was driving home late with a friend, and had reached the roundabout at the bottom of Royal Parade when he realised that he had a flat tyre. After stopping the car, he removed the punctured tyre without difficulty, but although he and his friend wrestled with the spare for about twenty minutes, it would not go on. A pedestrian, clearly a little the worse for drink after closing time, came up to them and offered his 'assisthance'. Their patience worn thin and they told him to go away. He politely refused, and in the end they let him have a go. He squatted down in the road, picked up the wheel, and fitted the tyre within seconds. Don't drink and drive, but...

June 10th

1965: A mysterious squeak had been puzzling Mrs Jones all day in her house in Efford. She had first heard it during the morning, and thought her cat must have caught a bird on the back porch. She asked her neighbour to come and look but the latter saw nothing and said she was imagining things. Later that day, Mrs Jones had friends visiting from America. By this time, the noise was beginning to worry her. It took her sharp-eyed 9-year-old niece Vicki to see the cause – a small beak protruding through the bolt hole in the door jamb. A baby starling had become trapped behind the hollow steel frame of the back door. Vicki fed it with pieces of bread, while neighbours and friends were invited round to see it. When Mr Jones came home from work, he had to cut a 6in-hole in the door jamb to release it. The bird was then bedded down in an old shoe box and given more food, before the Joneses' son fetched a ladder and climbed back on the roof so he could put it back in the nest with its siblings. By then it had become quite tame, and, when picked up, showed no signs of fear.

June 11th

1938: A package arrived at a Plymouth address, from Christiani & Nielsen, Reinforced Concrete Engineers of Marsham Street, Westminster. It had contained £200 in banknotes, sent by Registered Post, but when it arrived at its destination, the money had been replaced by pieces of chocolate. The police were alerted and asked to investigate.

1946: Two postage stamps, issued to commemorate victory in the war, proved particularly popular at city post offices. In addition to what was seen as customary demand, some collectors were purchasing whole sheets at a time. Within three days, £5,455 worth of the 2½*d* value had been sold, and £1,159 worth of the 3*d* value. One puzzled lady asked at a sub-post office, 'Is it all right to use these on letters?'

1956: An elderly resident, who had been a driver for over fifty years and was one of the first people in Plymouth to own a car, said he had given up driving altogether, as he had so much trouble parking, and it was easier to take a 3*d* bus instead. 'The other day I had to drive round the city centre twice in order to visit a shop. Finally I left my car on a roundabout.'

June 12th

1943: During an air raid on the city, a young Nazi airman bailed out of his aeroplane and landed in Lisson Grove, Mutley Plain. He was promptly captured by Mr Doidge, a warden, who was the only member of the service to capture an enemy airman in the streets of Plymouth during the war. The young German had been stricken with terror by the sound of a bomb dropping, and was seen to shudder at the flames as he was taken past Timothy White's shop, which was ablaze at the time.

When the news was released, one small detail was expunged by the censor and not revealed to the public until after the end of the war, almost two years later. In order to take the man captive, Doidge had found it necessary to remove a piece of string from his pocket, tie it firmly around the young man's wrists and lead him along the back lane by the loose end. It had been feared that knowledge of the string would have led to an international outcry, and consequent exploitation by the Nazi propaganda machine, about 'binding prisoners of war'.

June 13th

1956: A Plymouth lady had a Siamese cat which was very fond of playing with balls of wool, and frequently returned to the house with wool she had found on her travels. This was easy enough to tolerate within limits, but the owner felt these limits were breached when the pet came back one day with a partly knitted jumper, complete with needles.

———— • ✦ • ————

1982: Plymouth City Council charged Clark Construction £354 for parking, while the latter was working on a three-month conversion of the former Wadham Stringer building at Derry's Cross into premises for a new branch of Habitat. The charge was levied at time and a half parking rates – even though no vehicle had been left there – as the firm had placed security hoardings on two car parking spaces, thus enabling them to make the site safe for public access. Alan Coulter, Clark's regional surveyor, explained that they were enhancing a building which when finished would be bringing more shoppers into the city centre for parking. 'This is a completely unjustifiable charge and we don't think we will pay for it,' he said. John Mills, chairman of the Transport Committee, conceded that it was 'not encouraging industry very much'.

June 14th

1933: New facilities, in what was planned to be the final stage of modifications to the Tinside Pool on the Hoe, were opened by the Lord Mayor, Alderman R.R. Oke. The original bathing houses had been built and first opened in 1913, and limestone-fronted bathing houses and terraces on the western end of the bay were erected in 1928. Further developments, including additional terraces and dressing rooms, were completed two years later, with the fourth phase incorporating cliff paths, a promenade, sunbathing terraces, steps from Madeira Road, a concreted foreshore (for the benefit of young children who wished to paddle), public conveniences, and a circular extension to an existing groyne (so bathers could enter the water at low tides). After yet more modifications, the pool was opened again in October 1935 by the Lord Mayor, Lieutenant-Commander E.W. Rogers. Now open between May and September, it was designed in a semicircle 180ft in diameter, with a large central fountain and two smaller side fountains, and was floodlit at night with three decorative colour changes. After falling use and subsequent neglect, the pool closed in 1992, but demands led to its renovation at a cost of £3.4 million, and Grade II listed building status in 1998. It reopened in 2005. A lift and hoist were added in 2009 for disabled access.

June 15th

1982: There was a festive atmosphere at the Artillery Arms, Stonehouse, following news of the Argentine surrender which brought the Falklands War to an end. It was unofficially the marines' pub, and backed directly onto one of the Stonehouse Barracks gates. Marines who had remained in the city when the Task Force sailed for the South Atlantic, several wearing 'Keep the Falkland Islands British' T-shirts, raised their glasses in tribute as they joined with customers in preparing to give their colleagues a rousing welcome on their return home. Landlady Flo Hart started a collection at the bar to put towards a street party. One regular, Dave Robertson, had sailed on HMS *Intrepid*, but had had to return home earlier that month after injuring a foot during the taking of San Carlos, East Falkland. Wearing a 'Hands off – they're British' T-shirt, he said it was really boring to be back. 'Here I am filling in compensation forms when all that is happening over there. The atmosphere on the islands today must be pretty good.' Meanwhile, David Elliott, director of Atlas Flags, Commercial Road, said he could not keep pace with the demand for Union Jacks from those wishing to hang them out in celebration.

June 16th

1956: The Revd John Byrnell, vicar of St Matthias, caused mild controversy when he wrote in his parish magazine that he had told his wife he did not think washing dishes was a man's job. She had the perfect answer, quoting to him from Kings 2, Chapter 1 Verse 13, 'And I will wipe Jerusalem as a man wipeth a dish, wiping it and turning it upside down.' Now, Byrnell said, some of his male parishioners were complaining he had let them down.

1957: Norman Crayton, manager of the Palace Theatre, had had enough of thefts from the front of his premises. Pictures of the attractive ladies appearing in his shows were being torn out of their frames, and he announced that in future he hoped to install burglar-proof devices on them all. Rochelle Lofting, the star of the current production, said that four of her publicity pictures had been taken, and she must have lost nearly 100 altogether since she set out on her tour four months earlier. Nevertheless, she was prepared for it in Plymouth. Southampton, she had also discovered, was in what she called 'a collecting mood'. 'It's always worse when there are any sailors around.'

June 17th

1954: Mr F.D. Holman, manager of the Plaza Cinema, took out an insurance policy which covered any member of the audience for £500 in the event of their sudden demise from gelogenic rupture, or, in layman's terms, laughing themselves to death. The policy would remain in force for three days, 17-19 June, while the comedy *M. Hulot's Holiday* was being shown. Holman had been advised that it was so funny that he dared not take any chances. As the film would be shown at nine performances over three days, with seating for up to 1,000 each time, it was calculated that in the unlikely event of everyone falling victim to such a 'happy end', the total liability would be £4.5 million.

1982: A letter was sent from Argentina to Jimmy Hall, the president of Plymouth Rotary Club. Inside was a stamp worth about 10p, which the writer suggested could be auctioned for charity, and a pamphlet arguing Argentine claims to the Falklands. Headed 'Rotary Club de Montserrat', based in Buenos Aires, it was merely signed 'Charles'. Hall was surprised to receive this letter 'out of the blue'. It was strongly condemned by Rotary International, London, as a 'concerted campaign of political propaganda', to an organisation which by its constitution was non-political and non-denominational.

June 18th

1970: During an exceptionally warm, dry summer and subsequent heatwave, record sales were reported by the city and surrounding area's ice cream and soft drink manufacturers. Plymouth-based area representatives reported 2.5 million individual ice cream sales in Devon and Cornwall, an increase of about 1 million on the corresponding week's sales of the previous year. Soft drink sales had reached such a peak that glass manufacturers were temporarily unable to keep pace with the demand for further bottles. Mr R.C. Widdecombe, Managing Director of a city firm of mineral water manufacturers, said he had 'never known anything like it'.

In the general election held on that same day, which resulted in a Conservative victory over the outgoing Labour government, there was no change in Plymouth's parliamentary representation. Dame Joan Vickers (Conservative), who had sat for the Devonport constituency since 1955, increased her majority from 319 to 1,372, while Dr David Owen (Labour), first elected in 1966, was likewise returned, but with a sharply reduced majority, falling from 5,222 to 747. Dr Owen, who sat for Plymouth Devonport from 1974 to 1992 after a redrawing of the boundaries, later left the Labour Party to help found and then lead the Social Democratic Party. (*See* July 2nd)

June 19th

1901: Westwell Gardens was opened to the public when Archdean Wilkinson, on behalf of St Andrew's Church, handed over the silver key to the mayor, Mr R. Risdon. The site had formerly been a burial ground for St Andrew's Church. During the next forty years it would become a favourite lunchtime place for workers in the surrounding shops and offices. After the Second World War, the area was given over to temporary shops during reconstruction, the last being demolished in 1959.

———◆———

1949: On this, the hottest day of the year so far, a 12ft shark was seen off Millbay Docks. Police advised bathers not to swim off Plymouth Hoe, which was very crowded because of the heat. Many people could not understand why they were being warned off, as it was so calm. A number of people insisted on disregarding the red flag warning, and a lifeboat patrolled the area advising people to stay well out of the water.

———◆———

1958: A local resident called to see his doctor. While sitting in the waiting room, he picked up a rather inappropriate book, *Sixty Days to Live* by Dennis Wheatley.

June 20th

1916: Private Frederick Brooks, a soldier serving with the Worcestershire Regiment, gave himself up at the police station in Bedford Street and said he had just killed a young girl. 'I don't know what made me do it,' he explained. 'I must have been mad or in a fit of temper for a minute or two.' He then led them to the body of 12-year-old Alice Gregory, the daughter of a couple in Alexandra Road, Mutley, with whom he had lodged a few times. Mr Gregory had told his wife recently that he thought there was something rather peculiar about Brooks, and he did not want him in the house again. Earlier that day, the soldier had gone to Alice's school and told the teachers that her parents had given him permission to take her to a shop nearby. He had taken her out, hailed a taxi to Lower Compton, strangled her and thrown her body in a field.

Charged with murder, he went on trial at Exeter Assizes in November. Although the defence made much of his severe depression, fits, and 'attacks of unexplained violence', the jury found him guilty and he was hanged on 12 December.

June 21st

1840: Edward Stanley Gibbons, the world's most renowned philatelic dealer, was born (coincidentally, the same year as the first postage stamps were issued) at 15 Treville Street. His father, a chemist, allowed him to sell stamps from one of the shop counters and use a side window for display purposes. As the business grew, he expanded into a separate room above the shop. His most famous acquisition was in 1863, when he purchased a bag of triangular Cape of Good Hope stamps for £5 from two visiting sailors who had won them in a raffle. Edward sorted them and sold them in packets of twelve. His elder brother Alfred, a naval commander, helped the business by bringing back parcels of stamps from his overseas travels. In 1865, Stanley published his first monthly price list, the forerunner of today's catalogues, and changed the trading name from E.S. Gibbons to E. Stanley Gibbons. When his father died in 1867, he sold the pharmacy business to concentrate on trading in stamps, moving to larger premises at 8 Lockyer Street in 1872 and changing the name, yet again, to Messrs Stanley Gibbons & Co. The business moved to London in 1874.

June 22nd

1897: Celebrations were held throughout the country to mark the Diamond Jubilee of Queen Victoria. In Plymouth, sixty glorious years were marked – as were so many events of that nature down the ages – by bonfires on the Hoe which could be seen from some distance away. On this occasion, the bonfires had been built largely from old timber flooring from the recently demolished houses in Looe Street and the surrounding roads. What nobody had realised was that the wood was full of bugs. As the flames and temperature rose, thousands of them escaped and found their way into the clothing of the unsuspecting spectators. The mayor, members of the Corporation, and others who had been standing close by, were seen to be scratching themselves rather energetically afterwards as a result.

———— • ◆ • ————

1945: A small crowd in Exeter Street had gathered round a tank and were inspecting it with great interest. One elderly man said to another, 'It's a German tank.'

'How do you know?' asked his friend.

'The driver told me so.'

From behind them came an angry American voice, 'I said SHERMAN!'

June 23rd

1727: Richard Bickerton was born, probably in Bridgnorth, Shropshire. He became a distinguished naval officer, taking part in several naval engagements overseas as an officer, notably in the American War of Independence. Later knighted and subsequently ennobled as 1st Baronet Bickerton of Upwood, he served as Commander-in-Chief on the Leeward Islands station. After returning to England, he was promoted to the rank of Rear-Admiral. In 1790, he was elected MP for Rochester, and was also appointed Commander-in-Chief at Plymouth, flying his flag in the ninety-eight-gun second rate *St George*. He died in office in 1792.

1956: A worker at Devonport Dockyard was delighted when he bought a locally advertised 1953 Saloon car for just £2. There was nothing the matter with it, the bodywork was in excellent condition, and a garage workshop confirmed that the engine was in perfect working order. He even checked the registration with police in case it had been stolen. Eventually he found out the reason for his extraordinary bargain. It had been sold by a lady whose husband had just deserted her, telling her as his parting shot that she was welcome to sell the car and send him half the proceeds.

June 24th

1851: A train on the South Devon Railway line, which left Plymouth at 10.20 a.m., was nearing Totnes when it decapitated a man who had apparently lain down on the rail. He had been seen a few yards away from the line by the driver, who had sounded the whistle, but the train was going at full speed down an incline and was unable to stop. The deceased was identified as a Mr Bidlake, a middle-aged bachelor, who had a history of epilepsy. According to *The Times*, 'the mutilated remains were delivered to his brother', a farmer living near the railway.

———— • ◆ • ————

1965: According to the catalogue, Plymouth Central Library had 141 books on golf, but several callers complained that none were available. City Librarian Bill Best Harris reported that they were all out on loan, and this had happened since the opening of a new nine-hole golf course at Central Park. He said:

> When I first received these complaints, I could not understand them, knowing that we had a large stock of books on golf. But interest in the game prompted by the new course had produced this terrific demand, and now we hardly ever have any of these books on our shelves. The same occurs at the branch libraries.

June 25th

1880: James Reid, a 'burly Irish-American', asked the Plymouth Police if they would protect him against the Invincibles, a radical splinter group of Irish Republican Brotherhood members, who had already carried out several killings (some of the tit-for-tat variety) and who had a price on his head as well. According to a spokesman, he was 'in a state of the most abject terror'. The police surgeon who examined him regarded him as a lunatic, and ordered his detention, while contacting the Dublin Police for any further information about his recent activities.

——— •◆• ———

1916: William Hill, a taxi driver of Glen Park Avenue, was stopped and charged with driving too fast in Beaumont Road and Tothill Avenue. When he appeared in court, Constable Kerswell said that Hill's speed had been 30mph, and George Squire, a tramway inspector, said that but for the constable's prompt action, children would have been injured. Hill explained in his defence that he had been driving a wedding party that morning, and the groom was due to go to the front the next day. Superintendent Hitchcock conceded that they were all evidently anxious to get to the wedding breakfast, but nevertheless Hill was fined 20s.

June 26th

1907: Alexandra Park, Keyham, was officially opened to the public. Laid out on land given by John, Lord St Levan, who died the following year, it had provisionally been known as Keyham Barton Park during the planning stage, but was given its official name at a Devonport Council meeting in September 1907. Situated at the brow of the hill between Royal Navy Avenue and Keyham Barton, it gives an exceptionally good view over a wide area, including the naval barracks and the dockyard. It was used as a barrage balloon station during the Second World War.

◆

1958: Pupils in a class at a Plympton school were asked to write an essay about improvements which they thought were needed. One boy wanted Physical Training to be abolished. 'PT is rubbish,' he wrote. 'If you're fit you don't need it, and if you're not fit you can't do it.'

◆

1965: A Plymouth man went to see his GP about a back complaint, and was told that he should not sit for long periods at a time on a hard chair. 'Well, doctor,' he replied, 'that's precisely what I've been doing in your waiting room for the last hour and a half.'

June 27th

1925: The *Western Evening Herald* reported that on Alexandra Rose Day (a charity named after the Queen Dowager, widow of King Edward VII), Plymothians were 'besieged by a feminine army'. The women collectors had ensured that the day had…

> …been a massacre of the impecunious. The armies of the Pink Rose are vast, speedy and efficient. Although pedestrians are fleet of foot and cunning of brain, they have been annihilated … These brilliant, beautiful skirmishers know exactly when and where and how to adopt rank formation or to cover a large front most effectively with a comparatively small force.

———◆———

1981: Messrs S. Stephens Ltd, a long-established local bakery and confectionery business, closed its doors for the last time at its final branch in New George Street. It had announced that it could not afford the huge rise in rent charged by the City Council. The seven-year lease was about to expire and the annual rent would rise from £3,100 to £41,000. Solomon Stephens had opened the first shop in Hill Street in about 1888, and, by the outbreak of the Second World War, there were over a dozen branches throughout the Three Towns. Mr Stephens died in 1950 and next year the business, comprising seventeen shops and three bakeries, was sold to Messrs Rank Ltd.

June 28th

1916: George Hancock, of the Royal Garrison Artillery, was charged at the police court with stealing a purse containing four £1 notes, one 10s note, 7s in silver, and a train ticket to Birmingham from a handbag, the property of Martha French, on 17 June. Mrs Pollard, the wife of a naval stoker living at St Budeaux Terrace, said that in the morning Hancock had come to her door and asked for a drink of water. She had offered him a cup of tea, which he accepted, and showed him into the front room where she also gave him cake, ham, bread and butter. Mrs French, from Birmingham, was staying there at the time with her brother, and her handbag was in the front room.

When Hancock had finished, he had gone on his way, but Mrs French had become suspicious when she noticed him running away. Going to check, she found the purse had gone, and the next day her brother found the train ticket in the road outside. Detective Westlake received the purse from Private Elston at St Budeaux, and charged Hancock with theft. He pleaded guilty, and it was noted that he had been before the court on previous occasions. He was committed for trial at the next assizes.

June 29th

1874: John MacDonald battered his lover Bridget Walsh, with whom he had set up house while her husband was away at sea, at her home in Stonehouse. He then tried to poison himself and cut his throat, but was arrested and recovered in the prison hospital. When put on trial for murder at Exeter, he claimed that Bridget had been unfaithful to him – overlooking the fact that she was already married to someone else. He was hanged on 10 August. (*See* July 25th)

———•◆•———

1974: The sixty-first Tour de France, which took place from 27 June to 21 July, visited England – the first time the sport had been held here – for its circuit stage on the Plympton bypass. The organisers had had to approach the Secretary of State for the Environment for permission to close the road for the purpose. Plans had been made for 100,000 to watch, but rain the previous day was thought to have put some people off. Nevertheless, the sun shone as the roads were closed to traffic at 8.30 a.m. for a 10 a.m. start. Around 20,000 spectators turned out, braving the wind to watch 129 riders racing round the 7½-mile circuit up one carriageway and down the other, at an average speed of 26mph.

June 30th

1888: The Marine Biological Association headquarters were opened by Professor (later Sir) W.H. Flower, director of the Natural History Museum and president of the Zoological Society. Formed in 1884, Plymouth was chosen as the site for its laboratory and aquarium because of its rich flora and fauna. A site under the Royal Citadel (offered by the War Department) was chosen, as this made it possible to maintain direct salt-water contact.

— ◆ —

1921: Ernest Smith (24) appeared in court after having been arrested for begging in Greenbank Avenue the previous day. He wore a card which stated: 'I am a disabled ex-Service man trying to get an honest living. No pension.' When he was searched, a pension paper was found on him, showing that he received 8s a week. Shortly before his arrest he had been busking with a mouth organ. He was fined 10s.

— ◆ —

1949: Teachers at a private school in Plymouth decided to investigate the frequent absences of a boy. Like several others, he had been writing his own parents' notes and handing them to different masters. When they were compared, it was found that he had apparently had his appendix removed twice within the last twelve months.

July 1st

1890: HMS *Phoebe* was launched at Devonport Dockyard by Lady Dowell, watched by a crowd of about 3,000. A twin-screw protected cruiser with a speed of 19 knots, and a coal-carrying capacity of 300 tons, over the next few years she saw service during the colonial wars in Africa, and was later employed on duties in Australia and New Zealand. In 1906 she was sold at Portsmouth for scrap and broken up in Copenhagen.

———◆———

1900: Keyham station, between Devonport and St Budeaux stations, was opened. It was seriously damaged in the Blitz in April 1941 and closed to passenger traffic that November. In July 1965 it was closed to goods traffic and became an unstaffed halt in May 1969. The signal box closed in July 1973.

———◆———

1916: An inquiry was held at Devonport into the death of Charles Le Sanne, aged 52. This former French pilot and master of the ketch *Water Lily* was found in an open boat near Eddystone Lighthouse on 29 June. He lived at Perros-Guirec, and his vessel had left there for Plymouth on 27 June with a cargo of potatoes. There was no evidence that the ketch had been attacked, and a verdict of death from exposure was recorded.

July 2nd

1938: David Owen was born at Plympton. After studying medicine at Cambridge, he qualified as a doctor in 1962 and was elected Labour MP for Plymouth Sutton in 1966. Following boundary changes, he was elected for Plymouth Devonport in 1974. Having held several junior posts in government and opposition, he became a cabinet member in 1977 when he was appointed Foreign Secretary. Disillusioned with Labour's leftward drift, in 1981 he was one of the 'Gang of Four' who left to form the Social Democratic Party. He became leader in 1983, but wound up the party in 1990 after increasingly poor election results. In 1992 he stood down as MP for Devonport and became a life peer, Baron Owen of Plymouth. (*See* June 18th)

———————◆·———————

1958: A youth was flying from his Plymouth home to Ireland for a holiday, and he was rather anxious as it was his first time in an aeroplane. As he boarded the aircraft, he decided to take his mind off it by settling down with a good book. Only then did he discover that his mother, who did the packing, had included a copy of Agatha Christie's *Death in the Air*.

July 3rd

1954: A Plymouth man, who normally took his family to stay in a particular south Devon hotel every summer holiday, decided that they would be able to save money in the future if they bought a caravan instead. The hotel manager, a personal friend, was evidently disappointed to hear of this potential loss of income, and suggested that the man park the vehicle in the establishment's back garden. When the holidaymaker's wife was told, she was ecstatic. 'Splendid!' she said. 'We shall be able to spend all our time in the hotel.'

———◆———

1984: The *Western Evening Herald* published a letter from Plymouth town crier Ken Headon, under the heading 'Pompous twaddle', in response to another reader's letter which had differentiated between 'citizens of Plymouth' and Plymothians. In it, Ken claimed that he, and many more like him, were...

> ...sick and tired of interlopers moving in to live in our fair city and putting us down as simple 'janners' with straws sticking out of our ears. When I served in the Merchant Navy during the last war I was landed with the same image because I came from Plymouth, and was continually trying to live it down.

July 4th

1974: Rock group Sparks, of 'This Town Ain't Big Enough For Both of Us' fame, settled their bill for £400 at the Holiday Inn after staying there while playing a gig at Home Park two days earlier. The hotel innkeeper, Tony Forster, claimed that this was inadequate for the damage they and their entourage had caused. He demanded a further three-figure sum for repairs to a broken lift, damage to a colour TV in one of their bedrooms, and costs for cleaning a bedroom carpet. In addition, he complained that they had disturbed other guests with a rowdy party at 3 a.m. during their stay, and had attacked staff with water pistols. Their manager, John Hewlett, denied the alleged incidents and unruly behaviour, and said that the lift had been out of order when they arrived. The only damage they admitted causing was when some minestrone soup had been dropped on a carpet, and they refuted that it was vomit as the management had claimed. As for 'attacks' on hotel staff, Hewlett stated that 'water pistols are part of the fun of life. It is something of a cult for the group.' Nevertheless, it was clear that they would not be welcomed back there in future.

July 5th

1957: A resident of Furzehatt Road, Plymstock, was clipping his hedge when he was approached by a motorcyclist. 'Can you tell me the way to Underlane?' the motorcyclist asked. He was due there for dinner at 7 p.m., and it was now 8.45. 'I've been going round in circles. The joke is I'm living there.' The Furzehatt resident began to give directions, but the rider stopped him. 'I shall only get mixed up. Tell me how to get to the pub with the billiard room.' He was told how to find the Plymstock Inn and went away happily, leaving the other man wondering whether the hostelry was a suitable landmark, or perhaps, in view of the reception he might receive at Underlane, a better place for a convivial evening.

1992: RAF Mount Batten closed. Established as the Royal Naval Air Service at Cattewater in 1918, the base was recommissioned ten years later at Mount Batten. The departure of No. 19 Group Coastal Command RAF in 1968 had marked the beginning of the end for the station, and the ceremony for the disbanding of the RAF Marine Branch was held there on 8 January 1986. The land and buildings were handed over to the Plymouth Development Corporation.

July 6th

1797: Three marines, Lee, Coffy and Branning, were executed after being found guilty at a court-martial of incitement to mutiny at Stonehouse Barracks. They were marched from the Citadel to the Hoe by an escort of marines, with a coffin before each, preceded by a band playing Handel's Dead March from Saul. A contemporary newspaper report described how they were attended by two priests…

…who after praying with them near an hour, quitted them, and they all three knelt on their coffins for a few minutes, when an officer of marines came and drew the caps over their faces, and a party of twenty marines immediately came down and put a period to their existence by discharging the contents of their muskets through their bodies, after which all the regiments marched round them in solemn procession, the whole forming, perhaps, one of the most awful scenes that the human eye ever witnessed. They all behaved in a manner becoming their melancholy situation, and apparently very resigned and penitent. About thirty thousand people were supposed to be present at the execution.

Another marine who was tried for a similar crime, McGennis, was given 500 lashes, and then taken back to the barracks in preparation for being transported to Botany Bay for life.

July 7th

1837: On the occasion of King William IV's funeral, all shops and places of public entertainment in the Three Towns were closed. Services were held at churches, chapels and the synagogue as a solemn knell was sounded throughout the streets, and all ships in harbour fired salutes to his memory.

———•◆•———

1940: Plymouth had its first weekend of bombing during the Second World War. At 5.30 p.m., a German bomber flew over the east end of the city and discharged its explosives on houses at the junction of South Milton Street and Home Sweet Home Terrace, killing five people and injuring four, one of whom died in hospital a few days later. The post office was also destroyed. The previous day had seen the first of the enemy bombs, when a man, a woman and a boy were killed, and six others were injured, after a block of eight houses in Swilly Road, Devonport, was hit.

July 8th

1863: A well-dressed couple travelled from Plymouth to Truro by train this afternoon, to rob several drapers' shops. The woman asked to see a few dresses, order one, and have some trimming cut off for her, then requested that the parcel and bill be ready for her in an hour's time. When she did not return the dresses were examined, and it was found that various pieces had been stolen. The couple were recognised on their way back to the station, planning to return to Plymouth. Known to have committed similar thefts in Devonport, they were arrested and held in custody pending trial.

———◆———

1949: A man told reporters that he had a Plymouth telephone number similar to that of a local brewery and often received calls from pub landlords, as well as private customers, for the wrong reason. One woman landlord persistently called his number by mistake, until eventually he could not resist playing a joke. 'What have you done with all that beer you had last week?' he asked. There was a puzzled gasp, then he continued, 'Do you know you must be drinking too much, a lot too much? Have you any idea what all this drinking must be doing to your system?' The line went dead.

July 9th

1893: Walter Corry, a promising young professional operatic baritone vocalist, who had recently visited Plymouth while on a nationwide tour with the Burns-Crotty Opera Company, was found dead in bed in his Lambeth apartment shortly after midday by his neighbours. He had regularly suffered from severe neuralgia and insomnia, and took what was thought to be an accidental overdose of chloral. An empty bottle was found lying beside his bed.

———— ◆ ————

1938: A girl boarded a Plymouth bus, only to discover that the only money she was carrying in her bag consisted of a banknote and a ½*d* coin. She needed a 2*d* ticket for her journey, so she offered the conductor the ½*d* and a 1½*d* stamp. He looked at them and shook his head. 'I never write any letters,' he told her. 'You owe me the three halfpence. You'll be on these buses again?' She assured him she would be, and was allowed to travel on to her destination. Although she regularly took the same vehicle, and always made sure she had the right money with her in the future, she never saw the conductor again.

July 10th

1897: Walter Ward was charged on suspicion of being a deserter from the Royal Naval Barracks, Devonport. The constable who arrested him had seen his name in the *Police Gazette* as a deserter. It had since been found that Ward had been discharged from the service for misconduct in April after serving a term of imprisonment. The Chief Constable subsequently asked the Bench to discharge the case.

———— • ◆ • ————

1916: At a meeting of Plymouth Town Council, draft by-laws governing street trading were reviewed. The Special Purposes Committee recommended that no children under 12 should be employed or engaged in the practice. One member suggested that, in accordance with the findings of the education committee, the limit should be increased to 14 years, as 'the golden period of a child's education was 12 to 14'. On behalf of the trade unions, another said that the limit should be 15 years, as all children ought to have the opportunity of being educated up to that age, and it was in the interests of child and community that the age limit should be as high as possible. In a poll determining whether or not the minimum age should be raised, the notion was defeated by thirty-four votes to twenty-three.

July 11th

1908: Henry Francis Whitfeld, best remembered for his history, *Plymouth and Devonport in Times of War and Peace*, published in 1900, died at his home, Torrington Place, North Road. After leaving school he became a journalist at the *Western Daily Mercury*, where he became chief reporter and then editor of the paper – the circulation of which increased from 2,000 to 8,000 as a result. Unfortunately, the paper changed hands and Whitfeld found that he could not get on with the new owners, so he was sacked. In 1891 he formed a company in order to acquire the *Devonport Independent*, of which he then became editor. Deeply concerned by the slum housing conditions around Morice Square, he wrote and published a series of investigative articles under the by-line 'The Boy from the Back of Morice Square', followed by a pamphlet, 'The Curse of Devonport'. He was elected to serve on the town council and later became chairman of the Corporation's new Housing of the Working Classes Committee.

—◆—

1954: During the week, city householders received their rate demands. Accompanying these in the envelope was an illustrated folder recommending the Plymouth crematorium.

July 12th

1958: Mr A.M. Edwards, manager of the Gaumont Cinema, announced that, as from Monday 14 July, their main feature would be the horror film *Dracula*. In view of the nature of this picture, the cinema would provide special reinforcements of the St John Ambulance Brigade on duty in case patrons should pass out. While brigade members were always present, this time they would be at 'emergency strength' in case anybody should need first aid at the sight of the vampire at work.

———•◆•———

1999: The Institute of Management hosted a meeting of business chiefs at Seymour House, Mount Wise, under the banner 'Visions for Plymouth'. Each speaker reinforced the theme that the regeneration of Plymouth into a modern twenty-first century city was essential if it was to compete successfully in the world economy. One stressed the importance of extra funding for housing, in order to create sustainable communities for the 90,000 people living around the waterfront and to reduce pressure on the countryside. Another said that with the rise of globalisation, shrinking markets and worldwide reach as a result of the Internet, the city should consider itself as a world city, competing internationally for investment and grants.

July 13th

1892: Joseph Sowerby, formerly of the Leeds Police force, was appointed Chief Constable of Plymouth. At the time, a constable's wages were 19s per week, rising to £1 8s 6d for the most senior ranks. It was common practice for constables to have 1s deducted each week for the first forty weeks of service, in case they left suddenly and ran away with their uniform. Sowerby put an end to this, and £500 was distributed among his men. He retired in March 1917 and died at his home in Mannamead in 1919.

———◆———

1912: A 15-year-old girl was charged at the Children's Court, Stonehouse, with attempting suicide. Superintendent Crooke said that on the previous evening the girl had argued with her mother (who would not give her a new pair of boots), seized a bottle labelled POISON and drank the contents, but the liquid was relatively mild and would probably have been insufficient to kill her. Crooke had spoken to her this morning and was sure she never meant to kill herself, but merely wanted to frighten her mother. Her father was dead, and her mother promised to take charge of her daughter. The girl promised to give no further trouble, and was discharged.

July 14th

1827: Laira Bridge was opened by the Duchess of Clarence, later Queen Adelaide. Built privately by the Earl of Morley at a cost of £27,126 and thus subject to a toll, it replaced a rather unreliable ferry crossing. The first stone was laid in March 1825. Engineered by James Rendel in cast-iron, with foundations of granite, limestone and a water-resistant mortar, it consisted of five elliptical arches of iron on stone pillars. The bridge was purchased from the Earl of Morley by Plymouth Corporation, and tolls were abolished in 1904 for the benefit of farm traders bringing milk and other produce into the town from the South Hams. Work on a new bridge, comprising a dual carriageway, was begun in November 1959 and the completed structure, which cost £680,000, was opened on 1 June 1962 by Lord Chesham, Parliamentary Secretary at the Ministry of Transport. It was not the sweetest-smelling area in the city, and, around the end of the Second World War, a passer-by quipped that he had heard the water was going to be renamed the River Oder.

July 15th

1865: Charles Norrington, the Mayor of Plymouth, held an evening banquet at Sussex House for the officers of the French and English squadrons anchored in Plymouth Sound, as well as the heads of the public departments. The band of the South Devon Militia was present, and the mayor gave, in succession, the toasts of the Queen, the Emperor of the French, and the French Navy. Captain Le Bris of the *Magenta* responded to the latter.

——◆——

1931: The Prince of Wales presided over the opening ceremony for Plymouth Airport, Roborough. Because of bad weather, the royal party were unable to land at the aerodrome, and it had to be declared open from inside the Council Chamber in the Municipal Offices in the centre of Plymouth. As a souvenir of the occasion, His Royal Highness was presented with a silver model of his moth flying machine. Plymouth had been keen to have her own airport ever since a successful series of flights had been made from a site near RNAS Laira at Chelson Meadows. Sites at Staddon Heights, Chelson, and on land near Ernesettle Camp at St Budeaux, had all been considered, but Roborough was judged to be the most suitable location, and the council bought the site for £20,478.

July 16th

1723: Joshua Reynolds was born in Plympton St Maurice, son of the master at the local grammar school. He was apprenticed to Thomas Hudson, a London-based portrait painter, and went on to become Britain's most successful, in-demand portrait painter of the age. When the Royal Academy of Arts was founded in 1768, he was elected its first president and knighted. Although based in London throughout his career, he returned to the Plymouth area from time to time, mainly to paint the great and the good. He was a friend of the Parker family at Saltram House, where several of his portraits still hang on the walls.

———— •◆• ————

1948: A Plymouth doctor had just learnt that one of his patients preferred to remain on the private list rather than take free treatment under the National Health Service, which had been established earlier that month. 'All right,' he told him, 'and now you will receive treatment as the vermin that you are.' This was presumably a reference to the controversial speech by Aneurin Bevan, Minister of Health, who had overseen the creation of the NHS, in which he castigated the Conservatives as 'lower than vermin'.

July 17th

1916: Two Stonehouse women were summoned for failing to screen the lights in their rooms as laid down by wartime regulations. Constable Braund said that their lights were visible half a mile away after 11.30 p.m. on 10 July. Leah Penfold (20), of Water Lane, said that her husband had just joined up, she had not been home very long that evening, and the baby had fallen out of bed. Sarah Coe (59), of High Street, apologised, saying that she had forgotten about the blinds that night. Both were discharged with a caution, as the chairman of the magistrates said that they were living in small houses, and the occupants of larger dwellings were also infringing regulations.

1948: Wayne Sleep was born in Plymouth, where his stepfather was a clerk with Coates Gin. In 1961, he won a scholarship to the Royal Ballet School – at 5ft 2in the shortest person ever to be admitted to the institution. He later became a principal dancer with the Royal Ballet, as well as one of the most famous British dancers and choreographers of his time.

July 18th

1956: A couple returned home to Plymouth from a holiday on the Isle of Man. They had bought several souvenirs there, including two metal ashtrays with 'Good wishes from the Isle of Man' inscribed on the front. When turned over, the ashtrays turned out to be rather less local than had been supposed. Careful examination revealed a stamp, 'Made in Plymouth'.

———— • ◆ • ————

1984: Santa Claus was coming to town – five months early. That day, Father Christmas could be seen dancing outside the Good Companions, Mayflower Street, where parties were being held to celebrate his early return. Licensees Bill and Donna Hibbert said that they had decided to lay on unseasonal festivities for a joke and they were going down very well with their customers, who appreciated the restaurant being decked out with holly, Christmas trees and baubles in midsummer (and an unusually hot dry summer at that) as they tucked heartily into their yuletide fare. 'Why should everyone be boring and celebrate Christmas on Christmas Day?' they asked. 'It's much better to do it now and it's more of a surprise.' The only thing absent was real fir trees, found to be too expensive at this time of year.

July 19th

2008: On the fifth and last evening of Music of the Night, an outdoor spectacular of music, song and dance, there were fears that this might be the last ever. First staged in July 1992 and once every two years thereafter, the 2008 show was the ninth. It included hundreds of local performers working side-by-side with musicians from the Bands of the Royal Artillery and the Royal Marines, augmented by lasers, fireworks and gunfire, all presented by the 29th Commando Regiment of the Royal Artillery at the Royal Citadel. In 2008, the tickets were priced from £17 to £27, and the cast numbered over 300. During its sixteen-year history, the event had raised nearly £500,000 for various charities, including King George's Fund for Sailors, the Army Benevolent Fund, and SSAFA (Soldiers, Sailors, Airmen and Families Association). Organisers confirmed that they would take a break from the show due to pressures on military and civilian participants. Notably, the event depended largely on volunteers, the military were far busier in operational terms in the theatre of war by this time than they had been in 1992, and costs had been steadily rising. However, although there was no show in 2010, plans were in place to stage a tenth in 2012.

July 20th

1906: 'Chase over house tops' and 'Exciting scene at Stonehouse' read the *Western Evening Herald* headlines. They referred to the matter of Thomas King and Joseph Stanley, naval stokers from HMS *Vivid*, being charged at Stonehouse Police Court with being on the roof of premises belonging to Dr Waterfield with unlawful intent. Alerted to their presence by a neighbour who saw them on the roof shortly before midnight, Detective Rundle went into an adjoining garden and called to the men to come down and not cause any further disturbance. They ignored him, so he fetched a ladder with the intention of bringing them down. They then climbed onto another part of the roof, which was about 6ft higher, and walked further along the top of the house and hid behind the chimney. Rundle and another policeman followed them over the tops of several other houses, occasionally losing sight of them. At one stage, the men got into the backyard of a house, but they saw somebody there and consequently climbed back onto the roof. Finally they gave up, returned to the garden and were arrested. When charged, they merely said they were skylarking. Both men, who had joined the navy only two months previously, were given three months in prison with hard labour.

July 21st

1862: The Victoria Cross was conferred by Admiral Sir Houston Stewart, Commander-in-Chief at Devonport, on William Odgers, a leading seaman on HMS *Cambridge*. Odgers had been serving in the Taranaki Maori wars in New Zealand on 28 March 1860, and, according to the despatch from his commanding officer, displayed 'conspicuous gallantry' when a party of marines and officers from the ship stormed the settlement of Kaipopo Pa during a skirmish against the Maoris. He was the first to enter under heavy fire, and assisted in hauling down the enemy flag. It was the first VC to be awarded to any man serving in New Zealand. Later the action was dismissed as a 'fictional triumph' by a New Zealand historian. Odgers, a Cornishman by birth, later achieved the rank of quartermaster. He died in Saltash in 1873, aged 39.

———— • ◆ • ————

1948: The Bertram Mills Big Top Circus had been drawing large crowds to Victoria Park some six weeks earlier, and had put signs up along the route to the venue throughout much of the city, saying 'To the Circus'. After the circus left, all were removed except for one, at Prince Rock. A passer-by saw it on this day and was convinced it was directing him to Drake Circus.

July 22nd

1917: Aldo Genoni of the Swiss Café was alleged to have sold a bottle of cider to Lieutenant Mitchell, a military invalid, in contravention of a clause in the Defence of the Realm Act, preventing the supply of intoxicants to wounded soldiers. Genoni was fined 10s, and the magistrates remarked that the provisions of the Act, all too often disregarded, should be more widely known.

1949: One visitor to Plymouth, an elderly lady in her 70s, was unfamiliar with the local custom of friendly bus conductors and other public servants addressing people informally as 'my dear'. When she asked a museum attendant for directions to one particular gallery, he obliged. 'Straight on and turn to the right, my dear.' She exclaimed crossly that in all her life she had never been addressed in that way before.

2000: Terry Andrews, from Laira, completed a sponsored 45-mile walk across Dartmoor, 'a non-stop hike around the Royal Forest', in support of Safecare Aid to Romania, a fund for orphans in the country. Aiming to raise about £1,000, which his employers BP Amoco pledged to double, he started at the Plume of Feathers, Princetown, at midday on Sunday 23 July, returning twenty-four hours later.

July 23rd

1954: An elderly lady in a Plymouth home was worried about keeping up with the payments for her graveyard plot at Paignton. She was reassured that the matter was being attended to, but, concerned that she might be buried locally instead, she explained, 'You see, I don't want to go to Efford. I don't know anybody up there.'

———•◆•———

2003: Plymouth-born Michael Foot, who had been MP for Devonport between 1945 and 1955, later leader of the Labour Party and lifelong supporter of Plymouth Argyle Football Club, was given an unexpected present on his 90th birthday when he was allocated the club's No. 90 shirt as an honorary player. He had been an Argyle fan ever since his father Isaac started taking him and his elder brother Dingle to Home Park to watch matches, in about 1921. Later, he became a shareholder and director in the club. Interviewed in 2007, he said that the away supporters were 'the best in the world', and vowed that he would 'refuse to conk out until I have seen Argyle play in the top division!' Sadly his hopes were not to be realised before his death in 2010.

July 24th

1846: Two soldiers were flogged at Devonport. One, a Mr Higgins, of the 55th Regiment, had been found guilty of selling part of his kit, and of threatening to throw a pair of boots at his commanding officer, Colour Sergeant Williams. He was sentenced to 200 lashes, and the garrison was assembled in St George's Square to watch. According to one witness, while being punished Higgins 'never winked an eye', or let a sound escape him. However, the surgeon had the flogging stopped after 150 lashes, on the grounds that the soldier could not safely take any more. At least half a dozen men were carried out of the square, as they could not stand seeing any more. Another soldier from the same regiment, a Mr Lee, received 100 lashes and twelve days' imprisonment.

1877: An explosion at Keyham Gas Works caused some minor damage to local property, although nobody was injured. It was thought to have been caused by a piece of rock, which, having been dislodged by some blasting near the site on the previous day, had pierced and wrecked a large gasometer. There was an interruption to gas supplies for the rest of the afternoon, but they were restored by the evening.

July 25th

1440: Plymouth was granted its Charter, the first to be passed by an Act of Parliament. With this came certain privileges and obligations, among them:

> ...that the mayor was to be a justice of the peace ... that the borough was to have a merchants' guild as at Oxford ... that a coroner was to be elected ... that the borough was to hold two fairs each year, on the feast of St Matthew [21 September] and the conversion of St Paul [25 January], and two markets each week, on Mondays and Thursdays ... that the borough was to have the return and execution of all royal writs ... that no burgesses were to be summoned outside the borough ... [and] that it was to have freedom from tolls.

———◆———

1874: John MacDonald was put on trial in Exeter, charged with murdering his mistress Bridget Walsh at her house in Stonehouse on 29 June. Her husband was away at sea and she and MacDonald had lived together for a while, but after an argument he had beaten her to death with a bedpost, then tried to poison himself and cut his throat. His suicide attempts having failed, he was found guilty of murder and hanged. (*See* June 29th)

July 26th

1956: A Launceston taxi driver took a farmer's wife into Plymouth for a day's shopping. On the return journey, she held out to him what he thought was a bag of sweets. He took one, and found it was a lump of white sugar. 'What do you think I am, Madam,' he asked, 'a horse?'

———— •◆• ————

1962: The fourteen-storey Civic Centre at the end of Armada Way, previously the Council House and Municipal Office, was opened by Queen Elizabeth II, thus bringing together under one roof various civic departments which had been scattered throughout the city since the destruction of the old Municipal Office building in Guildhall Square. Work had begun on the building in 1958, and the final cost was £1.6 million, of which £100,000 represented the cost of purchasing the site. £400,000 had been raised by war damage compensation for the old Municipal Offices and the sale of some surplus land. A Rooftop Restaurant was added at the last minute on floor fourteen, with seating for eighty people. Access was only from the stairs below, and the rooftop and restaurant were closed in 1975 as they were a possible fire hazard. In 2007, to forestall threats to demolish the building, it was given Grade II listed protection by English Heritage.

July 27th

1849: A sailor was taken off a yacht at Devonport Dock, suffering from fever, and removed to the workhouse where he died. His body was placed in a coffin, ready for burial, and his widow in Yarmouth was notified that the body would be kept for a few days if she wished to attend.

Meanwhile, a Mr Gyder died the same day at Devonport during the cholera epidemic. His body was also put in a coffin and kept at the same place to await burial. His funeral was due to take place as soon as possible, with minimal delay – in order to prevent the spread of infection.

However, the bodies became mixed up with each other. The sailor and his coffin were taken away by accident, and at the funeral he was followed by Mr Gyder's family. The next morning, the sailor's widow arrived at Devonport, in order to say farewell to her husband. When the lid was lifted, she was horrified to discover the terrible mistake that had been made. She had her husband's body exhumed, taken out of the parish coffin, and placed in another at her own expense.

July 28th

1869: George Hatto, an engine driver at Millbay station, was killed when he was crushed by an engine and several trucks. Early in the morning, he had been oiling part of the engine opposite the coal platform. Coal was put into the engine, which was then driven back into the shed. Hatto was standing between the coal platform and the rail, when another engine came out. He tried to get out of the way, but it hit him and knocked him off his feet. With a line of trucks following behind, there was no chance of them stopping, and the wheels passed over him. A verdict of accidental death was returned at the inquest.

———◆———

1961: A professional photographer was visited at his studio by an engaged couple. They were planning their wedding and were interested in asking him if he would take the pictures at the ceremony. The only problem, it seemed, was the matter of payment. 'Can we have the pictures on HP?' (hire purchase) they asked. Never having had such a request before, and rather taken aback, the photographer politely suggested that he felt they had come to the wrong place.

July 29th

1924: The Plymouth Naval Memorial on the Hoe was unveiled by Prince George, later Duke of Kent. After the First World War, the Imperial War Graves Commission had decided to construct memorials at Plymouth, Portsmouth and Chatham – the three ports from which the Royal Navy's ships were manned. The memorials were designed by Sir Robert Lorimer, who was responsible for the design of the Scottish War Memorial in Edinburgh and several war cemeteries in Germany. In the afternoon, the Prince opened the Devon & Cornwall (Ex-Service) Tuberculosis Colony, Efford – an open-air hospital for servicemen and their families who had contracted the disease during the First World War. Accommodation was provided for forty-eight resident families and 102 trainees. It closed in September 1935.

———•◆•———

1948: After the ending of Double Summer Time (two hours ahead of GMT), which had been introduced the previous year because of fuel shortages, the council had planned to do without street lighting until 10 August as an economy measure. Following complaints about the inconvenience and dangers of unlit streets in the evenings, on 26 July councillors had voted to restore full lighting as soon as possible. This was the first night with full lighting since before the war.

July 30th

1938: The last day of Plympton Carnival was spoiled by heavy rain, 'a long line of grey raincoats and dripping umbrellas'. Even so it proved successful, with a programme including a baby show, gymkhana, and a ladies' football match between Plympton and Honicknowle, which ended in a 1-1 draw.

———◆———

1951: A man and wife were on the Hoe this evening, seated on the grass back-to-back, both knitting. The man remarked that he supposed he must look funny, sitting there knitting. Another person sitting nearby said, 'I don't know about that. Look, I'm darning my socks!' He held them up for all to see. Then a third man announced, 'And I'm doing my crochet,' likewise displaying his efforts to general view.

———◆———

1956: Joan Vickers, MP for Devonport, told the story of a woman who had dined in one of the city's Chinese restaurants. Admiring a set of characters on the menu card, she had taken a sketch of them and later embroidered them in red silk on a white jumper. Her delight with the result was cut short when a friend from Burma saw the jumper and nearly doubled up with mirth. Too late, the lady learned that the characters on her chest proclaimed 'Cheap but good'.

July 31st

1957: The Devonport Maternity Home, Cumberland Road, Devonport (formerly the Military Families' Hospital, built in 1890 as part of Raglan Barracks), was opened. The army had ceased to use it after the National Health Service took over running the hospitals in 1948, and between 1952 and 1956 it was used as a tuberculosis hospital.

———— • ◆ • ————

1967: One man found himself up the creek – Camel's Head Creek – when he was out worming, got 'that sinking feeling' and suddenly found himself waist-deep. City firemen were called to help him out, but he managed to extricate himself and they hosed him down. He was none the worse for his ordeal.

On the same day, William Piert (24), a labourer, pleaded not guilty in the Magistrates' Court to being drunk and disorderly in Vauxhall Street, and was fined £2. Constable Johnson said that Piert had been seen dancing along the white line in the middle of the road, shouting in a slurred voice, then had jumped on a car bonnet and emptied the contents of a Plymouth Corporation litter bin over the footpath. When approached, he had told the officer, 'I am an Irishman and proud of it.' In court he said he did not remember anything about being disorderly.

August 1st

1953: Miss Inga Gudmundsdottir from Iceland and Mr Gunnlangur Einarsson from Sweden were married at Revelstoke church, Noss Mayo. An engineering student at Gothenburg, Gunnlangur had met Inga shortly after coming to England in April to assist in salvage operations on the ship *James Eagan Layne*, which had sunk off Whitsand Bay. They had both fallen in love with the Plymouth area, and, after returning from their honeymoon, they intended to make their home at Plymbridge Road, Crownhill.

———•◆•———

2000: The Peninsula Medical School was established. Run in partnership with the Universities for Plymouth and Exeter, and the National Health Service in Devon and Cornwall, it aimed to expand the number of medical students in Britain. Professor Sir John Tooke, who had led the initiative to establish the school, was appointed as the school's first Dean, a post he held until autumn 2009. The first intake of 130 undergraduate students commenced their studies on 30 September 2002, an intake which rose to 167 a year later, to 214 from September 2006 and 230 from September 2010.

August 2nd

1945: President Harry Truman of the United States met King George VI aboard HMS *Renown*, moored in Plymouth Sound, after attending the Potsdam Conference at the end of the Second World War. Several thousand eager Plymothians turned out to welcome Truman, but left having seen nothing of him. The route had been changed at the last moment, and even the police were unaware of the exact plan. For a few hours, it appeared that the President was more closely guarded than the King. Only a few select representatives from the press were allowed within close range of Truman, who went to Victoria Wharves by way of Greenbank and Friary Bridge. There was disappointment that he saw very little, if anything, of the blitzed city centre, and the press claimed that, for the public, the visit was 'a fiasco'.

———————•◆•———————

1961: A French girl called at the Holiday Information Bureau and the Guildhall, but could not understand the assistant's answers to her queries. At length, she told the assistant sadly, 'I do not wish to be rude, but you do not speak English like they do at Okehampton.'

August 3rd

1769: After spending the previous day drinking, a captain and lieutenant in the marines, who had always been inseparable companions, fought a duel outside Plymouth. The latter was wounded, but, presumably anaesthetised by alcohol, made light of his injuries. They wandered back arm-in-arm to the barracks at about 3 a.m., at which point the lieutenant dropped down dead. The inconsolable captain was gaoled, insisting to others that he 'knows not how the affair happened'.

———— ◆ ————

2008: This evening, Chris Edwards (43) of Plymstock, a part-time magician, and his family saw an 'unidentified flying object' high above Staddiscombe, moving slowly towards the South Hams. He wanted to hear from anyone else who had seen an 'unusually bright white light' in the sky at the same time. Stepping outside for a cigarette at 10.30 p.m., he had spotted an object which was unusually dazzling – like a glowing orb or a small sun – with a glare coming off it so brightly that no other stars were visible. He watched it for about twenty-five minutes, as it moved away from him. When he looked again, at about 11.30 p.m., it had disappeared, but stars were once again visible in the night sky. A police spokesperson said they had received no reports of strange lights in the sky that night.

August 4th

1890: Queen Victoria's second son Alfred, Duke of Edinburgh, Admiral of the Royal Navy and former Commander-in-Chief of the Mediterranean Fleet, arrived at Devonport to take up his post as Commander-in-Chief. On landing at Mount Wise, he was escorted to Admiralty House (later Hamoaze House), which would be his official residence. Here his predecessor, Admiral Sir William Dowell, introduced him to the principal naval officers in the town. Afterwards they attended an official luncheon, then took the dockyard train to Keyham for a reception by a guard of honour and a ceremonial inspection of the barracks. Alfred then sailed to Cowes on leave, during which time Admiralty House was to be altered to make accommodation for additional domestic staff. He returned in September, but had to stay in the Royal Hotel at Devonport as the house was still not ready. During the two years and ten months of his appointment, the Duke was often seen in the town at naval functions and ceremonies, including the unveiling of the Armada Memorial. An enthusiastic (if not necessarily very proficient) self-taught amateur violinist, he joined the Plymouth Orchestral Society and played in concerts at the Guildhall. His appointment came to an end on 3 June 1893, the day he was promoted to Admiral of the Fleet. (*See* October 21st)

August 5th

1914: One day after the outbreak of the First World War, Salisbury Road Elementary School was taken over by the 4th Southern General Territorial Army as a temporary hospital. All the desks had to be unscrewed from the floors, and newly equipped with 280 beds, a treatment centre and a neurological department; it was ready to receive patients by 17 August. The first major intake of sick and wounded came on 31 August, with the arrival of over 100 soldiers who had been serving in northern France. A lift, a kitchen and mortuary were installed the following month. King George V and Queen Mary visited the hospital in September 1915.

———◆·———

1977: Plymouth was host to another royal visit, but under much happier circumstances – the day that Queen Elizabeth II and Philip, Duke of Edinburgh, came to the city as part of the Silver Jubilee celebrations. They were seen by thousands who came to greet them down (appropriately) Royal Parade, during which they signed the visitors' book outside St Andrew's Church, and inspected the Royal Marines on the Hoe. As the *Western Evening Herald* reported, 'Plymouth had seldom seen so much flag-waving' as on this day.

August 6th

1937: Philip Brenner, an antiques dealer from London who was on holiday in Plymouth, was fined 10s for being drunk, disorderly, and using obscene language, after he had been refused admission to a hotel because of his condition. 'I am thoroughly ashamed of myself,' he said afterwards. 'I have been coming to Plymouth for thirty years without any trouble, and it will not occur again.'

———— • ◆ • ————

1948: A Mannamead couple went to a cinema and queued for some time before the husband realised that he had changed his clothes just before leaving and forgotten to bring any money. They went home to fetch some, and the wife suggested that they have a quick cup of tea before returning to take their place in the queue again. Having done so, they were moving forward steadily – when they realised they had forgotten the money again. For them, the film was not to be, or not that day, at least. They went back home, and stayed there.

———— • ◆ • ————

1953: A woman took a telephone call at home and held the receiver in front of her 2-year-old daughter, asking her to speak to 'Auntie Muriel'. The little girl looked puzzled, then remarked, 'Poor Auntie Muriel. She can't get out.'

August 7th

1960: Two Belgian brothers staying near Plymouth on holiday tried to visit the dockyard. They heard that a guide normally showed parties round on weekdays, so they presented themselves at the dockyard gate to join an eager group of sightseers. When the guide on duty noticed from their accent that they were not British, he told them that, as foreigners, he could not show them around unless they had written permission. When they protested, he answered rather curtly, 'We have no time to argue with foreigners.' In vain they tried to explain that although they were Belgian, they had both served in the British Navy during the Second World War, and their father had held a naval commission in the war before that. Had they waited for one day, they could have entered during Plymouth Navy Days on payment of a fee of 2s 6d.

———— • ◆ • ————

1966: A couple from Cornwall visited Plymouth and were so dissatisfied that they vowed never to return. They said the city was too small, some buildings were spaced too far apart, the centre was devoid of entertainment during the day except for the cinemas, and when they had walked a few hundred yards they were completely out of the city centre.

August 8th

1862: During his first period of office as Mayor of Plymouth, William Derry presented the town with the clock named after him. It is officially a fountain, as the Corporation was allowed to build a fountain but had no legal authority to construct a clock tower, although it has never been linked to any water supply. It was built with four illuminated dials, each 4ft in diameter, with a 15ft pendulum. Until the Second World War it stood at a junction of George Street, Union Street, Lockyer Street and George Place, and was regarded as the centre of Plymouth. All trams and buses terminated nearby. It was said that marriages may be made in heaven, but in Plymouth they are arranged under Derry's Clock.

———— • ◆ • ————

1903: The South African War Memorial on the Hoe was unveiled by Lady Audrey Buller, wife of Sir Redvers Buller, Commander-in-Chief during the Second Boer War. A full 43ft high, the memorial comprised a shaft of red granite mounted on a green base, with steps and pillars of Devonshire granite. It was dedicated to Prince Christian Victor, a grandson of Queen Victoria, who had died of fever while serving in the war, and to officers and men of the Devonshire, Somerset and Gloucestershire Regiments who were killed during the conflict.

August 9th

1831: A sturgeon, weighing over 2cwt (over 100kg) and over 9ft long, was caught at Sutton Harbour. Thought to be the largest such fish ever caught at Plymouth at the time, it was offered for sale by Mr Walland, a fishmonger at Southside Street, for 9*d* per lb.

———————◆———————

1949: Heard from a barrow boy near Drake Circus: 'Here you are, lovely cherries, just arrived, tenpence per pound, lovely cherries.' For a few minutes he did no business, so he changed his pitch: 'Lovely cherries, only a few left, clearing out now, tenpence per pound, lovely cherries.'

———————◆———————

1956: Heard on the radio, and subsequently printed in St Matthias Parish Magazine: 'Statistics indicate that most accidents happen in the kitchen.' The vicar, Revd John Byrnell, had added a not very politically correct afterword: 'I think this may be true, and unfortunately most husbands have to eat them.'

———————◆———————

1961: A woman entered a shop in Cobourg Street as several youths roared past noisily on their motorbikes. 'There they go,' she said crossly to the assistant, 'on their way to the cemetery!' The assistant asked her to repeat it, and her customer did so. 'What's on down there this afternoon?' she asked.

August 10th

1403: A French fleet of thirty ships carrying 1,200 men, led by Sieur du Chastel of St Malo, sailed into the Sound up the Cattewater and landed about a mile north of the town. The invaders marched into the town towards the site of what is now Exeter Street, and spent the night pillaging, burning and killing. The townsfolk put up a spirited fight, and the French left the next day after setting much of the town on fire. Afterwards, that part of the town was named Breton Side.

———◆———

1925: A memorial to Captain Robert Falcon Scott ('Scott of the Antarctic') was unveiled at Mount Wise by Commodore C.W.R. Royds, who had been the explorer's first-lieutenant on his ship *Discovery*. Scott, born at Milehouse in 1868, had led an expedition to reach the South Pole in 1912, only to find that he and his team had been narrowly beaten by their Norwegian rival, Roald Amundsen. On their return journey, they had perished due to exhaustion and starvation in the severe weather. The memorial represents Courage, supported by Devotion and crowned by Immortality, whilst Fear, Death and Despair are trampled underfoot. A bronze medallion shows portraits of Scott and his fellow explorers, Oates, Wilson, Bowers and Evans, who all died with him.

August 11th

1967: Mrs Hilda England, of Crownhill Road, was using her sewing machine when her hand slipped and the needle went through the index finger of her left hand. She tried to carry the machine – with the needle still impaling her finger – to the phone to summon help, but could not. After she attracted a neighbour's attention, an ambulance was called. The men could not release her finger so they telephoned the fire brigade, who removed the needle and took her to Freedom Fields Hospital. No serious damage was done, and the finger was X-rayed for possible broken bones, after which Hilda was driven home. Presumably no further stitches were needed.

1999: The Hoe attracted large numbers of sightseers to watch the eclipse of the sun at the memorable moment, around 11.13 a.m. Walt Comber, a wood-turner from an arts and crafts street fair, caused a few startled looks and considerable laughter as he boomed through his loudspeaker, 'I warned you about Armageddon. You still have time to repent, do it now.' Most shops in the city centre had closed their doors to let staff go out and watch. The Grand Hotel had been fully booked since April, and other hotels reported a last-minute rush of bookings from those eager to be there.

August 12th

1898: Royal Assent was given to the Local Government Board's Provisional Order Confirmation Act 1898, which authorised the transfer of part of the parish of St Budeaux, and part of the parish of Weston Peverell or Pennycross, to the Borough of Devonport, to take effect on 9 November. Devonport Borough Council now had forty-five Councillors, an increase from thirty-six, and fifteen electoral Wards instead of twelve. In order to receive rates from the inhabitants of St Budeaux, Devonport Corporation was required to undertake various tasks, such as reconstructing Camel's Head Bridge; extending the tramway as far as St Budeaux railway station; and constructing a landing stage at Saltash Passage 'of sufficient size to enable passenger steamers of the size now plying between Plymouth and Saltash to land and embark passengers there'. Under the terms of the Order, the Corporation was also required to establish a new cemetery, open a public reading room, provide a fully equipped fire service, establish a police presence, lay down proper and sufficient mains for the supply of gas, improve existing footpaths and construct new ones beside the main roads, and build a footbridge from the Great Western Railway's viaduct over Weston Mill Creek. Additionally, the Order empowered them to take over the sewerage and drainage facilities in St Budeaux, which had formerly been the responsibility of Plympton Rural District Council.

August 13th

1874: The Prince of Wales, later King Edward VII, opened the Guildhall Square complex of buildings. It comprised the Guildhall on the southern side of the Square, opposite another building which housed the Municipal Offices and various local government departments (including the offices of the Borough Treasurer, the Town Clerk's office, a committee room, the office and boardroom of the Plymouth School Board, and the Lord Mayor's Parlour). Beyond was the Council Chamber, where the mayor sat on a raised platform which was covered with a canopy. Beneath the four large stained-glass windows was a door which opened out onto a small gallery overlooking Guildhall Square. From here, proclamations could be read and each new mayor was introduced to the population. A life-size statue of Drake, on the apex of the Council Chamber, watched over the proceedings. The remainder of the building, towards St Andrew's Church, comprised the offices of the borough surveyor and the water surveyor, while above them were rooms used by the Chamber of Commerce and the Plymouth Debating Society. The Municipal Offices were destroyed during the Blitz in March 1941.

August 14th

1948: A man took his young daughter to Plymouth Navy Days. As he was leading her on board the battleship *Vanguard*, they had to make their way through dense crowds and she briefly let go of his hand. He took hold of it again straightaway – or so he imagined – until an unfamiliar female voice rang out indignantly, 'What do you think you're doing?'

———◆◆———

1951: A boy who was taken to a concert at Prince Rock was told by his parents that it was in aid of the Lord Mayor's Christmas Fund. He looked at them in disbelief, as he said, 'I should have thought the Lord Mayor was rich enough already!'

———◆◆———

1956: At the People's Dispensary for Sick Animals, a young woman called in with her ailing parrot. The male superintendent showed both of them into the consulting room and closed the door. Within a few seconds the parrot, which clearly had no voice problems, whatever its other ailments might be, started squawking 'Don't! Don't! Leave me alone!' very loudly and clearly. An understandably concerned female assistant immediately came in to see what the matter was, and, as the man said afterwards, gave him a very odd look until she saw the bird.

August 15th

1945: VE Day was celebrated by official bonfires on the Hoe, Devonport Park and Central Park. Those on the Hoe were lit a day earlier by certain people who could not wait. The fires were unofficially stoked with park benches – even those embedded with concrete – which had been torn out of the ground. Other items used to stoke the fires included a pole, articles of uniform, an accordion, a café sign, trestle tables and a handcart. Corporation workmen spent much of the day clearing up the debris and rebuilding the bonfires.

That night and into the small hours, as almost 60,000 gathered on the Hoe to watch fires blaze and rockets in the sky, a civilian band marched through the streets blowing bugles, supplemented with makeshift cymbals removed from the City Engineer's pig food bins. One bin was used as a football, until it rolled under a police car. Girls from WAAF hostels, in their pyjamas with uniform coats on top, stormed cars as they begged for lifts into town to join in the celebrations. At 3 a.m. a car was seen parked across the road in Princess Square, as naval officers in pyjamas and dressing gowns leant over it drinking beer!

August 16th

1849: The *Plymouth & Devonport Weekly Journal* reported on this day that a severe epidemic of cholera was sweeping across the Three Towns. In the preceding week, it noted that in Plymouth there had been 154 cases, and 172 cases of choleric diarrhoea, resulting in eighty-four deaths. During the same period there were 125 deaths in Devonport and eighteen in the much smaller Stonehouse. In Devonport, the outbreak took its toll largely of those living in the poorly drained areas, but nevertheless the wealthy were not immune from the infection. William Pike, of Morice Square, survived an attack of cholera, only to succumb to congestion of the brain a few days later. Several soldiers and officers who were stationed at Millbay Barracks also died. In one property in St Andrew Street, in which bones and filthy rags had been stored, there were eight deaths.

Between 4 July and 2 October 1849, 717 deaths were recorded in Plymouth, 717 in Devonport, and 155 in Stonehouse. A small, temporary hospital was erected on Battery Hill, Stonehouse, providing twelve beds altogether: six for male patients and six for female patients.

August 17th

1898: Mr Rose, of Charles Street, was summoned for not having a dog licence for his terrier. When Constable Roberts asked him to produce it, Mr Rose asked his wife where it was. She said it had been put in a tin box when they moved house, and she could not find it now. It had been issued in Cambridge the previous year, but the Bench said it would now be out of date and fined Rose 7s 6d plus costs.

———•◆•———

1927: A party of boy scouts from the Swiss Cottage troop returned to London from Plymouth on the P&O liner *Ranpura*. They had left London on the liner *Khyber* on 28 July, and had arrived in Southampton the next day. From there they had walked to Plymouth, pushing their kit and supplies in a handcart. Covering between 12 and 15 miles per day, they camped at night in any convenient site en route. One of them was a blind boy, who still managed to repair fourteen pairs of boots and shoes for the others at various resting points on the way. They had reached Plymouth on 14 August, where they were welcomed and given hospitality by the St Andrew's scout troop, who allowed the boys to use their hall in Bank Street as a dormitory during their stay.

August 18th

1855: Alfred Wallis was born in Devonport. His parents came from Penzance, but they had moved to the Three Towns as his father Charles needed to look for work. Soon after the birth of Alfred and his brother, Charles, their mother died and their father took them back to his hometown. Alfred became an apprentice basket maker, then joined the Merchant Navy, sailing regularly between Penzance and Newfoundland.

After leaving the service, Alfred, his wife and stepchildren settled in St Ives where he became a marine stores dealer. His business closed in 1912 and he then went to work for an antiques dealer. After his wife died in 1922, Alfred took up painting – entirely self-taught. His pictures, mostly painted using a limited palette of paints bought from ship chandlers, on cardboard torn from packing boxes, were of his beloved ships, boats and seascapes, largely done from memory. His paintings were much admired by fellow artist Ben Nicholson, and some were sold in London, where he was hailed as one of the greatest English 'primitive' artists – ignoring perspective and scale – of his day. Nevertheless, he lived in poverty and died in the Penzance Workhouse on 29 August 1942, shortly after his 87th birthday.

August 19th

1885: A group of Scottish boys who had been serving on HMS *Lion*, stationed at Plymouth, were on the evening mail train to Scotland for a short holiday. As they neared Gloucester, two of them, Messrs Harper and McGraw, began to quarrel. Soon it descended into a physical fight, which culminated in Harper allegedly pulling out a knife and stabbing his opponent in the neck. A carriage window was broken in the course of the struggle. When the train arrived at Gloucester, Harper was arrested and charged. McGraw was sent to the infirmary, but the wound was not serious and he was discharged after treatment.

———— • ◆ • ————

1912: A cook's mate was summoned before Ivybridge magistrates, charged with gaming at Mount Batten on 11 August. Constable Isaac had seen eight lads come to the quarry to play a game of banker, with two acting as scouts, and had observed money being placed on cards and changing hands. Isaac had signalled to two other constables, and the scouts had promptly scattered in all directions. The defendant pleaded not guilty, and denied that he had been with the boys in question. He had been with the navy for two years and references were given as to his good character. The magistrates fined him 20s plus costs.

August 20th

1906: Samuel Saltern, of Wyndham Street West, was charged with animal cruelty. Inspector Royle of the RSPCA said he had seen Saltern driving an aged bay gelding, attached to a cab, along Union Street, on 31 July. He had tried to stop him but without success. Later, he saw Saltern in Citadel Road, when the defendant admitted that the horse was 'a bit groggy'. When examined, the beast was found to be lame in the near fore limb due to a diseased bone in the foot, with a raw wound on the fetlock joint. Saltern pleaded that he had been unaware that anything was wrong with the animal, and was fined £1 with the alternative of ten days' imprisonment.

1917: May Stone, of Oxford Avenue, was charged with loitering and importuning men in Lockyer Street in February. The case had been adjourned several times, in order to allow her ample opportunity to enter a situation or go into a home. Since her last adjournment, when she was given a caution and allowed to go back to her own home, she had stayed out for two nights, and, in the view of the Bench, she had gone back on her undertaking. She was sent to prison for fourteen days.

August 21st

1916: Rebecca Haddon, of Bayswater Terrace, was charged at the police court with failing to enter into a register the names and nationalities of four aliens who had stayed at her house – three Japanese and one American citizen – together with the dates of their departure and destination. She said she was unaware that an aliens' register was necessary, and was fined 20s.

———◆———

1948: This afternoon, heavy rain and winds reaching gale force in some coastal areas lashed the West Country. Holidaymakers were driven indoors for shelter, while farmers saw their cornfields drenched and waterlogged. Plymouth recorded almost an inch of rain at Mount Batten in only a few hours. Sutton Harbour Regatta and annual rowing races on the Yealm were among the fixtures which had to be postponed, while at St Budeaux the Conservative fête had to move indoors into a schoolroom.

During the next three weeks or so, fields on the outskirts of the city proved a fertile hunting ground for mushrooms, and pickers would return with baskets containing up to 14lb at a time. A few people asked why, when there was such an abundant supply for the taking, it was still necessary to pay 2s per lb for them in the shops.

August 22nd

1912: Edward Legg was charged with stealing £1 4s from the till in photographer George Bailey's shop in Union Street. Legg had been engaged as a doorkeeper. When the money went missing from the till, Bailey had contacted the police. Legg pleaded guilty, saying he had been drinking heavily and did not know what he was doing, and was sentenced to three months' hard labour.

1927: Able Seaman Robert Davison and Marion McAskill, of Alcester Street, Stoke, were charged with endeavouring to obtain a naval marriage certificate by false pretences. McAskill, the prosecution contended, was posing as Davison's real wife in order to obtain naval marriage allowance in respect of her child. Davison's estranged wife was living in Sunderland, and he had told McAskill all the necessary particulars of her history in order to help her obtain the allowance. Both pleaded guilty, and he was fined 40s while she was bound over for twelve months.

1965: During the holidays, a 4-year-old boy in Plymstock was staying in the countryside with his aunt, when he heard an odd noise coming from the grass in her garden. He asked what it was, and she told him it was a cricket. 'But I play cricket, Aunt,' he replied, 'and I don't make that noise.'

August 23rd

1957: A couple were driving along Union Street just after midnight, when they caught sight of a group of three policemen huddled outside the Palace Theatre, rather furtively shining their torches on the front of the building. The couple thought some major crime investigation must be underway, and had visions of a theatre safe being stolen or something of the kind, so they stopped and got out to offer their assistance. The rather embarrassed officers had to admit that no crime had taken place. They were merely making a close, torch-lit examination of the photographs of 'les artistes' mounted on the wall outside.

* * *

1970: Progressive rock trio Emerson, Lake & Palmer made their live debut in concert at the Guildhall, where they played to a capacity crowd of 3,000, featuring the material they would perform at the Isle of Wight Festival the following week. Featuring Keith Emerson (piano, organ, custom Moog, and a Hammond organ which had to work hard for its living), Greg Lake (bass) and Carl Palmer (drums), they played a set which included 'Rondo' and 'America' (both of which Emerson had featured with his previous band The Nice), and their arrangement of Mussorgsky's suite 'Pictures at an Exhibition'. Supporting them were local group The Earth.

August 24th

1951: At the Plymouth Festival Jewel Ball, held at the Royal Naval Engineering College, Manadon, the pianist Francis Hornbrook (55) was playing background music to the mannequin parade. When he had finished, he rose from his stool to rejoin Fred Hill's orchestra, which was going to play for the dance. As he was leaving the platform, he collapsed. He was discreetly carried out from the ballroom with very few people aware of what had happened, but he had died from a heart attack.

Hornbrook had worked in the Town Clerk's department as an archivist. He had been in charge of deeds and documents, was responsible for their custody and indexing, and had also been on the city reconstruction committee. His elder brother said afterwards that he had seen him only two days previously and he had seemed in perfect health. However, the show must go on – and it did. After a hurried whispered consultation among the officials, another member of the orchestra slipped into Hornbrook's seat at the piano, and the orchestra played on. Hill said afterwards that it had been a very emotional time; 'Francis had been in the band with me for ten years,' he commented. 'We were like brothers.'

August 25th

1858: Shipwright William Shilston launched the first floating dry dock in the south-west. Measuring 150ft by 40ft, it was capable of taking vessels of up to 800 tons. He kept it moored at Sutton Pool, adjacent to his shipyard near the China House. When required, it could be taken to the deeper part of the pool, where the gates would be left open; it would sink with the incoming tide, the vessel would be floated inside and secured on blocks as the tide fell. At low water, the gates would be closed so the dry dock could float on the incoming tide, and then be lowered to its moorings.

———◆———

1948: Frank Underhill died at his Plympton home, aged 81. A prominent figure in the Plymouth business community for over fifty years, he had been one of the main founders of Underhill's (printers, stationers, booksellers and bookbinders), in 1889 in Old Town Street. At various times he had also been chairman of the Mercantile Association and the Chamber of Commerce, and a Liberal member of the City Council. The business was purchased towards the end of the twentieth century by Latimer, Trend & Co., another long-established local printing house.

August 26th

1938: A woman left her car in a country lane on the outskirts of Plymouth and went for a walk. When she returned later, she found two large holes in the roof. At first thieves or vandals were thought to have been responsible, but after examining the damage the police told her that the culprits were probably horses, which had presumably made the holes while looking for any food that might have been inside the vehicle.

———— ◆ ————

1992: The Royal William Victualling Yard closed, and in April 1993 it was taken over by the Plymouth Development Corporation. After the latter was wound up, responsibility for the site devolved to the South West of England Regional Development Agency and it was converted into a mixed use development by Gilmore Hankey Kirke Architects and Urban Splash. Named after King William IV, in whose reign it was completed and first used in 1835, and whose statue can be seen over the entrance, the yard was designed for use by the Admiralty as a victualling depot for the Royal Navy. It occupied a site of about 16 acres, of which six were recovered from the sea by levelling the remainder of the site. Its impending closure had been announced by the Minister for Defence in 1985.

August 27th

1887: Plymouth had a royal visit when Queen Victoria's eldest daughter Victoria (the German Crown Princess Frederick William) and her three younger daughters, Princesses Victoria, Sophie and Margaret, arrived on board the royal yacht *Victoria and Albert*. After arriving early in the morning, the Crown Princess paid visits to Lord Revelstoke at Membland, the Mildmays at Fleet and the Bulteels at Pamflete, while the princesses were shown around the Three Towns. They spent the following day with Lord Mount Edgcumbe at his estate, then met with the Crown Prince – who was suffering from what ultimately proved to be the early stages of cancer and had been resting in Scotland – before returning to Berlin.

———◆———

1938: A frustrated motorist walked into a garage in the Mutley district and spoke to a man in overalls, who was hard at work on a faulty vehicle.

'I want you to start my car,' he said. 'There is a tinkle in the engine I don't like.'

The man continued with the job on which he was already engaged. After a pause, the impatient one repeated himself. 'I said my car had a tinkle in the engine.'

'All right,' sighed the other. 'What do you want, a mechanic or a piano tuner?'

August 28th

1954: During a very wet summer, a landlady at Morice Street, Devonport, overheard a conversation between two of her lodgers. 'I haven't seen any butterflies this year,' remarked one. 'Oh I have,' said her friend, 'twice this morning, with water wings on.'

———◆———

1961: Local councillor Stanley Goodman was astonished to receive an apparent unexpected gift – two 1cwt crates of dried eggs from Denmark. Marked 'From Van Olpen & Son', they arrived at Plymouth addressed to 'Stanley Goodman, Devonport'. After receiving a delivery note at home and going to inspect them at Millbay Docks, Goodman said he had no idea why they had been sent to him, as he had no contacts in Denmark. No other person of that name who might have ordered them could be traced either.

———◆———

1965: Julie Wallis, director of a blind-making business near the Barbican, married Norman Pooley, a teacher at Burleigh Secondary Modern School, at the Methodist church on Embankment Road. Some guests were surprised to read the following note on the silver-lettered service sheet: 'The bride and bridegroom would be grateful if guests would refrain from using confetti.' A friend of the bride explained that Julie felt very strongly about any kind of litter.

August 29th

1940: Beatrice Loveday Brown, sometimes known as 'Fair Jean', or 'Blondie', was found dead in her flat at Raleigh Street late at night. She had been strangled with her own silk stocking. Earlier that evening she had visited a pub in George Street where she was well-known, and, after leaving, she was seen being accompanied in the direction of her home by a man whom she had probably met that evening. Police enquiries were hampered by a blackout following an alert. The suspect, wearing a sports coat and flannel trousers, was said to have been seen leaving her flat. Nevertheless, nobody was ever charged with her murder, and the case remains unsolved.

———◆———

1953: Bandleader Ted Coleman was conducting an evening concert on the Hoe. Noticing a man on the fringe of the crowd who kept smiling and was obviously trying to attract his attention during the first half, Ted went over to see him during the interval. 'I just want to thank you for the splendid evening you and your band put on at Dartmoor in the spring,' the man said.

'Indeed, are you one of the prison staff?' Coleman asked.

'No,' was the answer, 'I've just done seven years.'

August 30th

1937: Percy Whitlock, borough organist at the Bournemouth Municipal Pavilion, and his wife Edna, attended an Incorporated Association of Organists Congress at Plymouth, which opened this day and lasted until 3 September. This visit provided some inspiration for Percy's 'Plymouth Suite', which he had begun composing in July and completed in December. It was published in 1939. The opening movement, 'Allegro Risoluto', was dedicated to Harvey Grace, the president of the Congress, and the closing movement, 'Toccata', to Dr Harold George Moreton, Plymouth borough organist, 'a sprightly fellow who has been shabbily treated by the Corporation, who are mercenary'.

———◆———

1956: A major city bookseller reported that whenever a film of a well-known title was shown at one of the cinemas in the city, far from boosting sales of the book, the sales tended to fall. He said it must be because readers had frequently been let down after buying the book and finding it very different from the film they had just seen. Occasionally there was a different, not to say unexpected, reaction, as with a middle-aged lady who was walking through the shop when she noticed a copy of *Oliver Twist*: 'Oh, look, they've written a book of the film we saw last week!'

August 31st

1966: Snowy, a while fallow deer, escaped from Plymouth Zoo. As she was exceptionally tame, she was often allowed to wander loose inside the grounds. The back gate of the zoo had been left open the previous night, and she wandered out into Central Park. She was found asleep and was almost coaxed back early in the morning, but there was nobody on duty at the gate and she ran past.

After crossing the main road, she reached the Milehouse area; manager George Houghton drove in pursuit of her, backed up by vans from the zoo and a police patrol vehicle. They found her in a garden in Segrave Road, but she leapt over the wall and into another garden in Scott Road. On escaping from the latter and crossing the main road, she collided with a slow-moving car. Unhurt, she returned to Central Park and was followed to the tennis courts opposite the swimming pool, where she stayed for an hour, chewing the leaves of a low-hanging tree as a crowd gathered to watch. The zoo staff borrowed a goal net from Plymouth Argyle and moved in on her, but she leapt away and eventually returned through the back gate again.

September 1st

1883: A gang of soldiers from the 52nd Regiment entered a pub and smashed much of the furniture. The landlord tried to summon help and stop them from getting away, but one of them knocked him to the floor. The rest were pursued by police across the roofs of several neighbouring houses, and put up some resistance when captured. One constable was so badly injured that he required hospital treatment. It was thought that the men had been ordered to serve in India, and resented the idea so strongly that they had decided to avoid going – by committing an offence for which they would surely be sent to prison.

———————•◆•———————

1954: A former soldier, now working as a taxi driver in the city, had a call from a man who had helped him – nearly forty years previously. When the Plymothian was serving near the front line during the First World War in 1917, he was having difficulty with his gun limber (a two-wheeled cart which allowed the gun to be towed) when another soldier came over to help. The first man had written his address on an envelope, handed it over and told the other man to look him up if he was ever in the area.

September 2nd

1882: Cetewayo, King of the Zulus from 1872 until 1879 (when he was deposed after being defeated in the Zulu War and exiled to London), left Plymouth Sound on board the Union Company steamer *Nubian*. Dressed in a morning suit and a hat covered with gold lace, the King went on board to inspect the accommodation allotted to himself and the chiefs travelling with him. As his own cabin was not large enough, he asked Captain Bainbridge to knock away the partition. On deck, he spoke warmly of the kindness showed to him in England by the Queen, her subjects, and Mr Gladstone, Prime Minister, and said that he was returning home a pauper, as he had owned many thousands of cattle before the war and had lived on the sale of them, but they had now disappeared. His people, though, would know how to receive and provide for him when he returned.

When the time came to leave, the method of electric firing was explained to him, and he was handed the firing key. When he pressed the communicator, the guns on the port side exploded loudly. For a moment he looked quite frightened, but after seeing that his entourage were safe, he burst into laughter.

September 3rd

1960: A woman bought a dirty, discoloured Victorian silver brooch for £3 in a Barbican antique shop, and took it to a jeweller to be cleaned professionally and reset. When she returned to collect it, he told her that the stone was a 22-carat diamond worth at least £150.

1989: The RAF and Allied Air Forces Monument on the Hoe, near the National Armada Memorial, was unveiled by Air Marshal Sir John Curtiss. Dedicated to men and women who served in the Royal and Allied Air Forces during the Second World War (both in the air and on the ground), it is thought to be the only international air monument in the world. The main body, of granite, is surmounted by a 6ft bronze statue of the Unknown Airman.

1997: A book of condolences was opened at St Andrew's Church after the death of Diana, Princess of Wales, Dodi Fayed and their driver Henri Paul, in a car crash in Paris four days previously. Thousands came in to sign and place floral tributes outside. A candlelit vigil was held two days later on the eve of the funeral, and a requiem mass took place at the Roman Catholic Cathedral of St Boniface, in addition to special services in several other city churches.

September 4th

1355: Prince Edward, 'the Black Prince', eldest son and heir of King Edward III, arrived at Plympton to prepare an expedition to France with his troops during the Hundred Years War. After waiting for suitable weather, they set sail from Plymouth early the following month.

1949: Robert Alfred John Walling, newspaper editor and historian, died at his home in Merafield Road, Plympton. Born in Exeter in 1869, he came to Plymouth, where he started the West Country's first football newspaper in 1891. Four years later, he became the first editor of the *Western Evening Herald*, and, in 1904, he became Managing Editor of the Western Newspaper Company – comprising the *Herald* and the *Western Daily Mercury*. In 1921 he was appointed editor of the *Western Independent*, Plymouth's only Sunday newspaper, which was circulated by agents because newsagents were closed on Sundays. Walling also wrote and published over twenty thrillers, and several books on the West Country. Furthermore, he was chairman of the Plymouth Magistrates' Court, chairman of the Plymouth Mercantile Association, and a member of the General Licensing Planning Committee. In 1949 he had just completed his best-known work, *The Story of Plymouth*, but did not live to see its publication; it appeared early the following year.

September 5th

1898: The New Palace of Varieties, Union Street, was opened. Admission prices were stalls 2s 6d, grand circle 1s 6d, and gallery 1s, with children in arms charged 5d. The opening show lasted three hours, the line-up including the Levey Sisters, who sang and danced Persian and hunting songs; the Six Craggs, a team of acrobats; Mr Walter Stockwell, 'a character vocalist'; Mr Fred Darby, roller skater; plus several other vocalists and comedians. To conclude, there was 'a collection of patriotic airs' from the Palace Orchestra.

———•◆•———

1953: Whitleigh Footbridge was declared open when the Lord Mayor and Lady Mayoress, Alderman Sir Clifford and Lady Tozer, each planted a tree at opposite entrances. The footbridge had been built at a cost of £17,000, to link houses on the new Whitleigh estate with Crownhill Road on the other side of the valley.

———•◆•———

1960: When a Plympton family's canary was found dead one morning, the mother broke the news gently to her 3-year-old daughter. 'Poor Dickie was very ill,' she explained, 'so the angels came and took him during the night.' After a good cry, the girl said, 'Mummy, it was good of the angels, but I'm glad they didn't take the cage as well, so we can have another canary.'

September 6th

1620: The Pilgrim Fathers sailed from Plymouth, at the point on the Barbican known ever since as the Mayflower Pier, to settle in what would become New Plymouth, Massachusetts. A group of Calvinists had moved from Britain to Holland in 1607, but later decided to move to the New World where they felt they would be free from religious persecution. With a licence from the London Company of Virginia, they chartered two ships, *Mayflower* and *Speedwell*, for an Atlantic crossing. They travelled via Southampton, and put into Dartmouth for repairs. They required more repairs at Plymouth as *Speedwell* was leaking badly. Only *Mayflower* was fit for the voyage and she sailed alone, with 102 passengers on board. They reached Cape Cod on 9 November and, after the first winter, during which about half of them died of disease or starvation, they established a permanent settlement.

—————•◆•—————

1828: It was announced that almost 600 Portuguese exiles had arrived in Plymouth. They included magistrates, physicians, merchants, and military officers – all liberals who felt persecuted under the reactionary regime of King Miguel. A large building was fitted up at Coxside to give them temporary accommodation until they could be taken by ship to Brazil, where they had been offered asylum by Emperor Dom Pedro.

September 7th

1951: A boy at the City Museum said to an attendant: 'I want to see the man with his meat off.' The latter was rather startled, until he realised that the lad was interested in the human skeleton.

———— • ◆ • ————

1953: Alec Wembury, a well-known Plymouth bookmaker, was at Home Park watching Plymouth Argyle playing Oldham Athletic, a match ending in a 1-1 draw. After the game, he succumbed to a heart attack. At the time he was wearing a much-loved, old, frayed and stained overcoat, which he always donned whether it was winter or summer. Friends and acquaintances had always said he would die in it. They were proved right, but what they did not know was that this garment was his bank as well. After his body was taken away, the sum of £3,600 was discovered, sewn carefully into the lining, mostly in fivers crumpled up into balls. It took three policemen three hours to unwrap all the notes, spread them on a large blanket and count them.

———— • ◆ • ————

1956: A man had been waiting to see his doctor for a long time in a crowded surgery in Plymstock. Eventually he got up, saying he was going home as he was not feeling very well.

September 8th

1764: Dame Hannah Rogers, wife of Sir John Rogers of Blachford, Cornwood, made a will in which she left £10,000 to establish a school 'for poor and unfortunate children from Devon and Cornwall'. In 1787 the Trustees of the school rented Bowling Green House, which became Dame Hannah Rogers School. Only girls living in both counties were admitted at first. In 1887 the school moved to Ivybridge and became the Dame Hannah Rogers Endowed Charity School for Girls.

1956: A death's-head hawk-moth was found at Prince Rock by Mr J.E. Dockree, a local bus conductor. It was shortly to prove an exceptional year for sightings of the very rare species, as only nine had been found in Devon during the previous ten years, the last having been at Teignmouth in 1954.

Within the next few days, another seven were reported, at St Budeaux, Tinside, Milehouse, Crownhill, Noss Mayo, in the grounds of Devonport High School, and about 30 miles to the east at Ashburton. A dozen specimens, kept in the natural history section of Plymouth City Museum, had all been caught in other areas of the county.

September 9th

1644: Widey House, Eggbuckland – the property of well-to-do farmer and staunch Royalist Yeoman Heale – was visited by King Charles I during the Siege of Plymouth in the Civil War. He stayed there for about five nights, during which time he unsuccessfully demanded the surrender of Plymouth to the Royalist cause. In December 1643, his nephew, Prince Maurice, used it as his headquarters when commanding the army in Cornwall. After the King left, his rooms were neither used nor disturbed by anyone else. After changing hands several times in the twentieth century, the house was requisitioned in 1941 for use by the Plymouth City Police until 1945, and by the City Stores Department thereafter. It was demolished in 1954 after being badly vandalised, and Widey Court Primary School was built on the site.

1895: Phoenix Wharf Pier was officially opened by the mayor, Mr W. Law. At 11 a.m. he headed a procession from the Guildhall to the pier entrance and unlocked the gate. The party then boarded the steamer *Eleanor* and enjoyed a short trip around the harbour, before returning to the Guildhall on the Corporation's horse-drawn trams. The Wharf, measuring 70ft by 45ft, is still open for boat excursions up the Tamar.

September 10th

1953: Melody, a Rhodesian ridgeback owned by Miss Maureen Rogers of Hooe which ate 2lb of meat daily, produced a litter of eleven puppies. It was rare for a bitch of that breed to have more than six at once, and the vet attending her advised Miss Rogers to keep them all, as they were in excellent health.

———◆———

1956: A pedestrian in Embankment Road was stopped by a Scotsman on holiday, who was travelling with his family on a motorcycle combination. 'How do I get back to England?' he asked.

———◆———

1959: A resident of a flat in Lockyer Street noticed that there were facilities for dog owners to buy drinks on the Hoe, but no facilities for dogs to drink themselves. She therefore put out a bowl of water for animals, and changed it every day while drawing the press's attention to the lack of canine drinking facilities. She said there was no need for horse troughs, some of which were now used for flowers, but there were more dog owners than ever before.

September 11th

1891: When the London mail train reached Plymouth, surgeon Edward Cook was found senseless in one of the compartments. He was taken to Stonehouse Naval Hospital where he died a few hours later, apparently from a large dose of morphia. He had been convicted of drunkenness not long before, and prior to that had been court-martialled on another charge.

———◆———

1960: A group of holidaymakers called in at the City Information Bureau, asking where they could see HMS *Victory*. The answer, sadly for them, was not Plymouth – it was Portsmouth. A foreign student also came to find out if he could see the Armada.

———◆———

2000: Members of the Plymouth Fishermen's Association, who had nearly 100 vessels between them, joined the campaign of fuel price protests which had been staged over the previous few days, led by hauliers and farmers. They joined forces in blockading one of the West Country's main depots at Cattedown Wharves, regularly used by Shell, Esso and BP, and prevented road tankers from leaving. In a development of the protest, the fishermen joined up with Farmers for Action, the militant pressure group set up the previous year.

September 12th

1956: Overheard on a bus to Yealmpton: 'We took them shopping, and it was the first time Uncle Bill had ever been up in the excavator.'

———◆———

1967: The Beatles made an unscheduled appearance in Plymouth, but not to play. On the previous day, they had arrived in Devon to make their movie *Magical Mystery Tour*. After planning to visit Widecombe Fair and film a scene there, their coach became stuck on a narrow bridge in Dartmoor. When John Lennon lost his temper, they gave up the idea, went to Plymouth instead and lunched at the Grand Hotel on the Hoe. As it was a fine day, in true tourist style they walked along the Hoe, undeterred by the possibility that they might be mobbed by fans as on their previous visit to the city on tour nearly four years earlier. Although they were easily recognisable, fans respectfully left them alone. A photograph of them sitting on the grass looking out over the Sound was taken by David Redfern, and an enlargement has for some time been a popular poster readily available for sale on the Barbican.

The movie was first screened on BBC TV on Boxing Day, but received a resounding critical mauling. (*See* November 13th)

September 13th

1887: An inquest was held on the body of George Herd, aged 5 months. He had been admitted to the Plymouth Workhouse in a very emaciated condition, and died four days later. His mother, the wife of a petty officer, was a heavy drinker and would often leave the baby in the care of her 10-year-old daughter for a week at a time, as she was incapable of looking after him. His bones were protruding, his eyes were sunken and he was less than half the normal weight. A verdict of manslaughter was returned against Mrs Herd.

1948: Seen on the door at Swarthmore Hall, a notice advertising a forthcoming dramatic production: 'FOOLS RUSH IN – all seats sold.'

1958: The manager of the Plaza Cinema remarked on the nuisance being caused by Teddy boys while films were being shown. There had been several instances of unruly behaviour, including a gang who had let off a stink bomb in the front stalls and moved around to other seats repeating such behaviour. Several names were on the 'banned' list, and the manager was considering employing judo experts to throw offenders out. Other cinema managers had reported similar trouble recently, some doubling their security staff.

September 14th

1908: The Hippodrome Theatre in Prince's Street, Devonport, opened with a revue, *Neighbours*. In January 1910 the theatre was granted a cinema licence, and in June 1929 it staged its final show as a theatre, with entertainers Layton and Johnstone starring in *In the Flesh*. During the next six months, the building was converted for use as a cinema only, with seating for 2,500, reopening on 23 December 1929 with the film *Broadway Melody*. An artist was employed to paint the name on the roof slates, but – too late – he found the name was too long for the width available, and only succeeded in painting HIPPO. The Hippodrome was destroyed during the Blitz in April 1941, and the remains were demolished in 1958.

———— • • • ————

1953: *House of Wax*, an X-certificate American horror film starring Vincent Price, began a season at the Royal Cinema. It was the first full-length 3D picture ever to come to Plymouth, and viewers were supplied with Polaroid glasses to watch. A correspondent from the *Western Independent* was invited to a preview the week before. He found the film so realistic that he could have sworn the cinema was full of smoke, and almost rushed to the phone to dial for the fire brigade.

September 15th

1873: While digging around the foundation of a cross wall, four men and three boys were killed in the Stonehouse area of Union Street when another wall, 45ft high and 50ft long, collapsed on them during a high wind. The wall had adjoined a property belonging to Mr Snowdon, which had been destroyed by a fire two months earlier. One man survived, but with severe head injuries. Mr Snowdon, who had been standing nearby, had a narrow escape. He was considered to be partly at fault, as he had received verbal and written warnings from the local board stating that the structure was unsafe.

———— ◆ ————

2001: Karen Gillard (27), a Plymouth City Council member and chairperson of TORCHE (Tory Campaign for Homosexual Equality) resigned from the Conservative Party, complaining that she had suffered years of prejudice within the party because she was gay, and announced that she was joining the Liberal Democrats. Her local party, she claimed, had blocked her from becoming a school governor as they thought it was an inappropriate job for a gay woman. 'I'm not asking for homosexuality to be compulsory,' she said. 'What I am expecting is a world in which people share the same basic rights.'

September 16th

1902: Henry Williams, a labourer from Pennycross, was charged with using obscene language and being disorderly on two separate occasions during the last fortnight. A neighbour giving evidence, Miss Fox, said Williams seemed to have a grievance against his wife, who had refused to give him something for their son, so he had thrown a teapot at her and sworn at her. In mitigation, Williams said it was merely a family squabble and pleaded for leniency. He promised that if the Bench was to give him one more chance, he would sign the Pledge and keep it. He was fined 6s plus costs, or seven days in prison, for each offence. When he asked for time to pay, this was refused, on the grounds that his conduct had been 'most brutal'.

———•◆•———

1949: During the last days of a particularly warm summer, Mr Watkins, of Peverell, found a Queen of Spain fritillary, a very rare migrant butterfly which had presumably come from Europe or the Channel Islands, at Stoke Beach. He took it back to his garden, provided it with garden pansies to feed on, and in due course it laid several eggs. According to records, the last time the species had been reared in England was in 1903.

September 17th

1902: Two bluejackets, thought to be patients at the Royal Naval Hospital, Stonehouse, eluded police on duty at the gates, and made off along Adelaide Street. They were chased by the police through Rendle Street and up Flora Street; they were finally captured in Union Street and escorted back. The sight of constables in hot pursuit gave foundation to rumours among those watching that a fire had broken out somewhere.

1956: A middle-aged couple were seen driving down Old Town Street, with a JUST MARRIED label on the back of their vehicle. They had not left their wedding reception, but their silver wedding celebrations. A small label underneath read: 25 YEARS AGO.

2002: Years after new technology and software had eliminated the tendency towards notorious typos, which had once resulted in the *Guardian* newspaper being nicknamed the *Grauniad*, the paper misinformed its readers with an admittedly rather common geographical *faux pas*. Writing about the flagship *Mary Rose* in its Education column, it suggested: 'If you can't get to Plymouth to see Henry VIII's favourite warship, pay a virtual visit instead.' Thanks to an eagle-eyed correspondent pointing out that somebody had the wrong city altogether, and it should have said Portsmouth, a correction appeared in the paper two days later.

September 18th

1893: Lessons started for the first time for 425 students who had enrolled at the new Plymouth & Devonport Technical School to study for courses 'applicable to the trades and industries carried on within the borough'. The institution was, at this point, housed in premises in George Street, Devonport. The premises were leased for five years at an annual rent of £65, pending the acquisition of a site adjacent to the London & South Western Railway's Devonport station. It was soon recognised that the George Street accommodation was quite inadequate. The foundation stone was laid at the new site in June, on Queen Victoria's Diamond Jubilee day, and building began shortly afterwards. Opened in 1898, it became a Technical College in 1926, and, on the opening of Plymouth College of Further Education at Kings Road in 1974, the building became an annexe for the business and commerce students. About twenty years later it was closed and sold off for development as apartments.

1954: A Plymouth couple took their two small children round Buckfast Abbey. At the time, a service was in progress, and at the sound of the deep organ notes, the 5-year-old piped out very loudly, 'Are you going to get married now, Mummy?'

September 19th

1953: An airman was in mufti at North Road station at 9.30 a.m. He was to be married, in RAF uniform, half an hour later, and had left the uniform with a navigator who was to clean it and put it on the morning train. By 9.45 it had not arrived. The airman was summoned to the stationmaster's office, where he was told that the navigator had miscalculated – the train ran an hour later on Saturdays and the uniform would not arrive on time. However, the stationmaster had contacted the groom's sister, who had arranged to borrow one from a firm specialising in service uniforms, and the airman would need to collect it from them. When he reached the place, the tunic needed to be altered as it had one ring too many. He arrived at the church five minutes late. Fortunately, the bride had also been delayed.

---◆---

1991: Plymouth Pavilions, built on the site of the former Millbay railway station, opened its doors for the first time. The granite pillars outside the main entrance were the old station gateposts. That evening's show included a classical concert by the Bournemouth Symphony Orchestra and a performance by comedian Frank Carson.

September 20th

1878: A statue erected in honour of the former mayor, Alfred Rooker, was unveiled in Guildhall Square by the then mayor, Joseph Wills. Rooker had held the position in 1851-2 and again in 1873-4, and had also stood unsuccessfully for parliament as a Liberal for Plymouth in 1871. As chairman of the New Guildhall Committee, he had welcomed the Prince of Wales to the town in 1874 when the latter opened the building. After his term as mayor came to an end, he and his family left Plymouth in December 1874 to make a pilgrimage to the Holy Land. A few months later, Rooker was stricken by Syrian fever and died in Beirut in May 1875, aged 61.

1948: Charles King (98) died in Bournemouth. He had spent most of his life in Plymouth, where he had been a regular at Tinside Pool, regardless of the weather, until the age of 90. Although not a good swimmer, he would cheerfully splash around in the water.

1956: A woman who had evidently had frustrating experiences in the past, telephoned a Plymouth store, opening the conversation: 'I want to speak to somebody who knows something about what I'm going to talk about.'

September 21st

1898: Burrator Reservoir, Plymouth's main source of fresh water, was officially opened by the mayor, Councillor J.T. Bond. It had been almost nine years since Edward Sandeman, the town's water engineer, had prepared a report on the local water supply, recommending Burrator Gorge on Dartmoor as the ideal site for a storage reservoir, from which a direct pipeline could be run to bring water into the town. The scheme was formally adopted in March 1892. The Plymouth Corporation Act (passed 9 June 1893) authorised construction of the project near the villages of Sheepstor and Meavy, and a pipeline from there to the service reservoir at Roborough. Work on the dam at Burrator had started in August 1893, and at Sheepstor a year later. The total cost was £178,000, with the two dams costing £102,000 and £24,000 respectively. Later it was reported that, as a result of the construction of the reservoir, the revenue from the water property had increased from £13,000 to £15,000 per year while expenditure had decreased from £4,000 to £3,500. Although the reservoir was completely frozen over during the very cold winter of January 1917, when the top was covered with a layer of ice 10in-thick, there was no interruption in the supply of water to the town.

September 22nd

1886: A man who jumped from a moving railway carriage going from Leeds to Grantham was believed at first to be James Curteis (a missing solicitor wanted for questioning), but was later identified as another man. Curteis, who had worked for the Stonehouse Local Board, had absconded earlier in the month after being suspected of fraud. In January 1887 he was arrested in Calcutta, where he had been living under the name of Ridgway; he was extradited and brought back to Plymouth in April. Pleading guilty to embezzling more than £14,000 over a period of six years, he was sentenced to five years' penal servitude. It was feared that his financial misdemeanours had ruined several Friendly Societies.

———◆·———

1899: Alderman John Pethick, Mayor of Plymouth, opened the Plymouth Corporation Electricity Works, which would inaugurate the new electric tramway route from Prince Rock to the town centre. Construction of the Works had started two years earlier, although electricity had been used to provide lighting in Plymouth since 1849, when an arc lamp was installed at the top of Devonport Column. Town officials and guests who had been invited to the ceremony were given a guided tour of the Works, and then travelled in tramcars to the Guildhall for a celebration luncheon.

September 23rd

1920: Cyril Saunders, a lance-corporal in the Royal Engineers, went to stay with his cousin Dorothy May Saunders and her cousin Elizabeth Lawrence, who kept a shop at Percy Terrace, Lipson Vale. Cyril had been unofficially engaged to Dorothy, but she had written to him several times telling him that it was all over between them. She feared she had become pregnant by him, and did not want to see him again. He took a train to Plymouth with the intention of persuading her to reconsider, and arrived on 22 September at their house. That evening, she reluctantly agreed to go to the cinema with him, and after they had returned she told Elizabeth how tiresome he had been. The next morning he went out and tried to buy a revolver, but, as he could not obtain one, he bought a hunting knife instead. He returned to the shop where Dorothy was serving at the counter, seized her and stabbed her to death. He then stood outside, admitting he had 'done her in', as he waited for the police to come and arrest him.

At his trial in Exeter on 9 November, the defence pleaded insanity as Cyril had suffered a severe blow to the head earlier that year – but he was found guilty and hanged three weeks later.

September 24th

1954: Peter Lanyon, the renowned St Ives painter, opened the Plymouth Society of Artists exhibition at the City Art Gallery. There were 254 works on display altogether. A journalist, who was looking at the show, met another well-known local artist, who suggested that exhibitors ought to wear an identity label while they were on the premises, in order to avoid the potential for any *faux pas*. As he explained, 'I am always afraid that when I say, "Heavens, that's awful", the artist may be standing by my side.'

———•◆•———

1980: The 'Drake 400 Suite', commissioned by the City Fathers from Plymouth-born composer, orchestrator and conductor Ron Goodwin, to mark the Drake 400 Commemorative Festival, received its first public performance in the Guildhall this evening. Goodwin conducted the Bournemouth Symphony Orchestra through the six movements, each of which depicted – in music – various facets of the area's seafaring traditions. The titles included: 'Song of the Mewstone', 'The Hoe on a Summer Night', and a 'Plymouth Sound March', which had been inspired by Goodwin's childhood memories of hearing military bands on the Hoe on Sunday evenings. Eight years later, Goodwin was commissioned to write a companion piece, the 'Armada 400 Suite'.

September 25th

1907: Sidney Parnell (12), of Grenville Road, was charged at Plymouth Police Court with breaking and entering Thomas Monk's sweet shop, and stealing chocolate valued at 4s 6d. Monk had found everything in order on checking his premises at 7.30 a.m. on 22 September. In the evening, though, he noticed that the rear doors were unbolted, and, when stock was checked the next morning, the chocolate theft was noticed. William Williams said he had seen Parnell in the evening. The latter had told him that his father had brought some chocolate home, and they immediately had some. The next day, Parnell distributed fifty-two chocolate cakes among the other boys at his school. Constable Down spoke to him the following day and charged him with theft. Parnell denied knowing anything about it, and said his uncle in Claremont Street had given him some chocolate on Friday, and he had won some from a machine. Later he pleaded guilty, and was sentenced to nine strokes of the birch.

———•◆•———

1948: A Plymouth man picked up a bargain while on holiday in Birmingham. Looking in an antique shop, he spotted an unusual-looking old flask priced at 1s, which he considered cheap for the item. When he got it home, he found it was full of whisky.

September 26th

1941: The Plymouth Citizens' Advice Bureau was opened at 5 Marlborough Road, off Tavistock Road. The first Citizens' Advice Bureau in Britain had been established on 4 September 1939, the day after the declaration of the Second World War. The National Council of Social Services had decided that centres of free advice 'should be established throughout the country, particularly in large cities and industrial areas where social disorganisation may be acute'. However, many members of the public misconstrued the purpose of the CABs. One of the earliest enquiries made at the local office was a request for the recommendation of a reliable pettifogger, or a less-than-ethical lawyer. The caller was a schoolboy, who had been set the question as part of his homework. Or had he been sent by a schoolmaster, who would rather not admit to asking for such information?

1949: The speaker at Plymouth Harvest Thanksgiving arrived very late this evening. A puzzled congregation was told that he had misunderstood the message on his phone asking him if he would meet the minister at the Harvest Home. Only after waiting outside the renowned pub of the same name had he realised his mistake.

September 27th

1840: A fire broke out at Devonport Dockyard, probably caused by a spark falling on to the timbers of *Talavera*, a ship that had been treated with coal tar to prevent her from contracting dry rot. Nobody was killed or injured, but the ship and one other were destroyed, as were several dockside sheds and collections of timber supplies. The most serious loss was the Adelaide Gallery, a small museum containing several trophies, including the flag under which Nelson died at the Battle of Trafalgar.

———◆———

1957: Some Hungarian refugees in the area were thought to be a little choosy when it came to seeking employment. A Plymouth factory manager interviewed one who had just come from the north of England, and offered him a post with all expenses paid and a basic wage of £10 a week. The man said he could easily get £15 for the same job in his own country. When the manager pointed to the suit the refugee was wearing and asked how much it would have cost in Hungary, the answer was 'about £30'. 'You can buy it here for £10 to £12,' he pointed out. Nevertheless, the interviewee insisted that the pay was not good enough and said he would return north.

September 28th

1948: The Lord Mayor welcomed a party of twenty-two town planners from local government authorities in Austria, Czechoslovakia, Colombia, Denmark, Finland, Italy, Norway, Pakistan, Poland and Sweden. They spent four days looking at the city (which was under reconstruction), paying particular attention to the city centre and new housing estates.

1951: A couple at Mount Gould had had an argument, after which the husband put his hat on and walked out of the house. His wife, furious at first, then said to herself, 'Why should I stay at home?' She had heard that a good film was showing at the Royal, and thought it might take her mind off things. As the usherette showed her to her seat, she realised that her husband had had the same idea and had taken his place in the chair next to her. Instant reconciliation followed.

1956: A housewife asked for six apples from a fruiterer in the Pannier Market. 'Do you want them for a harvest festival?' the stallholder asked her. The woman shook her head and he selected half a dozen as asked. Putting them into a bag, he told her, 'If they had been for a harvest festival, I should have picked out the best.'

September 29th

1807: Plymouth Market was opened by the mayor, Thomas Lockyer. It stood in a field adjacent to Old Town Street, officially known as Saunders Meadow, but unofficially known as Blood Field, as a boy had drowned in a pond on the site. The market was enlarged in 1840, with the addition of separate markets for corn, fish and cattle – although the fish and cattle markets moved to separate premises later in the century. Most of the market survived the bombing of March and April 1941, and several major retailers whose premises had been destroyed were allocated stalls in the building. This stretch of booths was known as 'Tin Pan Alley', a line of corrugated iron temporary stalls. The market buildings were gradually demolished from 1952 onwards, during the post-war reconstruction, to be replaced by the new market which opened on 7 September 1959.

1945: Plymouth's last tram, festooned with bunting and Union Jacks, started its final journey, leaving Old Town Street with 135 passengers on board, destined for Peverell Corner. It was estimated that, since 1872, Plymouth's trams had travelled 70 million miles and carried over 800 million passengers. The gradual changeover from trams to buses had begun in the early 1930s.

September 30th

1889: The foundation stone of what was initially known as the Victoria Memorial Science, Art and Technical School was laid by the mayor, Mr H.J. Waring. By the time the building was completed three years later, it had been named the Municipal and Technical School.

———•◆•———

1954: The Plymouth Transport Manager received a report from an inspector:

> Sir, I have to report that bus no –, route no –, driver – was out of service from 2.14 at Crownhill until 2.50 at Mutley Plain, owing to a mouse running loose in the lower saloon of the bus. Lady passengers took a dim view of the incident.

The Transport Chairman, Alderman Medland, was unimpressed: 'It took thirty-six minutes to kill a mouse!'

———•◆•———

1965: One of the pupils at Plympton County Secondary School was supposed to have been sent to a school for backward children, but it had been decided by the authorities that his intelligence was superior to several others whose names had been considered. The headmaster overheard a conversation that the boy had with one of his friends in the playground:

'I thought you were to go to that school for the daft ones.'

'So did I, but I failed the entrance examination.'

October 1st

1878: Keen to provide a superior and comfortable alternative to pubs, which were considered a threat to the health and family life of the working men who spent far too much of their spare time and money drinking, the Plymouth Coffee & Cocoa House Co. opened the Borough Arms Coffee Tavern in Bedford Street at 7 p.m. In his opening speech, Dr Prance said – with tongue in cheek – that the only people who would suffer from the opening of such establishments would be the doctors, as sober people did not generally need treatment after injuring themselves and doctors, who always charged their patients for treatment, would therefore lose business. The coffee house's regular hours were 5-11 p.m. every day except Sunday, and it provided a takeaway service, known as the 'jug and bottle trade'. On the first evening, 96 gallons of tea, coffee and cocoa were served to the public, with takings of more than £10.

Although it was very successful at first, it closed about twenty years later and the premises were taken over by a branch of the Union of London & Smith's Bank, later the National Provincial Bank.

October 2nd

1501: Princess Catherine of Aragon landed at the Barbican, after travelling from Spain. One contemporary wrote: 'had she been the saviour of the world, she could not have had a more enthusiastic welcome.' She went to St Andrew's Church to give thanks for the safe ending of a stormy and unpleasant voyage, then stayed in a local merchant's house before leaving for London, where she married Arthur, Prince of Wales and subsequently his brother, the future King Henry VIII.

———•◆•———

1969: Plymouth Hospital Radio Studio was opened by the Lord Mayor, Alderman George Creber. The city's hospital broadcasting service had begun in 1955 when the Toc H organisation had transmitted a programme, using the GPO telephone network, to all nine hospitals on Saturday afternoons when Plymouth Argyle were playing at home. This was followed in 1967 by a music programme, broadcast by Plymouth Lions Club, to patients at Mount Gould Hospital on alternate Wednesday evenings. In 1969, a weekly show proved so popular that larger premises were needed. Equipment at the new Barbican Studio was provided by the BBC, with their technicians undertaking the installation work. The studio moved successively to Lockyer Street, Nelson Gardens in Stoke, then to Greenbank Hospital, Freedom Fields Hospital and eventually Derriford Hospital.

October 3rd

1907: Florrie Prete and Georgina Parfetti, two ice cream vendors, were charged at the police court with having caused an obstruction in Union Street on 21 September. They ran a business jointly and were selling ices outside St James' Hall. An altercation took place between them, and an argument became a fight. A crowd, doubtless finding the spectacle rather entertaining, gathered to watch. Trams were unable to pass until the way had been cleared, and a constable issued them with a summons. They were each fined 2s 6d.

———◆———

1923: The Exmouth Hall, Exmouth Road, Stoke, was opened by Alderman J.P. Brown, Deputy Mayor of Plymouth. It had been built to provide a venue for dances, entertainments, scout meetings and wedding receptions. The main hall had room for 700, while an adjoining room could be used for smaller meetings and events such as whist drives. Three club rooms were also available for smaller functions. The hall remained in use until about 1990, after which it was demolished so the site could be used for a new housing development.

October 4th

1885: The Belgian steamer *Hermann*, sailing from New York to Antwerp with a general cargo, broke her low-pressure crankshaft just westward of the Isles of Scilly. She was towed into Plymouth Sound by SS *Chicago* for repairs.

1948: A Plymouth solicitor went to see a client in Tavistock. Having completed his business, he walked out of the man's front door and saw a Plymouth-bound bus just about to leave, so he got on. Shortly after returning to his office, his client telephoned him to ask how he got back. The solicitor explained about the bus. 'Splendid,' was the reply. 'But tell me this – what am I supposed to do with your car?'

1950: A city fishmonger put out an advertisement asking members of the public to give him any old, clean, newspapers in which he could wrap his fish. A number of customers nearby were happy to oblige, including one man who rang up to offer him a bundle, saying in all seriousness that he had not included any sporting editions as he did not want the fish to know that Plymouth Argyle had been relegated to the third division.

October 5th

2006: The Drake Circus shopping centre was opened at 9 a.m., replacing the old centre which had opened in 1971 but was demolished after tests detected the presence of concrete cancer. Comprising 560,000 sq ft and costing £200 million, it was twenty years in the planning. According to one reporter, the scene at the opening 'resembled New Year's Eve in Times Square'. Staff outside Primark, one of the largest stores, offered glasses of Buck's Fizz and handed out lobster pot-shaped baskets to customers. The shop stayed open till 9 p.m., and sold an estimated 4,500 items of clothing – eighty per cent more than expected. Other retailers also claimed similar good business. An executive from Marks & Spencer had a verbal complaint from a woman about the size of the lavatory cubicles, and he informed her that a few weeks ago there had been no toilets at all. 'Now we have lavatories and two restaurants.'

The centre's appearance behind the civilian war memorial at Charles Church provoked some controversy. Some believed that its unsightly appearance did injustice to the dead of the Second World War, while defenders claimed that its picturesque backdrop to the church created a striking combination of traditional and modern architecture. It received an ironic architectural 'award' for being the single worst building in the United Kingdom.

October 6th

1945: An inquest was held on Arthur Martin of Peverell, a burner employed at Devonport Dockyard, who had died in a tragic accident the previous day. He had been working on the aircraft carrier *Atheling*, and had switched on his torch as he prepared to cut a plate in the outer bottom of the carrier. Then an explosion occurred. Petrol had been leaking from the tank, which was ignited by a spark from the torch; a great jet of flame had then shot up against the ship's side, and he was killed instantly. Smoke rose in dense thick pillars and could be seen all over the dockyard, while the brow alongside the ship and the side of the carrier were scorched by the heat. The Royal Marine Police and ambulances rushed to the scene and put the fire out.

———————◆———————

1967: Clive Williams, a city centre store manager, took the revolutionary step of announcing that free tea would be served in the balcony cafeteria to shoppers during the first hour of opening. He said later:

> We gave away about 100 cuppas. I look upon these 100 customers as ambassadors, who will spread the word that early shoppers can get a warm drink before shopping. It could encourage more early shopping and greater use of the cafeteria.

October 7th

1995: A large-scale bridge slide took place at Marsh Mills. Viaducts supporting the sliproads for the A38 trunk road had to be replaced, as the concrete had been rotted by alkali-silica reaction. The method of sliding was chosen in order to minimise traffic disruption and save £12 million in carriageway lane rental charges, as well as the cost and delays that would have been incurred by demolishing and replacing the roads with new structures – this would also have caused major disruption for eighteen months. The new deck initially carried traffic while resting on temporary supports. When the old viaduct was demolished, eight new concrete piers and two abutments were built to support the new deck. Road closure was limited to a weekend: eight hours for the slide, twenty-four hours to allow bearing grout to set, and the remaining time for asphalting and traffic re-routing.

The operation began at 2 a.m, and the deck was realigned several hours later. It was inched into position early in the afternoon, completing civil engineering's biggest ever bridge slide. The repositioned bridge was reopened to traffic at 6.30 a.m. on Sunday 8 October, completing an operation costing £12.25 million.

October 8th

1784: 'I am afraid Lord Boringdon has had a bad meeting, by the Papers,' Boringdon's sister-in-law wrote this day to her brother Frederick.

> However, I flatter myself he won't have many more … He is really and seriously going to have to part with all his horses as soon as he can, he finds it so very inconvenient to come so far [to Newmarket] every year to see them that the trouble is not worth the pleasure and I am sure if they are no pleasure they are not worth keeping for the profit.

John Parker, 1st Baron Boringdon, the squire of Saltram, was devoted to his horses and his racing. But, with failing health and increasing debts, he was going to have to cut his cloth accordingly in order to leave his wife and family properly provided for. He died in April 1788, aged 53.

———◆———

1948: A woman from Cornwall sent a letter to a correspondent in St Budeaux, but forgot to add Plymouth to the bottom of the address on the envelope. Someone at the sorting office evidently misread it, and in due course it was returned to the sender, bearing some French pictorial stamps, and marked 'Inconnu à Bordeaux'.

October 9th

1960: The Revd Clifford Davies, chaplain at the Royal Naval Barracks, Devonport, was a guest speaker at the Plymouth Rotary Club. He told a story about a sailor and his girlfriend who were killed in the Blitz and found themselves awaiting admission to heaven. They told St Peter that it was their dearest wish to get married at once. St Peter told them that, if they insisted, he would see what he could do. The sweethearts waited for several years, but no banns were put up, and they went to St Peter to remind him. 'Yes, I know it's a long time,' he said. 'But to tell you the truth I've been waiting for a naval padre to come up so that we can get the job done properly.'

1964: Rowland Crabb, the Labour candidate for Devonport in the general election, was out canvassing. When he knocked at one particular front door, it opened to reveal a lady with her arms full of beautifully laundered sheets. Breathlessly, she gasped, '--- washes whitest.' Only when she saw his rosette did she realise with disappointment that he was not a sales representative about to present her with a free gift.

Although Labour normally won the election on a national scale, Crabb failed to take Devonport from the Conservatives.

October 10th

1907: Ten boys, all aged between 12 and 16, were summoned for behaving in a disorderly manner in Embankment Road on 25 September. A witness said that they had used disgusting language to pedestrians, and had run around the paths, inconveniencing others, invading people's gardens nearby and trespassing over their flowerbeds. Two of the boys, charged with bad language and misconduct, were fined 5s each. Four, who had previously been cautioned, were each fined 3s 6d, and four who had not previously been cautioned were fined 2s each.

1922: Agnes Clarke (23) was charged at Ker Street Police Court with being drunk while in charge of a baby aged 7 weeks. A constable, who had found her lying completely intoxicated across her child's pram in the street, said that she had, until then, always seemed like a perfectly respectable woman, and her child was well cared for. The Bench dismissed her with a caution.

1958: A hairdresser attending a ball in the city bought some raffle tickets. Looking at the list of prizes, she remarked to her partner that she would be happy to win anything except for the free perm. One of her tickets was pulled out of the hat and she won … the free perm.

October 11th

2002: Nigel Meadows, City Coroner, revealed the long-running mystery of what had happened to the embalmed body of Edwin McKenzie, or 'Diogenes'. McKenzie, who died in 1984, had been named Diogenes by painter Robert Lenkiewicz, after he found him living in a concrete pipe at Chelson Meadow rubbish tip. He had promised the tramp that he would be preserved after his death as a 'human paperweight' rather than being handed over to the authorities for burial. Lenkiewicz refused to tell Plymouth City Council officials where the body was kept, despite the Environmental Health Department's determination to have McKenzie buried. Lenkiewicz invited them to his studio, where they found a coffin which they expected to contain Diogenes' body – until Lenkiewicz himself jumped out. A spokesman said the affair had degenerated into music-hall farce, yet they still meant to find the body.

One year later, the council admitted defeat. McKenzie was found in a concealed drawer in a cupboard in the Barbican studio of the artist, ten days after the latter's death. The body was eventually allowed to be retained by the Lenkiewicz Foundation. Nigel Meadows stated that: 'Provided they comply with health and safety regulations and don't outrage public decency it is possible that they could retain the body on some sort of public display.'

October 12th

1956: A Plymouth schoolboy was telling his parents about his teacher's enthusiastic account of his summer holiday on the Continent. His father asked if the teacher was married. 'I shouldn't think so, Dad,' said the lad, 'because teacher said he had had a wonderful holiday.'

———— ◆ ————

1967: Sluggish-looking pigeons, seen lying around in the city centre, were thought to be dying by concerned members of the public – but they had been heavily drugged instead. The Health & Welfare Services Committee was assured that no pesticides or insecticides had been used. The City Council had employed a private firm to try and remove some of the birds from the city, as they were proving a health hazard. The chairman, Percy Washbourn, said that the procedure was to narcotise the birds with bait so they were temporarily drugged. Representatives from the RSPCA, and a public health inspector, were in attendance when the birds were collected and later painlessly destroyed. The bait used would drug the birds for up to four hours, and those which were not caught would recover unharmed. Eight sparrows were also found drugged, but were released on recovery. Altogether, ninety-one pigeons were painlessly put to sleep, and every effort was made to ensure the absence of any cruelty.

October 13th

1902: A boy, Percy Griffiths, was charged at Plymouth Petty Sessions with stealing wood from a shed at Prince Rock, the property of Matcham & Co., two days earlier. His mother said that he had told her an old toolhouse had been demolished, and the timber was being given away. Percy was discharged after being given a caution.

1938: A member of the Industrial Welfare Society, addressing Plymouth Rotary Club, referred to a conversation heard between a schoolboy and a teacher during a history lesson: 'If Alexander the Great was alive today, what would be his politics?' With barely a pause for thought, the schoolboy had replied, 'If Alexander the Great was still alive today, he would be too old to be interested in politics.'

1948: Ten years later, another member of the Rotary Club was speaking at a meeting. He recalled a story told to the delegates at a district conference he had attended recently at Carlyon Bay. Arthur Mortimore, vice-president of Rotary International, had spoken at the conference about a farmer bewildered by the ever-increasing number of returns he had to make to the government. 'With all them blinkin' forms I fill in,' he said, 'I shall soon have to engage a shorthorn typist.'

October 14th

1870: Captain Andrew Henry died at his home in Plymouth, aged 46, and was buried at Ford Park Cemetery. A veteran of the Crimean War who had fought as a young man of 20 at the Battle of Inkerman on 5 November 1854, he was the first member of the Royal Regiment of Artillery ever to be awarded the Victoria Cross for Gallantry. Despite being heavily wounded, he had successfully defended his gun from capture by the enemy. Nevertheless, he never completely recovered his health. To this day, the Plymouth branch of the Royal Artillery Association holds an annual ceremony of remembrance for him.

———— ◆ ————

1921: The US cruiser *Olympia* arrived at Devonport, en route for France, to convey the body of America's Unknown Warrior for burial in Washington. Rear-Admiral Lloyd H. Chandler and his staff landed at Plymouth, where they were received by Admiral Sir Montague Browning, Commander-in-Chief and his staff. They were greeted by a guard of honour of Royal Marines, with Colours and band – an honour rarely paid to visiting dignitaries. The visiting party was entertained to dinner in the evening.

October 15th

1929: Lord and Lady Astor presented a Hall of Residence – the Astor Hall – to the University of the South-West at the Manor Lodge, Devonport. They invited George Bernard Shaw to give an address at the opening. He accepted the invitation, delivering an address to a crowded Devonport Guildhall with some typically eccentric and tongue-in-cheek remarks. 'The extraordinary devotion of my friends Lord and Lady Astor to the City of Plymouth has always been a source of astonishment to me,' he started, 'because I have never been able to understand in what way the citizens of Plymouth have ever deserved it.' He then said that English university education was destroying civilisation, and for centuries had been making decent government and life for the people impossible. He advised that no citizens of Plymouth, or of anywhere else, should send their children to study at Oxford or Cambridge, as the only thing to be done with those venerable institutions, despite the beauty of their buildings, was to raze them to the ground and sow the foundations with salt.

After he had sat down, Lady Astor thanked him and said that there were few people who could speak as he did, and perhaps it was as well for the world that there were.

October 16th

1759: Smeaton's Tower, erected on rocks a few miles south-west of Plymouth, was lit for the first time. It had been completed in August at a cost of £40,000. John Smeaton had modelled the shape of his lighthouse on an oak tree, and construction began in 1756 at Millbay. The lighthouse remained in use until 1877, when it was found that the rocks on which it stood were being eroded. The upper part was dismantled and rebuilt on Plymouth Hoe in 1882.

———— • ◆ • ————

1886: Plymouth Argyle Football Club, formerly Argyle Football Club, played its first match against Caxton, a Cornish team, and lost 2-0. Later that week they played their second match, beating Dunheved (now Launceston) College 2-1. After several poor performances they were laid to rest in 1894, but returned three years later as Argyle Athletic Club. In 1903 the club became fully professional and adopted the present name, their first professional game being on 1 September, a 2-0 win over West Ham United.

Several theories surround the adoption of the name Argyle, the most probable being that the club was named after the nearby street Argyle Terrace, or the local pub the Argyle Tavern.

October 17th

1907: Edward Edmonds, a plasterer from Morley Place, was charged with being drunk and disorderly, breaking a pane of glass in the New Town Hotel, York Street, and assaulting two policemen. He had been involved in an argument about a game of dominoes there, where three others were playing and did not want him joining in as he was so drunk. It led to a fight in which the glass was smashed and he attacked the policemen who were called. He was fined 5s or five days in prison for drunkenness, and 20s or fourteen days for the assaults.

1928: The County Borough Council of Plymouth was granted City status on the recommendation of the Home Secretary. A tablet to commemorate the event was placed on the northern wall of the Guildhall.

1951: One of the regulars at a pub in Stoke brought in a copy of a local evening paper dated 1904, and passed it round for the other customers to see. Another man said he had an older newspaper than that, and the next evening he came along with a copy of the same title dated 1898. As he handed it round, one drinker looked at the births column and exclaimed in astonishment that his own arrival was among those announced in that issue.

October 18th

1877: After an inquest in Plymouth on Private William Laskey, aged 25, of the Royal Marines, Corporal Joseph Hector and Private John Mutter were charged with having killed him. It was alleged that Laskey had gone to bed rather the worse for drink on 14 October, and they had set on him, striking and kicking him, leaving him with serious injuries – including a fractured skull, from which he died early the next morning. Other marines in the same room were threatened with similar treatment if they gave the alarm. The defendants were tried at Exeter Assizes on 31 October, found guilty of manslaughter and sentenced to twelve months' hard labour.

———— ◆ ————

1965: A Plymouth antiques dealer had a call from a lady in east Cornwall, a widow with a few pieces she needed to sell. After she had described some of them, the antiques dealer drove to her house to inspect them. He estimated the total value at about £25 and made an offer accordingly.

'Of course,' the widow told him, 'I'll have to consult my husband first.'

Taken aback, he said, 'I thought you were a widow.'

'Yes I am,' was the reply, 'but I always get in touch with him through the spirit world before doing any business.'

October 19th

1866: Alfred Parrington, a clerk, was attending a play at the theatre, when he felt a sudden jerk at his watch chain and then noticed that it was gone. A respectably dressed man near him suddenly moved away. The man, Henry Harris, a Plymouth gas fitter, was charged with theft. He pleaded not guilty, saying that he had been at an inn all the time. Enquiries were made there, and nobody had ever seen him on those premises, but as the evidence against him was insufficient, he was discharged.

———— • ◆ • ————

1938: The English Classical Players presented two plays at Plymouth High School for Girls. Afterwards, they were discussing the different schools at which they had played and the number of autograph hunters at each, concluding that boys were much less likely than girls to ask for them. With evident relief, one said, 'I got away with only two this time.'

———— • ◆ • ————

1947: At a meeting in Plymouth for trade unionists, one delegate was taken ill. The chairman rose to his feet, asking, 'Is there a medical man here?' As the British Medical Association was not yet affiliated with the Trades Council, no answer was forthcoming.

October 20th

1869: Mrs Margaret James (30), wife of Captain James, formerly of the 20th Regiment, cut her throat. For the last three years she had suffered from depression, and neighbours had often heard her in her Devonport lodgings dancing around the rooms as she muttered to herself. She generally seemed to be much worse when her husband was away on military business in London, as he had been on this occasion. At the inquest the next day, a verdict that she had taken her own life while 'temporarily insane' was recorded.

———— · ◆ · ————

1951: A Mannamead housewife bought a cake at a corner shop. When she took it home she tried to cut it, but found it was so hard that she was unable to get her knife into it. The cake went back to the shop and the assistant apologised profusely as he gave her a Swiss roll instead. This time, when she put the dessert on the table at home and inserted the knife, she found it was easier to cut – until the blade came into contact with a ball of string in the middle. Once more she went to the shop – and, thankfully for all concerned, it was a case of third time lucky.

October 21st

1873: The body of a baby boy, aged about a month, was found in a field at Stoke, with an apron string tied tightly around his throat and the apron forced down his throat. A woman who had been seen loitering near the spot was summoned to give evidence at the inquest, but, although her behaviour had been rather suspicious, she was cleared. Nobody was charged with killing the infant.

———•◆•———

1890: The Armada Tercentenary Memorial on the Hoe was unveiled by Alfred, Duke of Edinburgh, Commander-in-Chief at Devonport. The foundation stone had been laid on 19 July 1888, the 300th anniversary of the sighting of the Spanish Armada. The memorial is in the form of a granite pedestal, surmounted by the 11ft 6in-high figure of Britannia, with a lion by her side. Granite from Gunnislake Quarries was used for the pedestal, which is 40ft high. It features various busts and arms – including those of Sir Francis Drake and Lord Howard of Effingham, and various other naval commanders – plus the shields of other cities and towns which sent ships to aid the English fleet in 1588. On the first step is a small cannon mounted on a carriage, and on the opposite side is a pattern anchor, enclosed with light chains.

October 22nd

1931: The Beacon Castle Greyhound, Whippet & Sports Ground at Lipson, near the top of Efford Lane, was opened. Whippet and greyhound racing was scheduled for Tuesday and Thursday evenings, and on Saturday afternoons. Whippet races (of up to 300 yards) and greyhound races (of up to 1,000 yards) could be run with the use of a trackless hare. There were to be seven races in each programme, with eight dogs in two of them and six in the others. A club on the premises had been furnished by men from the Efford Ex-Servicemen Colony. Meetings took place on Tuesday, Thursday and Friday evenings, and every Saturday afternoon. Admission was 7d, while entry to the sweepstakes and trials was free of charge. The club later became the Beacon Castle Sports & Social Club.

October 23rd

1965: Two youths called at an undertaker's office in the city, saying they had come to arrange a funeral. 'Who's dead?' the undertaker asked them.

'My aunt at Plympton,' said one. The man then noticed a knowing look pass between his visitors.

'It isn't sudden death, is it? Because if so, you should notify a policeman.' The man added that there was a constable in the office upstairs. One of the boys then said he was feeling dizzy and had to go outside for air. The other then went outside to see how his friend was. Neither of them returned.

———◆———

1986: The Gdynia Fountain in the centre of St Andrew's Cross roundabout, which was created to symbolise links between Plymouth and Gdynia, was switched on jointly by Dr Cezary Ikanowicz, Polish Consul-General, and Bill Glanville, Lord Mayor. The central jet, surrounded by smaller ones, is capable of reaching a height of 30ft.

———◆———

1987: A nearby resident, whose property overlooked the view, was horrified when six trees flanking the amphitheatre in Saltram Park were cut down. Head gardener Ray Briggs explained that the Douglas firs had lost all their lower branches and were 'looking like lavatory brushes'. Replacement cedars had been planted as closely as possible, in order to grow quickly and fill the gaps.

October 24th

1950: Two devoted female fans of singer Al Jolson, in floods of tears, rushed into a Plymouth record shop after hearing that he had died the previous day. 'We've just heard that he's gone,' they sobbed, 'and we simply must get some of his records before they die out.' They left with three discs each, doubtless leaving a few for other grieving admirers who felt the same way.

———— •◆• ————

1953: Plymouth was drenched by a sudden cloudburst, accompanied by thunder and lightning. The weather station at Mount Batten recorded 1.13in of rain. Over 16,000 watched Plymouth Argyle play Notts County and draw 3-3, despite the pitch at Home Park being flooded, but several other city football matches were called off. The worst flooding was in Wolseley Road, where almost 2ft of water rose above the level of the ground floor of some council flats.

———— •◆• ————

1973: Bob Weston, born in Plymouth in 1947, was fired from Fleetwood Mac. A guitarist, harmonica and banjo player, he played on the group's albums Penguin and Mystery To Me, both released that year, but was asked to leave after he was found to be having an affair with the wife of the band's drummer, Mick Fleetwood.

October 25th

1910: The City Museum & Art Gallery, and the Central Library on Tavistock Road, were both officially opened in a joint ceremony. The mayor, Alderman J. Yeo, opened the library with architect Lionel Thornley, while Alderman T. Brook (chairman of the Museum & Art Gallery Committee), Alderman R.W. Winnicott (the deputy mayor), and Mr Rooke, opened the museum part of the building. The Corporation had decided in 1887 to create a museum and art gallery to mark Queen Victoria's Golden Jubilee. A site was donated in Tavistock Road, and, in 1890, Beaumont House and grounds were purchased as a temporary place of storage for paintings and other items. The building was opened as a museum in 1898. In 1906, Dr Andrew Carnegie, the Scottish philanthropist, offered the council £15,000 towards building a new public library. A site was found – on the opposite side of Tavistock Road from the original library – and the decision was taken to put a museum alongside the library. The library, museum and art gallery form part of the same block of buildings, and the foundation stones were laid in October 1907, with building work beginning two months later. The final cost of the work was £15,627 14s 6d for the library and £13,313 9s 9d for the museum.

October 26th

1957: At Freedom Fields Hospital, a nurse found two 9-year-olds in the waiting room, reading. Assuming that they had come for treatment, she asked what was wrong with them. 'Nothing, miss,' answered one. 'We just came in to read the books.'

———◆———

1986: Plymouth CityBus took over the running of the bus services from the City Council. The history of local buses had begun in 1900 with the Plymouth Motor Co., which soon had competition from the Great Western Railway (which opened a motor road service from Millbay station to Roborough) and from the Peverell Road Car Co. Plymouth Corporation Tramways Department started to run motor buses in 1920. Several successive companies took over services, among them the Devon Motor Transport Co., the Plymouth & District Motor Co., and the Western National Omnibus Co. In December 1959, Plymouth's last independent bus operator, the Heybrook Bay Motor Services Co. Ltd, was sold to Western National, and its services were integrated into the Plymouth Joint Services. Plymouth CityBus was sold to The Go-Ahead Group plc, of Newcastle-upon-Tyne, in December 2009.

October 27th

1954: The Revd Douglas Jago, vicar of Honicknowle, reported that one of his parishioners was ill and wanted to take Communion at home. Jago had a very heavy diary that week, but said he would be able to pay her a visit on Friday morning.

'That won't do,' was the reply, 'I don't suppose I shall last until then.'

'Then what about Thursday morning?'

'Oh no. I might be gone then.'

'All right,' the vicar suggested, 'I'll make a special point of looking in on Wednesday evening.'

'In that case,' she said, 'don't come until after 7 p.m., because I want to listen to The Archers.'

———— ◆ ————

2007: Professor Alan Southward, one of the leading marine biologists of his day, died, aged 79. A native of Liverpool, he began his scientific career in 1953 at the Laboratory of the Marine Biological Association in Plymouth. His expertise was much in demand after the Torrey Canyon oil spill contaminated much of the Cornish shore. He was also one of the leading scientists on the team which monitored the environmental impact on the animals and plants on the coastline, demonstrating that the toxic chemicals that were used to disperse the oil slick were generally more harmful to wildlife in the long term than the oil itself.

October 28th

1913: Amanda Bradfield (18), wife of a naval stoker serving on board HMS *Monmouth*, died in hospital. James Honeyands had been lodging with Amanda's mother, Mrs Perry. On 18 October, he and Amanda had been quarrelling in the Courtenay Arms, and continued to do so after they left the premises. Honeyands then pulled out a revolver and aimed three shots at her, two of which hit her in the chest. He then tried to shoot himself but the weapon jammed, and, on attempting to run away from the scene of the crime, he was apprehended by passers-by. Amanda was badly wounded but still conscious, and lingered in agony for a further ten days, during which time she coughed up one of the bullets.

Honeyands was charged with murder, sentenced to death at Exeter in February 1914, and hanged on 12 March.

1964: A woman who had been to watch a film at the Plaza Cinema asked an attendant if she could help her find her arm, which she had dropped under the seat. She had been wearing an artificial limb which had become unstrapped. It was soon recovered. The picture the woman had just been watching was the science fiction thriller *The Crawling Hand*.

October 29th

1917: At Carmarthen Assizes, Mary Elizabeth Orchard (17), a postmistress from Milford Haven, was sentenced to eighteen months' imprisonment with hard labour for stealing a mailbag containing £3,000, after being arrested in Plymouth. £2,876 of the missing money was recovered.

———— ◆ ————

1947: Royal Parade, the first major road to be built during the post-war reconstruction of the city centre, was opened in two portions. The western end, from Courtenay Street to Westwell Street, was declared open by King George VI and Queen Elizabeth.

It was a bitterly cold day, and among those who had come to watch was a former air-raid warden who had come through the war unscathed. On this occasion the weather was too much for him, and after eight hours in the bitter autumn wind he went straight home to bed, saying it had got to him where the Luftwaffe's bombs had failed. The rest of the road, extending from that point to St Andrew's Cross, including Derry's Cross roundabout at the western end, was opened on 27 September 1948, when the Lord Mayor, Alderman H.J. Perry, removed the Road Closed signs and drove through in the official car. Construction had begun in August 1947 on the 150ft-wide road, built at a cost of £180,000.

October 30th

1891: Two fishing boats, *Sunbeam* and *Alonzo*, were sunk near the Breakwater by shots fired from the gunboat *Plucky* during target practice. Mr Hisbent, a fisherman on one of the boats, was drowned. In the preceding months there had been several near-misses during similar firing exercises, and some thought it an accident waiting to happen. An inquiry was held, and Lieutenant Fremantle, commander of *Plucky*, was court-martialled but acquitted, as the tragedy was 'attributed to an error in estimating the distance, due to the peculiar condition of the atmosphere'.

1954: A man attended several meetings of a faith-healing campaign in Devonport, enthusiastically telling his colleagues at work about each meeting on the following day. At the end of the week, he contacted the staff to report that he was off sick.

1976: The ABC Cinema closed its doors for a conversion, the last films being two television spin-off comedies, *The Likely Lads*, starring Rodney Bewes and James Bolam, and *Steptoe & Son*, starring Wilfrid Brambell and Harry H. Corbett. The cinema reopened in May 1977 as a triple-screen cinema – with seating for 578, 367 and 122 – and a bingo hall with capacity for 1,200.

October 31st

1880: The ship *Glamis*, a 1,150-ton vessel built in Dundee, chartered by the agent-general for New South Wales, sailed from Plymouth for Sydney with 370 emigrants on board.

———◆◆———

1907: Ernest Oram, a shipwright, was charged at Devon Assizes, Exeter, with stealing post and letters from a Devonport post office on 21 August. Postman Day had found Oram at a pillar box acting in a suspicious manner. He had run away, but was soon caught, and, when searched, four letters and a postcard all addressed to different persons with the stamps not cancelled were found on him. A stick and metal weight, which he had used for abstracting the letters, was found lying nearby. A sticky substance was detected at the aperture of the letterbox and on the letters themselves. In his defence, Oram said that the letters had been given to him. He was sentenced to fifteen months' imprisonment.

———◆◆———

1922: Mrs Mary Sennett, of Pym Street, Devonport, was taken to court by Lily Ford, who lived at the same address, on a charge of assault. 'It is false lies,' Mary protested. 'I am a mother of fourteen children, and wish to live peaceably.' The magistrates adjourned the case for two months, to give defendant and plaintiff a chance to live harmoniously under the same roof.

November 1st

1954: From time to time, city councillors held their meetings in the museum and art gallery. On this day, they met in the precincts of an exhibition featuring the work of sculptor Gerhard Marcks. Some of those attending showed a distinct lack of respect for the artefacts by using them as hatstands. The *Western Independent* commented that it was 'hardly a cultural attitude to important work and surely a poor example to set to "lesser" citizens'.

———◆———

1962: Sharron Davies was born in Plymouth. She learned to swim at the age of 6 and set a record by swimming for the British national team at the age of 11. Breaking both wrists after falling out of a tree did not deter her from training. In 1976, aged 13, she represented Britain at the Montreal Summer Olympics. Two years later, she won two gold medals at the Commonwealth Games in Edmonton, and was a silver medallist in the 1980 Moscow Olympics. By the time Sharron retired from competitive swimming in 1994, she had broken several British and World Masters records. Awarded the MBE for her services to sport, she subsequently worked as a TV presenter and became a patron of several charities for disabled children and fitness.

November 2nd

1949: At the start of what was generally regarded as the Christmas shopping season, on this day it was announced that Plymouth toy shops were proud to be offering what they considered to be their best selection since before the war, as well as better value, with some prices cut by fifty per cent or more on those of last year. There was a wide choice of good quality dolls and box games in particular, while cowboy and nurse play outfits – which had been unavailable the last few years due to rationing – were now back on sale at 30s each. Lead toys, which had also been unobtainable for some time, were around 2s each, and the year's latest craze, plastic unbreakable music balls, were 2s 6d each.

———◆———

2010: Messrs Western Garage Ltd, previously Messrs W. Mumford Ltd (founded as Mumford & Sons in around 1860), went into administration and was acquired by Vospers. The firm had been one of the largest car dealers and hire firms in Plymouth for many years, and was, for a time, the Rolls-Royce and Bentley agent for Devon and Cornwall. In January 1972 it opened in new premises in Marsh Mills, and was hailed as 'Plymouth's biggest ever car sales complex'.

November 3rd

1880: As this day was the tercentenary of Drake's return home after circumnavigating the globe, the mayor, Alderman Derry, said that Plymouth should erect a fitting monument to his memory, and he himself would contribute £50. Comic magazine *Fun* published a joke (all right, this is Victorian humour) to say that the leader of the voyage was at once 'Drake' and 'dux', and gave his brave crews a chance of making 'ducks and drakes' of the contents of the Spanish treasure ships they captured.

1942: Plymouth-born Duncan Alexander Croall Scott-Ford (21), of the Merchant Navy, was hanged for treason at Wandsworth Gaol after being convicted of supplying information to the Germans on the movement of shipping. Details of his trial were kept secret until after his execution. Newspapers reported that he had betrayed his country for £18, and had paid the ultimate penalty as a warning to other Merchant Navy sailors who might have been similarly approached.

1950: A couple of friends were discussing the bad quality of radio reception in Plympton. 'When you think of it, it's bound to be poor when everybody is listening at once,' said one. 'The load gets so heavy that somebody's bound to suffer.'

November 4th

1910: The Plymouth Ambulance Service was founded, chiefly through the initiative of some of the young men attending first-aid classes in the George Street Baptist church. Brothers Hedley, Wilfred and Walter Miller set up the George Street Ambulance Corps, using rooms at the church as their headquarters. Members got called out to accidents and gave basic first aid to members of the public. In 1921, the George Street Ambulance Corps became part of the St John Ambulance Brigade, with headquarters at 35 Notte Street; the ambulance station was next door. The Corps later became the Plymouth & District Ambulance Service.

1956: Boys were out in force collecting 'a penny for the guy'. When asked if he was collecting to buy fireworks, one lad said his father was bringing some home, so he would use the money to take to school and buy savings stamps. In Royal Parade, a pedestrian told a group of boys that he would not give them anything unless they could tell him who Guy Fawkes was. They all looked blank, except for one who thought and said, 'He's a bloke on a bonfire.'

November 5th

1954: A smartly suited man called at a chemist in Westwell Street for some methylpentynol capsules to remove the 'butterflies' from his stomach. The reason? 'I'm proposing tonight!'

1957: Two small boys in cowboy outfits, carrying toy six-shooters, met the Revd W.H.A. Cooper on the steps of St Andrew's Church, and asked if they could go inside to look round. 'It is not usual to go into church armed,' he told them.

'Will you look after our guns, mister?' one of them asked. The Revd duly obliged, and waited outside, holding the weapons while they went in.

1965: Seven hundred churchgoers in St Francis', Honicknowle, received their parish magazine. Inside was a supplement from the *National Christian News*, produced in Birmingham, featuring an article about how life may appear to a returning ex-serviceman, warning them that 'N*****s have moved in next door and the value of your house has dropped by hundreds.' The vicar of St Francis', the Revd Anthony Watson, resolved to complain to the publishers that such comment was racist and grossly offensive. A fortnight earlier, Jamaican-born leading sick berth attendant Samuel Kennedy had been told that his potential purchase of a bungalow in Carew Grove, Honicknowle, had been cancelled, as some neighbours objected to his ethnicity.

November 6th

1939: John Commins of Plymouth appeared in court in Torquay, charged with obtaining £6 from Gwendoline Wiles, a hotel worker, by false pretences. He had told Gwendoline that he was an RAF pilot officer engaged in secret work, including flying aeroplanes to Romania, for which he received £10 weekly and a bonus of £50 for the successful delivery of each plane. He claimed that when he met her he had been shot down in flames off the French coast, and had lost his chequebook and wallet. When arrested, Commins admitted that the story was false. Outstanding charges of obtaining money for advertisements in a directory – which he said he intended to publish – were also taken into consideration, and he was sentenced to six months' imprisonment.

1947: A Czech student who had helped to dig the area where Royal Parade was being built during the summer, and had then returned home, sent a large package to the Plymouth family who had given him accommodation, as a thank you present. It contained a magnificent glass fruit bowl, beautifully packaged and in perfect condition. The sting in the tail for the recipients was the charge of £9 19s 4d customs duty and purchase tax, payable on delivery.

November 7th

1949: Devonport Dockyard workers were given a day's holiday, although many of them did not know why. Three were stopped while they were shopping in Royal Parade, but none could answer the question as to why they were enjoying a day off. A fourth was unsure, but said he thought it might be something to do with 'industrial fatigue'. It was, in fact, a goodwill break awarded to them by the dockyard management to compensate for the long period without any bank holidays between August and Christmas.

2001: Addressing the University Vocational Awards Council in London, Professor Roderick Floud, president of Universities UK, defended vocational degrees against criticism from those who felt that degree courses were being dumbed down as a result of a government pledge to get fifty per cent of young people under 30 into university. Floud commended initiatives such as the Surf Science & Technology degree at Plymouth University. Two years earlier, the *Sun* had voted this the most bizarre degree course in the country. Despite what preconceptions tabloid readers might have had about a 'surfing' course, it incorporated 'rigorous academic disciplines', including coastal and ocean sciences, materials and equipment technology, clothing design and business studies.

November 8th

1912: Kate Butler was murdered at her house in King Street. She was separated from her husband and had moved in with George Cunliffe, who had recently left the navy. Earlier that month, Cunliffe had been sent to prison for five days for being drunk and disorderly, and was angry as Kate had refused to pay his fine. On his release, he said he planned to return to his hometown of Wigan, and asked her to give him his fare. She told him that she did not have the money, whereupon he seized her and slashed her throat with a razor. Within half an hour, she had bled to death. Cunliffe was convicted and hanged three months later.

1921: The Royal Marine Memorial on the Hoe was unveiled by Earl Fortescue, Lord Lieutenant of Devon. The pedestal is surmounted by a 7ft 6in-bronze figure of St George. It was erected at the suggestion of Mr W.C. Storr-Barber, who had served in the Royal Marines during the First World War, and who sculpted the stone figures at the side of the pedestal.

1957: A very honest 7-year-old boy was overheard at school asking his teacher: 'Could I be let off my homework because we are going to Bournemouth and Mother doesn't think she'll have time to do it.'

November 9th

1927: W.H.J. Priest became Mayor of Plymouth on his 32nd birthday, thus becoming the youngest person ever to hold that office – a record which remained unbeaten at the time of his death on 24 April 1957. When he died, he was the deputy leader of the Conservatives on the City Council.

1949: Rabbits were reported, having been seen on the Hoe by a woman while she was out exercising her dogs. The rabbits (which were an unusual sight on the Hoe) were thought to have escaped from people doing greyhound coursing in the area.

1956: Walter Hopkins, of Ernesettle, was probably the luckiest man alive on this day. He fell 80ft while painting the railway bridge across Camel's Head Creek, but his commando training during the war had taught him how to fall without injuring himself. He fell into 2ft of water, which acted as a cushion. If he had fallen off the other side of the bridge, he would have struck the rocks. He also missed, by a dozen feet, falling into soft mud (which would probably have engulfed him), a brick pillar supporting the bridge, and an old wooden stake sticking up from the bed of the creek. He got up and walked away without a scratch.

November 10th

1904: Weston Mill Cemetery was opened. The land had been purchased in 1899 for £25,000, from Edward St Aubyn, Lord of the Manor, and the foundation stone of the chapel was laid in June 1903. The Church of England plot was consecrated by the Bishop of Exeter on 22 November, during a heavy fall of snow, and the first burial took place there four days later. By the end of the year, twenty-five burials had occurred there. It is also the site of a large number of Commonwealth War Graves.

1961: The annual 'Rag Mag', produced by Plymouth Technical College students, went on sale, with all profits going to the Torr Home for the Blind. The previous year's publication had been condemned by a clergyman for its dirty jokes. However, the current issue, according to a local newspaper, while remaining 'bright and full of fun', contained 'fewer borderline jokes and none which really cross over'. One innocuous gag was: 'Tell your wife you love her daily. If you haven't got a daily, advertise for one through this magazine.' As well as humour, it included much 'sensible material', including an article on the Torr Home.

November 11th

1918: The sound from ships' sirens and whistles, joined by factories and warships in harbour, signalled that four years of war were over at last. One 9-year-old schoolboy, walking along College Road in Mutley, feared he would be late for class – until he heard the sirens, arrived at school and found the others being sent home. A teacher, patting him on the back, told him that there would not be any lessons that day. Although there had not yet been any official announcement in the town, flags were being hung from windows everywhere, as well as from the main buildings in the centre, and strings of bunting were hung across the roads in celebration. Church and school bells rang out at intervals, and continued to do so for the rest of the day. Thousands congregated in New George Street, outside the *Western Morning News* offices, for the official announcement, which came at 11 a.m. when the Admiralty at Mount Wise contacted the newspaper staff, and a formal proclamation was made by the Mayor of Plymouth in Guildhall Square.

Amid the rejoicing, two lorries containing German prisoners of war passed by and had to halt because of the crowds. The prisoners looked pleased as they realised what was happening, and everyone waved to the men who had, until then, been their enemies.

November 12th

1948: Seen on a village hall notice just outside Plymouth: 'A lecture on Happy Married Life will be given to the Mothers Union by Miss ----'

———•◆•———

2010: A Royal Navy bomb disposal team successfully detonated an unexploded 70kg bomb, dropped on the city during the Second World War, off Cawsand Bay. It had been discovered by builders at the NAAFI demolition site in Notte Street the previous day, Remembrance Day, and had been driven slowly under police escort towards Millbay Docks, where it was transferred to the unit's diving boat. Police had to clear the frontages of every building – including offices, shops, hotels, and restaurants – which the van passed in case the device detonated. A massive underwater explosion, propelling a 15-metre jet of spray into the air, signalled the end of the operation.

November 13th

1963: The Beatles appeared in the city as part of their autumn tour. They were interviewed by Stuart Hutchison for local music TV show, *Move Over Dad* on Westward Television, and, to avoid being mobbed by waiting fans, they were taken through a tunnel into Derry's Cross to record the interview. Afterwards they played two sell-out shows at the ABC Cinema, on a bill which included supporting acts The Kestrels, Peter Jay and the Jaywalkers, The Vernons Girls and comedian Frank Berry. The Beatles' performance was inaudible as the – mainly female – audience screamed continuously throughout their set. Chief Constable Skittery said that the young audience were 'highly excited but perfectly well behaved'.

After leaving the building, the group spent the night at Burgh Island Hotel, Bigbury-on-Sea. Their single 'She Loves You' was No. 3 in the charts that week, having slipped from No. 1 – although it would return there later that month after a seven-week gap, and their second LP, With The Beatles, was released nine days later. (*See* September 12th)

November 14th

1892: Fernley Wallis was born in Plymouth. After qualifying as a chemist, in 1914 he acquired a recently failed pharmacy business, Martin & Palmer, and incorporated it into his own, which had been based at East Street until the Second World War, when he had moved to the market. Some of the buildings were damaged during the war, but Wallis managed to keep trading there until shortly before they were demolished in January 1952. He then moved to New George Street, sold the business in 1980 and died at his Plympton home the following year.

1947: During a season marked by outbreaks of fowl pest in south Devon, stock at Lower Dunstone Farm was inspected by the Ministry of Agriculture. About 100 birds, including poultry, ducks and geese, were found to be infected, and all had to be destroyed.

1957: A lady from Mutley Plain bought a golden hamster in a pet shop for 7s 6d, and decided to call him Champagne Charlie. About three days later, she woke up in the morning and found she had had a bargain, for there were four in the cage. By lunchtime the total had increased to nine. 'He' was promptly renamed Clara.

November 15th

1577: Francis Drake and his fleet left Plymouth on an expedition against the Spanish along the Pacific coast of the Americas. A storm caused damage to the ships and forced the fleet to stop at an island off the coast of Morocco to carry out repairs. They set sail again early the following month. The journey took them through the Magellan Strait, up the west coast of South and then North America, and then via the Pacific and Indian Oceans and the Cape of Good Hope. They returned to Plymouth, well laden with treasure, years later.

———•◆•———

1954: A city schoolgirl was set an exam question: 'What do you know about Sir Francis Drake?' In answer, she wrote, 'He was a great sailor who sailed round the world and discovered Drake's Island.'

———•◆•———

1860: Another voyage abroad ended when Albert Edward, Prince of Wales, sailed into the Hoe at dawn and landed at the Royal William Victualling Yard on HMS *Hero*. He had departed from the same place four months earlier for a very successful tour of Canada and the United States. The Plymouth and Devonport Corporations presented addresses, but, because of cold weather, they were handed to the Prince without being read aloud first.

November 16th

1949: At Hooe, a hawthorn tree was seen in its full summer bloom. Some weeks earlier a couple of oil tanks had caught fire in the neighbourhood, generating intense heat and destroying a large amount of undergrowth in the vicinity. The unnaturally high temperatures were believed to have caused this unusually late flowering, and also that of a nearby ash tree which had put out new foliage.

———— • ◆ • ————

1974: Teen sensations, the Bay City Rollers, played two shows at Plymouth Guildhall this evening. Pandemonium erupted at the first concert as several girls, some only aged 7, had to be dragged off the stage, fainting, and six were taken to Freedom Fields Hospital with suspected broken or crushed ribs. In order to avoid a repetition of such incidents, the second concert was stopped for ten minutes while order was restored. The Public Services Committee later suggested that parents ought to ban young children from attending such shows. About 1,000 fans were at each performance, while nearly 2,000 had waited outside in the cold to catch a glimpse of their idols, and a few from Halifax had been camping on the Guildhall steps since 3.30 a.m.

November 17th

1908: Clara Jane Hannaford (15) was murdered by 19-year-old Edmund Walter Elliott. They had lived nearby for some time, and she regarded him as a friend but nothing more. He had become obsessed with her and had taken to following her around, even breaking into her bedroom window one night. Clara's parents regarded Elliott as a bad influence on her, and at length she told him that she wanted nothing more to do with him. During the evening, she went to the Theatre Royal with her new boyfriend. Elliott had been shadowing them; he called Clara out into the street and cut her throat with a razor, which he had been carrying around with him for the purpose. He gave himself up at the police station, was tried for murder in Exeter in March 1909, and, despite pleas for clemency on account of his youth, he was hanged.

———— • ◆ • ————

1956: Sandy, a cat which belonged to a family living in Efford Lane, was successful at the Sutton Conservative bazaar. His owner had entered his name on a ticket and he was one of the lucky winners whose name was drawn out of the hat – he won two cinema tickets. Yet he would doubtlessly have considered himself luckier if he had secured one of the other prizes – a cold chicken.

November 18th

1909: Arthur Conan Doyle (a member of a deputation from the Congo Reform Association, which was committed to raising awareness of the ill-treatment of the Congolese population by King Leopold II of Belgium) spoke at the Guildhall on the subject of the 'Congo Atrocity'. John Yeo, Mayor of Plymouth, presided over the packed meeting, and the speaker was thanked by the Mayor of Devonport, William Littleton. Conan Doyle was no stranger to Plymouth, having been a junior medical partner in a surgery in Durnford Street, and having lived at Eliot Terrace for a few weeks in 1882 before beginning a successful career as the creator of Sherlock Holmes.

———— •◆• ————

1954: An artist, painting on the Barbican, suddenly noticed that a small boy was standing beside her and watching as she worked. In order to strike up a friendly conversation with him, she asked him if he was a good boy and helped his mother. 'Oh yes,' he assured her, 'I file down the ha'pennies for the gas meter.' Naturally, the artist reported this to the authorities in order to alert them to the problem. An antiques dealer in the same area of the city said that he had had regular visits from small boys, who had been sent by their mothers with shillings to find pieces of the same size in his tray of cheap foreign coins.

November 19th

1840: The *William Bryan* sailed from Plymouth – the first ship to sail under the auspices of the Plymouth Company of New Zealand, enabling people from Devon and Cornwall to set up a colony there. There were twenty-one married couples, twenty-two single adults and seventy children in the expedition, led by George Cutfield, a former naval architect from Devonport Dockyard. They landed at a bay off the west coast off North Island on 31 March 1841. On writing home, Cutfield said that they had reached...

> ...a fine country with a large quantity of flat land, but every part is covered with vegetation, fern, scrub and forest. The fern, on good land, is generally from four to six feet high. There are thousands of acres of this land which will require but a trifling outlay to bring into cultivation.

The community was named New Plymouth, and the main thoroughfare was called New Street.

—— • ◆ • ——

1900: At the height of a local epidemic of enteric fever, seven cases were reported in the last twenty-four hours, bringing the total of patients to fifty-five. Sixteen cases had been reported the previous week. The outbreak was traced to milk which had been supplied by a dairy just outside Plymouth.

November 20th

1907: Emily Pobjoy, 'an unfortunate', was charged at Stonehouse Police Court with being drunk and incapable. It was the third time she had been before the Bench that year for drunkenness – quite apart from summonses for other offences – and she had only just been released after seven days' imprisonment on another charge. There had been thirty-three convictions against her already in Bristol and Cardiff. The chairman of the court called it 'a fearful and unbearable case', and her conduct 'was too bad'. He fined her £1 or fourteen days' imprisonment.

1922: An application was made to Plympton magistrates by Superintendent W. Chammings, about a ladder which had been stolen in April 1921 from the wolfram (tungsten) mines at Hemerdon. Police enquiries only succeeded in locating a small portion of the ladder, and a larger part was later obtained from a man who had bought it, unaware that it was stolen property. The ladder's owner declined to prosecute, as he wished to hear no more of the matter. It was now in police possession, and the superintendent needed an order as to its disposal, as the original owner refused to go into court and identify what remained of his property. After expressing the view that the original owner's attitude in refusing to assist the police was most unsatisfactory, the Bench decided to return the ladder to the purchaser.

November 21st

1931: The Regent Cinema, Frankfort Street, threw open its doors for the first time with *City Lights*, starring Charlie Chaplin, on the opening programme. It had seating for 3,500, with 1,390 in the balcony. There was a large waiting area, furnished with deep-sprung couches, which meant that tickets could be sold in advance to 2,000 people, who could then be let into the auditorium with the minimum delay as the audience for the previous house was leaving. Three fairy water fountains stood in front of the curtain, while incidental music was provided by an HMV Panatrope system (based on the electric phonograph). There were facilities for an orchestra as well. Chaplin was visiting Plymouth at the time as a personal guest of Lord and Lady Astor, and welcome publicity was provided for the opening by unfounded rumours that he would be making a personal appearance.

The business was bought in September 1939 by Odeon Cinema Holdings, and on 17 June 1940 it reopened as the Odeon Cinema.

Five years later, after a showing of *Henry V*, starring Laurence Olivier, a disgruntled female customer emerged from the cinema, muttering, 'I don't think much of that film. It didn't tell us anything at all about his wives!'

November 22nd

1922: Charles Smith, a labourer from Gunnislake, was charged at Crownhill Police Court with using obscene language and annoying fellow passengers while travelling on the London & South Western Railway from North Road station to Tamerton Foliot on 30 September. The other occupants of the carriage, Mrs W.J. Martin, her friend and two children aged 5 and 3, had entered the train at North Road station, and Smith and a female companion had joined them at Devonport station. On entering the carriage, Smith had complained to Mrs Martin that her baskets were taking up too much room on the seat, which meant that he could not sit down. Mrs Martin said that the defendant and his companion had quarrelled and used very bad language to each other on the journey. Later, Smith had begun to annoy her, and, on entering Tamerton station, she was so frightened that she had pulled the communication cord and stopped the train. When she got on the platform, Smith had sworn at her and tried to strike her. Corroborative evidence was given by the guard and foreman of the train as to Smith's behaviour on the platform. Smith admitted to being under the influence of liquor at the time, and was fined 40s and 10s costs.

November 23rd

1950: A Mutley resident, just out of hospital with a peptic ulcer, was puzzled by her instructions: 'Eat your foot slowly and chew thoroughly. You should have sufficient teeth for efficient mastication.'

———— • • ————

1965: During Rag Week, a crowd of about 100 students with collecting boxes marched into the ABC Cinema while a film was showing, reached the upper lobby, and tried to gain access to the circle as they shouted and banged on the floor with staves. Several of the staff were horrified – some white-faced, having had no warning of the invasion – and were concerned for the audience, which included several elderly cinemagoers. The students were turned out but they tried to repeat their performance at the Drake Cinema; however, the ABC staff had had the forethought to warn the other cinema in advance and the group were turned back without being allowed to set foot inside. One large department store in the city centre was equally displeased when a smaller group of students burst in and demanded protection money, and the manager sent for the police. This firm had previously given donations of several hundred guineas to the students for Rag Week, but this year they had sent none, as the Rag Committee had not asked them. 'And it only needed a letter,' the manager commented.

November 24th

1902: Annie Pearce, of Queen Street, was charged with stealing a gold ring from Thomas Moorshed, a shipwright, of HMS *Flora*, at Summerland Place. Moorshed told the court that the ring must have been taken from his finger during the night. Annie alleged that he had been drunk at the time, and in any case she had not taken it – he had given it to her in lieu of money. The Bench presumably considered it unnecessary to enquire further into the details of this transaction and any services rendered; they dismissed the case, saying that there was no corroborative evidence, and reminding Moorshed that he had brought the loss on himself as a result of getting into bad company.

———— ◆ ————

1949: During the evening, an American sailor at a pub in Union Street bought himself a drink, and put the change from a £1 note into his pocket. A shower of silver immediately poured out of his trouser leg. As he reached down to pick the coins up, there was laughter at the bar, as one customer remarked, 'That, I suppose, is what is meant by the dollar gap.'

November 25th

1880: After a day or two of strong weather, a heavy gale at sea struck the Anchor Line steamer *Utopia*, which had left London for New York on 20 November with 253 steerage and twelve cabin passengers, and had reached a point somewhere west of the Isles of Scilly. By about 4 p.m. winds were at hurricane force, and all passengers were sent below. Later that day, sea came over the starboard bow, struck the funnel, and carried about 40ft of it overboard; three seamen were seriously injured. The next morning, a decision was taken not to continue the journey to New York as the vessel was in such a poor state, and the *Utopia* sailed for Plymouth, where she arrived on 29 November for repairs.

———— • ◆ • ————

1947: At a Toc H meeting in Crownhill, one of the delegates told the story of a young schoolgirl who had been told to write a 200-word essay on cars. Her effort read: 'My daddy had a car. He was run into at Crownhill one day, and he used the other 180 words on the way home.'

November 26th

1999: At Plymouth's second American Thanksgiving Festival, the guest of honour, Captain Stewart Barnett III, the US Defence and Naval Attaché in London, unveiled a bronze plaque on Island House at the Barbican, naming all 101 pilgrims who had sailed on the *Mayflower*. The festival, hosted by the Chamber of Commerce, was believed to be the only one held outside the USA.

Neill Mitchell, the Chamber's chief executive, said that Thanksgiving was something that Plymouth had a genuine reason for celebrating, because of the city's particular link with the story of the Pilgrim Fathers. 'We also have a rich naval heritage and if we have any visiting US ships at sea, they can come to Plymouth and enjoy a bit of home culture.' Captain Barnett said in reply how amazed and impressed he was that a quintessentially US holiday was celebrated so far away, and saw it as a great opportunity to build on links between Plymouth and America. The Stars and Stripes were hoisted outside the Civic Centre, and on the following day there was a full programme for the city centre of line dancing, jazz bands and other American entertainment.

November 27th

1948: A 3-year-old girl was taken to a dedication service at a church in St Budeaux. She was puzzled when the congregation knelt in prayer. 'Who are we hiding from now, Daddy?' she asked.

———•◆•———

1956: A couple came back to their house in Noss Mayo at about 11 p.m. to find their pet hen waiting for them inside the garden gate. During the winter, she usually roosted in her nest of dead leaves in the corner of a shed at about 4.30 p.m. They went to investigate, and found a hedgehog coiled up in her usual place. The couple wrapped him in thick newspaper, and deposited him in the garden so the hen could go to bed.

———•◆•———

1964: Mr S.C. Markey, a visiting delegate to the Boilermakers' and Shipwrights' Dinner, said that when passing the dockyard, he had asked how many people worked there. 'The reply I got was "About thirty per cent!"'

November 28th

1919: The voters of Britain elected Nancy Astor a Member of Parliament. She was the first female MP to actually take up her seat at Westminster (the first elected woman MP, Countess Markievicz, belonged to Sinn Fein and never took her seat).

A by-election had been held in Plymouth Sutton after the elevation of the sitting Coalition Unionist member, Waldorf Astor, to the peerage; he had become a viscount when his father died, and therefore had to resign his seat in the House of Commons. His wife Nancy stood as candidate and won 14,495 votes, against 9,292 for Mr W.T. Gay (Labour) and 4,139 for Isaac Foot (Liberal), giving her a majority of 5,203. 'Although I cannot say that the best man has won, I can say that the best policy has won,' she declared in her speech after the result was announced at the Guildhall. Taking the oath of allegiance and her seat in the House of Commons on 1 December, with her sponsors being the Prime Minister David Lloyd George and the previous Conservative Prime Minister Arthur Balfour, she represented Sutton as a Coalition Unionist and then as a Conservative until the dissolution of parliament at the end of the Second World War in 1945.

November 29th

1842: A woman in Devonport was convinced that somebody in the house was stealing from her candle box. She told her husband, who decided that the most effective way to prevent further theft would be to connect the box to the poles of a galvanic battery. After preparing the device, without her knowledge, he sat down to his supper – to be interrupted by the sound of a horrified female voice. He went to see what was happening, and found his wife standing by the box. She said she had seen a mouse get in, and had tried to catch it, but promptly felt such an 'all-overish sensation' that she felt compelled to cry out. What happened to the mouse is not recorded, but she did not lose any more candles after that.

———— • ◆ • ————

1947: A customer at a café in the city centre ordered an ice cream, and when the waitress enquired brightly how he had liked it, he told her ruefully that there was 'not very much flavour'. She went out to the back, and returned somewhat apologetic. 'I'm sorry, but it wasn't ice cream,' she explained. 'They made a mistake in the kitchen.' He had been given a concoction of frozen milk instead.

November 30th

1949: Two children, a brother and sister, were sitting in a single-decker bus on the Hoe circular route. The girl asked if they could go upstairs. 'Don't be silly,' her brother answered. 'Don't you know this is a bungalow?'

———— ◆ ————

1956: As a result of the Suez crisis and subsequent fuel shortages, petrol rationing was due to be introduced on 17 December. People were anxious to complete their Christmas shopping in good time, and a number of shops in the city centre noticed that people from other areas of Devon and Cornwall were doing their shopping there earlier than usual. Some predicted that if this trend continued, most of the present-buying – except by those who lived within walking distance of the shops – would be more or less over by mid-month. At one store, five assistants who had to travel some distance to work handed in their resignations with regret, as they feared they would be unable to use their cars soon. Once rationing began, some garages decided to close either part of the day, or even whole days at a time, as they were quickly running out of rationed petrol. Shoppers continued to come to Plymouth – but by coach instead of car.

December 1st

1848: The Ford Park Cemetery, sometimes known as 'The Old Cemetery', was opened, and the first interment took place on unconsecrated ground three weeks later. The cemetery had been established to serve the Three Towns, as there was no longer enough room in the parish churchyards. Within a few months, part of it was earmarked for over 400 victims of the cholera epidemic. In 1857, part of the burial ground was set aside for those of the Roman Catholic faith, and the area was consecrated by the Bishop of Plymouth. In 2000, the management was taken over by the Ford Park Cemetery Trust.

1862: The Royal Albert Hospital in Devonport, named after the late Prince Consort who had died a year earlier, was opened. In addition to the general wards, it included a Female Lock Ward in the eastern wing – by order of the government under the Contagious Diseases Act. Part of the hospital was taken over by the Admiralty during the First World War, and was retained in peacetime as a war college and port library. In 1963 it became the Plymouth General Hospital, Devonport section. It closed in June 1981 on the opening of Derriford Hospital.

December 2nd

1947: A girl of 16 applied for a job at a Plymouth firm and was asked what salary she required. She asked for £5 a week. 'That's a lot of money for a beginner, isn't it?' suggested the manager. 'But think how difficult it will be for me, doing work I know nothing about,' she replied.

———•◆•———

1972: 'Despite the decibels, fans captivated', was the heading of Miles Edson's review in the *Western Evening Herald* of Slade's evening performance at the Guildhall. Edson wrote that 'for those who prefer listening to music as opposed to having it rammed down their throats', the most comfortable position would have been outside the main doors, over 100 yards from the stage. Quiet they were not, but they went down a storm 'as they carried out a policy of rock, scream and roll', with their hits and tracks from Slayed?, their new album. Their supporting acts were Thin Lizzy and Suzi Quatro. At the time, Slade was the most successful group in Britain since the heyday of the Beatles, having just achieved three No. 1 singles within less than a year. Demand for tickets had been heavy, and the show was sold out a fortnight in advance.

December 3rd

1643: The people of Plymouth, who had supported parliament during the Civil War while most of the south-west were fervent in their adherence to the cause of King Charles I, successfully fought off an attack by the army of Prince Maurice, who had asked them to surrender. The Prince and his party had advanced around Lipson Creek from Compton Village, and then down the narrow valley from Eggbuckland. The defenders at Lipson Fort were outnumbered and drew back to Freedom Fields, but the town quickly rallied and, with Colonel Gould leading a counter-attack, the Royalists were forced to retreat. The withdrawal soon became a panic – especially as high tide had now filled Lipson Creek – and several horsemen put to flight were drowned or washed away as they attempted to cross. The occasion is commemorated by a memorial in Freedom Fields Park, bearing an inscription noting 'the hard fighting for several hours' and stating:

> For many years it was the custom to celebrate the anniversary of this victory, long known as 'The Sabbath Day Fight,' & recorded as 'The Great Deliverance' of the protracted siege, successfully maintained by troops & townsfolk on behalf of the Parliament against the King under great hardships for more than 3 years.

December 4th

1948: It was rumoured that a street cleaner had been killed at Hender's Corner, Mannamead. What had actually happened was that a 15-year-old Honicknowle boy had been thrown off his bicycle, and sustained facial injuries. A cleaner had taken off his coat to wrap it around the boy as he was taken to hospital, and the coat became stained with blood.

———◆———

1957: A woman was buying 2lb of potatoes in the Pannier Market. 'Please give me small ones,' she requested, 'as I have a long way to go, and they'll be lighter to carry.'

———◆———

1961: At a council meeting, Councillor Ken Adams had a heated exchange with the Lord Mayor, after which Adams got up and walked out. Six of his Labour colleagues followed him. It looked as if they had walked out in protest, but, as he explained later to the press, 'It was all a mistake. I simply went to keep an appointment.' He had made an appointment elsewhere for 7.30 that evening and the meeting had slipped his mind. Having mentioned to his neighbour that he needed to leave early, he had looked at his watch and realised it was time to go. The other members had followed him in a gesture of solidarity.

December 5th

2006: The City Museum & Art Gallery acquired a painting by J.M.W. Turner entitled Plymouth, from Mount Edgcumbe. It had been purchased at Sotheby's for a hammer price of £80,000, with funding from the Heritage Lottery Fund and a grant from The Art Fund. The artist's first watercolour of the area to enter the museum's collection, it was painted in 1814 as one of a series of views of Plymouth which he produced for the publication *Picturesque Views on the Southern Coast*.

The subject of the picture is a lively social gathering on Mount Edgcumbe, at which a group of smartly dressed ladies, gentlemen and sailors are dancing and waving at a fleet of ships anchored in the docks at Devonport. It is said to capture the mood of triumphant celebration which was felt throughout the area with the abdication of Emperor Napoleon that year, and with it the lifting of the threat of a French invasion.

Turner visited Plymouth three times between 1811 and 1814, staying in the area for three weeks and making several expeditions to Mount Edgcumbe with sketchbook and watercolours in hand. He had often spoken highly of the natural beauty of the Three Towns and the surrounding countryside.

December 6th

1907: Eugene De Lagarde, a language teacher, was charged at Plymouth Police Court with being 'a lunatic wandering abroad'. On coming to Plymouth a year previously, he had become engaged to a lady in Portland Villas, but, as he had financial problems, she refused to marry him until the money issues were sorted out. The previous night, Constable Down had been walking along Portland Villas when he saw Lagarde jump into the air. He had gone to his assistance – but Lagarde had tried to strangle him. Lagarde was held on the ground until an ambulance arrived, and detained in hospital overnight. After being examined in the morning, Lagarde was judged by a doctor to have become excited and to have lost his balance for a while. He said he wanted to return to his father in Paris, but in the meantime he was handed over to the care of his fiancée.

———— •◆• ————

1923: In the general election, Leslie Hore-Belisha won Devonport for the Liberals, with a majority of 1,841 over the previous MP, the Unionist Sir Clement Kinloch-Cooke. Born in Devonport, Hore-Belisha later held cabinet office, becoming Secretary of State for Transport (thus giving his name to the Belisha beacon used at road crossings), and subsequently for War. He was defeated in 1945 by another locally born man, the Labour candidate and future party leader Michael Foot. (*See* July 23rd)

December 7th

1735: The organ at St Andrew's Church, which had been built by James Parsons and paid for by subscriptions totalling £391 16s, was used for the first time. John Evans, the first organist, was paid an annual salary of £14. The instrument was maintained and enlarged at regular intervals, and it had just been completely rebuilt by Messrs John Hele & Co., only to be destroyed when the church was bombed during the Blitz in spring 1941.

1956: A teenager called at a house in Stoke; she was collecting money for the Hungarian Relief Fund which was hoping to raise at least £5,000 in the Plymouth area. The door was answered by a little girl, and the collector asked her to tell her mother the purpose of her visit. 'Mummy, mummy,' the girl called, 'the first of the Hungarian refugees is here.' A woman and four children, all in nightclothes, came downstairs immediately, took their visitor eagerly by the hand and invited her indoors. Their excitement soon turned to disappointment as they learned that she was not a fugitive from Eastern Europe, but was only a local and had merely come to ask them for a donation.

December 8th

1964: Shops in the city centre had just started to put up their Christmas decorations, and one large store at the bottom of New George Street had a giant plastic Santa Claus which it arranged to hang on to the roof. A small boy passing below with his mother pointed to it, asking her what Santa was doing up there, as 'it isn't time yet.'

'No,' she answered, 'but I expect that he has to see the chimneys are clean.'

———•◆•———

1969: A married couple appeared at Plympton Magistrates' Court after a bitter argument about each other's driving had led to physical violence. Louisa Davey admitted assaulting her husband, a scrap metal dealer, by slapping him in the face, and she was bound over in the sum of £20 to keep the peace for a year. Her solicitor, Mr J. Carter, said she had been driving the car and her husband had been behind the wheel of the lorry. They had had a minor collision, and, though neither was hurt, Louisa was furious with her husband for driving in 'an unsafe way'.

December 9th

1742: Long before MPs' expenses came under scrutiny, it was permissible to buy votes at election time, or provide 'hospitable inducements' for the electorate. According to C.W. Bracken's *History of Plymouth*, a list was available of 'Things used at the Election of Mr Richard Edgcumbe, Esq., ye 9th day, of December, 1742.'

Edgcumbe was a member for Plympton, and his accounts included over eight dozen bottles of red port wine at 18*s* per dozen; a hogshead of cider, £1 10*s*; seven wine glasses and two quart mugs, 4*s* 6*d*; pipes and tobacco, 1*s*; and a can of white ale, 7*s* 9*d*. The party following his election (and it must be assumed that few people entitled to vote in those days would have even considered backing a rival candidate) must have been a good one.

———◆·———

1929: After several days of severe storms in the west, with loss of life, high winds, heavy rainfall and structural damage, 'famine prices' were today being paid for fish on Plymouth Barbican. One box of plaice cost 5 guineas, and one lot of ray £18. The fishermen were stormbound – eight steam trawlers had been in harbour since the previous week, and smaller boats had been unable to put to sea for a month.

December 10th

1947: Residents in Collings Park Villas, and other terraces between Hender's Corner and Eggbuckland village, had been busy putting new numbers on their front doors during the last few days. If they had not done so by today, they faced the possibility of a £2 fine. The street name was being changed to Eggbuckland Road, so all house numbers needed to be altered within the week, or Plymouth Corporation would do it for them and 'claim damages' from the householders. The latter were advised that they could easily obtain 2in-metal numbers from any ironmonger for the purpose. At the same time, the road stretching from Tavistock Road, flanking Hartley Reservoir to Eggbuckland Road, would from this day be known as Higher Compton Road.

———•◆•———

2004: HMS *Bulwark* entered service at Devonport Dockyard as part of the Devonport flotilla. Built and launched in Barrow-in-Furness, she was part of Britain's newest class of assault ships, designed to provide a much-improved and potent amphibious capability for the Royal Navy. From 2006 onwards she saw service around the Horn of Africa, the Persian Gulf, and Lebanon, returning to Devonport in 2010 for a six-month refit.

December 11th

1929: An inquest on Joyce Lilian Hill, aged 5, of Grenville Road, was held at Plymouth Mortuary. Joyce had been given anaesthetic prior to what should have been a routine operation for tonsillitis at the General Hospital. When she unexpectedly went black in the face afterwards, the doctor administered oxygen and artificial respiration for nearly half an hour, yet to no avail.

———◆———

1957: A tornado swept across the Hamoaze in the afternoon. A naval officer reported seeing a column of spray, which looked like a 50ft funnel, rising from the approaches to Devonport Dockyard. It raced across the water and hit the yard, sucking up dust and leaves. Heavy rain caused flooding, with awnings and wires slightly damaged. The Air Ministry's meteorological station at Mount Batten called it 'a tornado type storm' – a rare occurrence in Britain. It followed a fierce gale the previous night, in which trees and advertisement hoardings had been blown down throughout Plymouth, and some roads had been blocked overnight. A Christmas tree in the city centre – which had been fixed with steel cables – fell on its side, over 300 buildings were damaged, and power failures were widespread. Train journeys and ferry crossings were delayed as high winds made travel too dangerous.

December 12th

1800: The brig *William and Mary*, heavily laden with butter, cheese and brandy, had been sailing from Bristol to Portsmouth to join a convoy to the West Indies, when she was captured on 10 December by a French privateer. On this day she was retaken by an armed Plymouth vessel and brought back to port, but was wrecked on Mewstone Rock, and was 'entirely gone to pieces', although all of the crew were saved.

———◆·———

1947: Under finance regulations in force after the Second World War, bank notes could not be sent to the Dominions, and were liable to be confiscated en route if opened in the course of checking. Postal Orders could be sent to South Africa and New Zealand, and Money Orders up to £40 to any of the sterling group Dominions, Australia among them. This morning, a woman with family in Australia asked at the Plymouth post office counter whether she was allowed to send money there. 'If you do, you'll go to gaol,' the clerk quipped. She did not realise he was joking. As a newspaper reporter commented later, because of somebody's ill-considered joke, someone else might well have been deprived of a Christmas gift.

December 13th

1898: The liner *Avondale Castle*, part of the Union-Castle shipping line which operated a fleet of passenger liners and freighters between Europe, Africa and America, sailed into Plymouth at around midnight. On board was the twelve-strong crew of *Glenhuntley*, a barque which had left Liverpool for New York earlier in the year. While sailing through the South Atlantic, they had fallen foul of stormy weather; the vessel had hit a rock and sprung a serious leak, and the pumps had failed to work. No lives were lost, but the crew had had to abandon their vessel in the first week of June near Tristan da Cunha, 'the most remote inhabited archipelago in the world', and take to their boats for the island shore. They had remained there for 154 days with no provisions, existing almost completely on a diet of birds and birds' eggs, until they were rescued by the gunboat *Thrush* and taken to Cape Town. They had then been transferred to the liner for the return voyage to England.

December 14th

1929: The *Western Evening Herald* reported that, on this Saturday, the Plymouth streets were unusually quiet and devoid of festive shoppers. Traders had been eagerly hoping for 'a certain liveliness' as from today. However, there was less money around, and, in addition, the bad weather had been a deterrent – damage caused by recent hurricanes and downpours meant that property owners would be faced with considerable bills, often running into several hundred pounds, for putting the damage right. The paper noted that: 'Such an expenditure will probably mean depleted purses for the coming festivities. Liberality is likely to be displaced by care.' In view of the disappointing trade so far this season, shops were planning to remain open for the whole day on 18 December, prior to the annual three-day closedown.

———◆———

1956: A Yealmpton farmer who had a holly tree on his property, covered with berries, did a deal with some travellers who had asked him whether they could buy it for Christmas. A price of 15s was mutually agreed, and they promised to call round the next day with the cash. That night, as a newspaper put it, 'somebody got at the tree and did the George Washington act'. There was no sign of the travellers the next day.

December 15th

1898: A battleship, HMS *Nile*, was practising in Plymouth Sound with dummy torpedoes, while a Brixham trawler *Victor* was putting out to sea. The crew of the latter experienced a shock, and the vessel was found to have been torpedoed below the waterline and was leaking. A party of bluejackets assisted the trawler's crew at the pumps, while she was towed back to land and safely beached for examination and repair.

At a naval court the following week, it was established that the accident had occurred because the steering mechanism of the torpedo was out of order, as it had been fixed to go 100 yards astern of the trawler. The crew of the *Nile* were exonerated from blame, and the Admiralty was ordered to recompense the owner of the trawler for the damage done.

———— •◆• ————

2001: ITV Digital, the pay-TV platform, announced the loss of 550 jobs from its 1,000-strong workforce at the customer service centre in Plymouth, as part of a nationwide effort to reduce costs.

December 16th

1874: The outward-bound Cape mail steamer *American* was visited by detectives from Plymouth. They had received a telegram from Penarth, stating that a navvy called Charles Martin, who was wanted for attempted murder, was among the passengers. All 145 people on board, including about seventy navvies and labourers going to work on the railways, were paraded, but the police had been given only a very vague description of Martin and failed to find him; they were hissed at as they left the ship. Martin's name had not been on the passenger list, but he was later apprehended and sentenced to prison for serious assault and wounding a policeman.

1949: Soon after the main post office opened this morning, a young woman approached the stamp counter and asked if she could have two Cup-tie tickets at 5s each. The clerk told her that she could not buy them there, as it was a post office. 'You've got it up there,' she insisted, pointing to a notice on the grill advertising tickets at 3s and 5s. Others had also seen it and a queue was beginning to form. The offending notice, thought to have been put there as a practical joke, was quickly removed.

December 17th

1954: Television had just come to the West Country, and the first VHF transmissions in the Plymouth area were made on this day from North Hessary Tor, near Princetown. Although this was undoubtedly a boon to viewers in the city, it was not regarded as a benefit by all. One small group of businessmen rapidly became so bored with the subject of television that they found a way to banish it from conversation. They decided to introduce a rule at their morning coffee breaks that any member of the party who dared to start a conversation with the words, 'What I saw on TV last night', had to pay for the coffee.

1956: Triplets Rosemary Ellen, Christine Ann and Gillian Mary were born to Mrs Reginald Kelly. The young Mrs Kelly and her husband had been living in a rather cramped three-roomed flat in Embankment Road for five years, and they had a 2-year-old son. They had been on the waiting list for a council house for a long time. Once their daughters arrived, in effect doubling the family at a stroke, it proved the decisive factor, and they moved eagerly into their new home at Blandford Road, Efford, on 3 January 1957.

December 18th

1948: Overheard in a Mutley Plain shop where a mother had taken her small son to see Santa Claus:

'Is he really Father Christmas, Mummy?'

'No, dear, he's only imitating him.'

'But won't Father Christmas mind?'

1953: People were warned not to walk across Hartley Pleasure Grounds after dark – the surface was very rough and poorly lit, and there was a risk of them falling. Several pedestrians had taken to using it as a short cut. They were advised that it could be a short cut to Freedom Fields Hospital instead.

1957: On this, the last Wednesday before Christmas Day, contrary to their usual practice, all of the shops remained open all afternoon. By 4 p.m. Royal Parade was beginning to look deserted, as most people had assumed that the shops would be closing early. One big store had planned to shut, but the management changed their minds at the last moment. No announcements as to the change of policy had been made beforehand, and it was said by the press that those shoppers who ventured forth probably had the most comfortable and peaceful afternoon's shopping over the festive season that they would ever know.

December 19th

1861: The opening celebration for the Catholic Church of St Michael and St Joseph, Devonport, was led by Bishop Vaughan. Since the establishment of a cathedral in Plymouth, he had wanted to build another for the people of the sister town and for sailors who were regularly in port. Prince Gardens, Mutton Cove, was made available. Work on the building began in 1859, and the foundation stone was laid in June 1860. It became the military chaplaincy for the army and navy. The chancel, aisle and North Chapel were added in 1884. Exactly a century later, the church was sold and then demolished; a modern church, dedicated only to St Joseph, was built in 1985 at Raglan Road, on the site formerly occupied by Raglan Barracks.

———— ◆ ————

1948: The Plymouth office of an insurance company received a claim for a set of artificial teeth. It came from a woman who had removed her upper denture while peeling an apple, and had then thrown the core into the fire with her peelings. When she realised that her dentures had gone into the flames with the remains of the fruit, she thought there was no need to worry as it would be covered by her policy.

December 20th

1954: A man was seen driving over Stonehouse Bridge in the direction of Devonport, with a live goose in his car. It was assumed that he was not taking the bird home as a pet. However, the goose was evidently aware that its destiny was the Christmas table. As the window was slightly open (a little rash of the driver, perhaps), it managed to make a bid for freedom, escaping from the car, landing on the road and holding up the traffic. One driver just behind had to jam his brakes on very hard to avoid it. Meanwhile, the owner of the runaway – or flyaway – pulled in at the side of the road, got out and tried to grab the bird. It proved more than a match for him and soon flew off in the direction of Durnford Street.

---◆---

1961: A woman shopping at a store in New George Street unwisely left her purse in full view on top of her shopping bag full of purchases. A store detective politely advised her to take more care, in view of possible thieves; he was rewarded with a terse: 'Mind your own business.' A few minutes later, the purse had indeed been taken.

December 21st

1955: Among the crowds who had gone out Christmas shopping in the city, two men were spotted taking their dogs out in a novel way. They both had dachshunds curled up comfortably in the hoods of their duffle coats, thus leaving them with two hands free for carrying bags and parcels.

———— • ✦ • ————

1956: One Lipson family said that they had found the perfect way around the problem of being woken up too early on Christmas Day. They always told their children that Santa Claus was terribly busy, and could not reach their house until about 11 a.m. This ensured a good night's rest, and allowed the turkey to be put in the oven and other presents to be unwrapped first. The stockings were hung in a separate room, which was not unlocked until the magic hour.

———— • ✦ • ————

1957: A large, well-built American in a city pub was talking loudly to his friends about his experiences in the frozen wastes of Alaska. This was a region where, he told them, one really knew what cold is like. Suddenly he broke off his narrative. 'Will somebody close that door?' he asked. 'It's draughty in here.'

December 22nd

1960: A story was being spread, which was a minor variation on one which had been circulated in Plymouth about ten years previously. Reportedly, one local family had relatives in the East who made them a gift of various ingredients each year which they could add to the Christmas pudding. The package arrived this year as usual, and in addition to the dried fruit, nuts and other delicacies, there was a small tin of powder. Everything was mixed into the pudding, which was put away until it could be enjoyed at lunch on Christmas Day.

Not long afterwards, the family received a letter from the sender of the parcel, explaining that the tin – which, it had been assumed, contained some kind of exotic spice – actually held the ashes of Uncle George. The letter requested that they honour his last wish and scatter the ashes in Plymouth Sound.

The tale is perhaps a myth, as with the similar story of a food parcel which had arrived in the city from Australia during the food shortages, shortly after the war, when an unmarked tin of powder had been used for making soup.

December 23rd

1815: A large canvas of Napoleon Bonaparte, shown standing on the deck of HMS *Bellerophon* while the ship was anchored in Plymouth Sound, went on exhibition at a picture gallery in Frankfort Place. The picture, about 8ft long by 6ft wide, was painted by Charles Lock Eastlake. Eager patrons flocked to view it at an admission price of 1s. In order to make the picture as lifelike as possible, the artist had made sketches of Napoleon, with his full approval. The latter had willingly posed on board the ship, and had sent the artist parts of his uniform to ensure that the picture would be as accurate and detailed as possible.

Eastlake, who had been born in Plymouth, was aged only 22 at the time he completed the work. He went on to enjoy a successful career not only as an artist but also as an art historian, the first keeper of the new National Gallery in London, and president of the Royal Academy.

December 24th

1945: Christmas Eve sales were reported to be good this Monday, although choice was limited. Among non-coupon goods, Christmas cards were very scarce, especially the cheaper lines; diaries were sold out at most shops; calendars were in short supply; and, although handbags were plentiful enough in the cheaper and more expensive lines, those from the 'in between' range were running short. Expensive toys and novelties were readily available, but more modestly priced ones less so, and a shopper wanting a cheap wooden car might have to make do with a wooden boat instead. Children's and adult books were limited, and traders advised purchasers to give a book token instead. As for coupon goods, handkerchiefs were still available but mostly in white – with a few in coloured silk – while fancy boxes were entirely sold out. Most shops were out of long-sleeved cardigans and pullovers, but a few polo-neck sweaters, sleeveless pullovers and a good variety of ties were available. For many, said the *Western Independent*, it would be 'a matter of fancying what one gets, rather than getting what one fancies'.

———◆———

1948: A small boy in a bus queue dropped a package containing a bottle of champagne that the family had saved up for. 'That's finished Christmas for you!' his mother joked, provoking raised eyebrows from other passengers.

December 25th

1880: North of the border, the *Dundee Courier* reported (during an abnormally temperate festive season) that:

> On Christmas Day some gentlemen taking a ramble in the neighbourhood of St Budeaux, near Plymouth, picked no less than seven different varieties of wild flowers, all in full bloom; and in front of a cottage, and altogether unprotected, a fuchsia was noticed in full bloom.

1955: Barbara Downing, a member of the Ballet Montmartre (which was busiest over the festive season), was in Plymouth with her family for at least part of Christmas Day – for the first time in seven years. On 21 December, she had flown to Iceland to join the *Bob Hope Show* for four shows (the first almost as soon as she stepped off the plane). She was also there to entertain American troops, and to make a TV film for the US networks. She had flown back to London on Christmas Eve, coming home just in time for tea.

1960: The residential welfare home at Queen's Gate Nursery allowed its thirty children an hour on Christmas morning to bang their drums and blow their trumpets as loudly as they liked. The children then had to put the instruments away, and allow the grown-ups to enjoy a traditional family Christmas in peace and quiet, with presents from the tree after lunch.

December 26th

1889: The Grand Theatre in Union Street, Stonehouse, opened with the pantomime *Cinderella*, and there was such a rush that the performance started thirty minutes early. Under new ownership, the theatre closed briefly and reopened in March 1909 as the Grand Theatre and Picture Palace. In 1930 it became a cinema, but was destroyed in March 1941; the remains were demolished in March 1963.

1945: Charles Pollard (79), a retired builder living at Tavistock Place, Stoke, received a telegram advising him that his wife Caroline (76), who was in hospital, had taken a turn for the worse. Within minutes he collapsed and died from a heart attack. His wife passed away the next morning.

1955: A Plymouth man with two Siamese cats was surprised when one of them refused a piece of roast turkey. A search in the garden revealed a roast chicken carcass with no meat left on it. A few months later, the man was chatting to his next-door neighbours, who asked if one of the cats had eaten their cold chicken on Boxing Day. They had had a roast for Christmas lunch, and had put the rest of the meat in a safe in the courtyard, planning to eat it cold the next day. One of the feline predators was particularly skilled at opening doors, unless they were latched.

December 27th

1809: Under the heading 'The Plymouth Monster', the papers reported that:

A long-eared gentleman has been assiduously and meritoriously engaged, during the past and present week, in personating the wretch, whose title we have designated at the head of this article, and who justly merits the epithet with which he has been dubbed. Several unprotected females have been grossly insulted by this 'less than man', but were we to give credence to the various tales which have been conjured up by 'female terror', our friends would, and perhaps justly, class us among the disciples of Munchausen. We have heard the names of three females who have been ill-treated, but none of them are seriously injured; and, as a sharp look-out is kept, it is presumed the monster, whoever he may be, will not long evade the castigation he merits.

———— • ————

1944: A contingent of United States marines in Plymouth pooled their resources and got together to hold a festive party for children at the naval base in Manadon. After Father Christmas had distributed the presents and sweets, one youngster, aged about 6, muttered scornfully to his friend, 'I don't believe he's real, do you? He sounds to me like a Yank!'

December 28th

1955: The pillar box at the end of Westwell Street was moved to a new position – about 150 yards along the street on the same side. Within a few hours, a Post Office van pulled up at the old site, and a postman got out carrying an empty mailbag. On seeing the empty space, he was heard to ask, 'Who's pinched my blinking letter box?'

1957: A group of children in a Plymouth home were seated in front of the TV one afternoon. One remarked sadly, 'If only we didn't have television we could go out and play.' Luckily, an adult in charge took the hint and switched it off.

1961: A recently married couple spent Christmas at a guest house just outside Plymouth. One day the wife complained of indigestion, and the landlady recommended that she visit the local chemist. Her guest did so, and found the tablets very effective. 'I told you our chemist was a good chap,' said the landlady afterwards. 'He's better than any doctor.' To her horror, only then did she discover that the young couple were recently qualified doctors themselves.

December 29th

1949: Having paid 17s 6d for a club dinner ticket, a Plymothian donned evening dress, and, looking his best, took a bus to the hotel. Anticipating a splendid meal, he walked in through the glass door – and caught sight of his reflection. To his horror, the clip-on bow tie he had put on so carefully before leaving the house was missing. He retraced his steps, looking outside the door and on the pavement all the way back to the bus stop – but without success. He glumly took another ride home, but there was no sign of the bow tie there either. As he had no spare and the shops were closed, he felt he had no alternative but to cancel his plans and stay at home.

———— • ◆ • ————

1964: Alan Fulbrook, a piano teacher in his 70s who used to lead an orchestra which played at Palm Court, the Royal Hotel, and later at Pophams in the 1930s, was asked why Plymouth restaurants no longer employed orchestras to entertain the patrons. It was purely a matter of economics, he said. 'Before the war the restaurants paid £3 a week. Now it's 10s an hour.'

December 30th

1882: An inquiry was held on the death of Mr Woodfin, a stoker at Coxside gasworks, who was killed when part of one of the chimney stacks fell on him. The jury returned a verdict of accidental death, adding that they hoped the company directors would ensure that an improvement was made in the cornice when it was repaired.

———— • ◆ • ————

1955: According to city cinema box office records, the films attracting the biggest crowds that year were *The Dam Busters* (Royal Cinema); *White Christmas*, in VistaVision, closely followed by *Doctor at Sea* (Odeon); *Vera Cruz* (Gaumont); and *Three Coins in the Fountain* (Plaza). The majority of the Royal's most successful pictures were musicals, including *Seven Brides for Seven Brothers*, and *The Student Prince*. Elsewhere, adventure and action movies like *20,000 Leagues Under the Sea*, *The Colditz Story*, and *Above Us the Waves* were the biggest hits.

———— • ◆ • ————

1956: Plymouth headed the sunshine table this year, according to Air Ministry records collected weekly from twenty places (all regarded as representative of different regions) in England, Wales and Northern Ireland. Despite some spells of heavy rain, the city recorded 1,752 hours of sunshine, narrowly beating Falmouth which had 1,749. In 1955, Plymouth had headed the table most of the year, and was only surpassed by Falmouth in the final week.

December 31st

1954: The invitation for a private New Year party in the city stated: 'Carriages at 12.15.' One reveller told his host at midnight that he had missed his last bus to Plympton, 'but I see you've got something laid on.' Only then did he learn that it was a joke.

1999: Plymothians let their hair down to celebrate the Millennium, and supermarkets reported a roaring trade. Sainsbury's superstore at Marsh Mills closed at 4 p.m., and, during the previous hours, last-minute shoppers had caused over a mile of traffic queues on the roundabout and approaching roads. The on-duty manager reported that party packs and wines were selling well, saying, 'It seems as though people think the end of the world is coming.'

In the city centre the newly restored Derry's Clock was unveiled, and a tea dance was held at the Guildhall. At sunset, about 10,000 people saw the Royal Marines Band beating the retreat, with a selection including 'Rule Britannia', 'Land of Hope and Glory', 'Life on the Ocean Wave', and 'Auld Lang Syne'. Nightclubs and pubs were packed, while others held private parties at home.

On the Hoe, about 20,000 watched a display featuring £40,000 worth of fireworks, visible from a considerable distance, which were spoiled only slightly by a shroud of mist and drizzle.